THE ORIOLE'S SONG

THE ORIOLE'S SONG

An American Girlhood in Wartime China

BJ ELDER

EastBridge
Norwalk

EastBridge
Signature Books

Cover calligraphy by Harrison X. Tu. End photo of BJ Elder by Petranella J. Yisma.

EastBridge is a nonprofit publishing corporation,
chartered in the State of Connecticut and tax exempt under
section 501(c)(3) of the United States tax code.

EastBridge has received a generous multiyear
grant from the Henry Luce Foundation.

Library of Congress Cataloging-in-Publication Data

Elder, BJ, 1933-
Oriole's song : an American girlhood in wartime China / BJ Elder. p. cm.
-- (Signature books)
Summary: The author relates the experiences of her first sixteen years
growing up in Changsha, the capital of Hunan Province, during the
turbulent years of the Japanese invasion through World War II and the
civil war that followed.
ISBN 1-891936-34-4 (alk paper) -- ISBN 1-891936-33-6 (pbk. : alk. paper)
1. China--History--Republic, 1912-1949--Personal narratives, American.
2. Elder, BJ, 1933---Childhood and youth. [1. Elder, BJ, 1933---Childhood
and youth. 2. China--History--Republic, 1912-1949--Personal narratives,
American. 3. Americans--China--History--20th century. 4. Women--
Biography.] I. Title: An American Girlhood in wartime China. II. Title.
III. Signature Books (Norwalk, CT)
DS774.E44 2003
                                                    951'.215--dc21
2003011356

Printed in the United States of America

*For Winifred and Dwight,
my parents*

There is a style of Chinese painting in which isolated areas of fine brushwork depict mountains in the mist or islands on a sea. The more closely one looks at the mountains and the islands, the more one sees — trees and rocks, boats and bridges, pavilions and people. But the mist and the sea are not shown explicitly. They are empty spaces on the paper. We know what the spaces are because the areas of brushwork give them meaning and give shape to the painting as a whole. I remember my growing up as though viewing such a landscape. The closer I look at a memory, the more I remember about it. And each recollection, each remembrance, gives shape and meaning to my past.

CONTENTS

ACKNOWLEDGMENTS

Perhaps more than most, this book owes its existence to other people. First, there were two gifted teachers, Janice Booker at the University of Pennsylvania and Connie Thompson of Germantown Friends School, whose comments on my work and whose support persuaded me to get started. Then there were those who, as the work progressed, generously gave their time and attention to read and critique what I had written—Lady Borton, Laurence Sigmund, Peg Calabrese, Pat Macpherson, Adam Corson-Finerty, my daughters Jenny and Renee, and my writers' group: Ralph Allen, Anne Farnese, Bill Hengst, Hal Lynch, and Caroline Reeves.

But it was Danny Ashkenasi, my nephew by marriage—composer, actor, and teacher—and Dave Elder, my husband, whose enthusiasm, attention, and unfailing support over the long haul carried me through to completion. From the beginning, Danny's professional skill and insight were invaluable in helping me shape the book. His patience and repeated reading of the manuscript, his nagging and boosting me when I flagged were actually what pulled—or shoved—me through to the end. To him I am profoundly grateful. Also to Dave, who read countless excerpts countless times, who made excellent suggestions which I almost invariably followed, even though I may have disagreed with them at first, and who patiently put up with the very odd hours I kept when seized by spasms of writing.

In 1996 I returned to China in order to make sure that my memories of Lushan and Yuanling were accurate (to my surprise, they were). Dave's sympathetic interest and enthusiasm made that trip the most rewarding of all the journeys I have taken. The trip would not have been a success, however, without the guidance and interpretive skill of my friend, Jiang You-qin, who took time out from her work as head of the ophthalmology department at Hunan Medical College to accompany us, with her husband, Liu Yung-de, who came with us part of the way.

The book could not have reached its conclusion without the members of the Changsha and Yuanling Yali Alumni Associations. With their kindness and hospitality, with sharing their stories with me, and with their joy at our reunion after so many years, they restored my ties to China and my past. To them I wish to express my deep admiration for their unflagging spirit in the face of great adversity and for their steadfast loyalty to Yali and the values on which it was founded. Among those men, You Dajun, in particular, has provided me with essential information and details about Changsha and Yuanling which otherwise I would not have known.

Finally, I have to thank Douglas Murray, formerly of the Yale-China Association, and Gayle Feldman, journalist, for putting me in touch with Doug Merwin of EastBridge—the final and most necessary act which made this book possible.

To all of the above, my heartfelt thanks.

Xie-xie.

BJ Elder

THE
ORIOLE'S
SONG

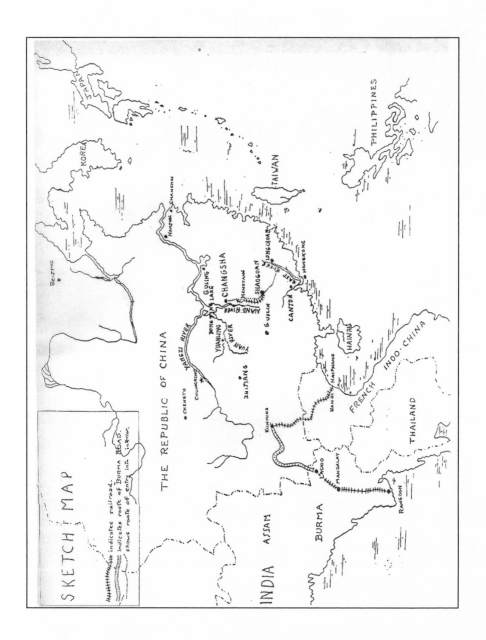

SKETCH MAP

+++++ indicates railroad.
•••••• indicates route of BURMA ROAD.
- - - - shows route of entry into interior.

THE REPUBLIC OF CHINA

INDIA

ASSAM

BURMA

THAILAND

FRENCH INDO-CHINA

HAINAN

PHILIPPINES

TAIWAN

HONG KONG

CANTON

KOREA

JAPAN

BEIJING

CHENGTU

CHUNGKING

YANGTZE RIVER

GULING

DONG TING LAKE

CHANGSHA

YUANLING

YUAN RIVER

ZHIJIANG

XIANG RIVER

CHENGYANG

SHAOGUAN

GUILIN

LONGGUAN

NANCHANG

CHANGCHN

HAIPHONG

HANOI

KUNMING

LASHIO

MANDALAY

RANGOON

PART I
1973–1974

HONG KONG

"You're speaking with a Hunan accent!" Madame Liu says, wrinkling her nose fastidiously. The room is hot, the window shut against the noise and fumes of Prince Edward Road, where I have just alighted from one of those ubiquitous double-decker buses that ply the busy streets of Kowloon and Hong Kong. Now, in this upstairs room, Madame Liu is undertaking to revive my Mandarin. I look up from the lesson, secretly pleased that I have retained my Hunan accent after twenty-four years of nonuse.

"What about Chairman Mao?" I ask. Whatever else I think of him, I am proud of the fact that the Chairman and I both were born in Hunan— no matter that it was several miles and many years apart. "What about *his* accent?" It is a trick question. Madame Liu is a member in good standing of the Communist Party. Will she defend the Great Helmsman when everyone knows his accent is so thick that only his fellow Hunanese can listen to him without acute discomfort? Or will she tell the truth and admit that he isn't perfect?

Madame Liu's expression of disapproval deepens, her Mandarin even more crisp and clear. "Chairman Mao? His accent is terrible! You don't want to talk like that!" She shakes her head. "Please read that again and watch your tones." Meekly I resume the lesson, trying to copy her Beijing accent by occasionally adding an exaggerated "rrr" at the end of a word.

The year is 1973, and the Vietnam War seems to be drawing to a close. President Nixon made his historic trip to Beijing last year after more than two decades of relentless enmity between China and the United States. With my husband, Dave, and our two children, I have come from Philadelphia to live in Hong Kong for a few months while Dave, working for an American Quaker organization, investigates possibilities for helping the nations of Southeast Asia recover from the war. I was born, an only child, forty years ago in Changsha, the provincial capital of Hunan, where my parents had come from the States to teach in a boys' school called Yali, founded by the Yale-in-China Association. Now, with China only thirty minutes by slow train from downtown Kowloon, I have decided to try to return to the city of my birth.

It is an outrageous idea. For an ordinary American to visit China at this time is like trying to climb Everest—practically impossible. Besides, I don't want to go back. There is no smooth joining between the early years of my life as a foreigner at home in China and the rest of my life as an American not quite at home in America. I have packed those disconnected years in China at the bottom of my memory, not forgotten but left undisturbed. To bring them out now would be too painful. The truth, I admit to myself, is that I am afraid—afraid of some inner catastrophe at what I would find if I returned. I don't want to go back to the place where my father was denounced as an enemy of the people. I don't want to survey the residue of what had once been my entire world; I don't want to face the fact that the imprint of my parents' lives and mine has been purposely wiped out from that most precious location—the place where we started as a family. And yet I feel impelled to go for the memory of that family, for the sake of my parents, and for the sake of my unwilling self. I suspect it will be good for me, like swallowing bitter medicine.

So it was from a sense of duty rather than desire that I had mentioned my idea at the head office in Philadelphia, when we were being oriented to Dave's assignment. "While we're in Hong Kong," I said, "I'd like to try to get into China."

Stated out loud, it sounded ridiculous. The executive secretary and the secretary of the International Division turned their gaze thoughtfully to the window; Dave's immediate supervisor looked at me with the studied calm of a psychotherapist listening to a slightly deranged client. "I thought maybe I could return to where I was born," I explained, "and learn something about the health care system in Hunan." It still sounded absurd. Despite Nixon's visit, only a few politically correct or highly prestigious Americans had been admitted to "Red China." What's more, some of the nations in Southeast Asia were not on friendly terms with China. If it became known that Dave's wife was going there, that might jeopardize his mission. I brought up this last possibility hopefully—perhaps it would be best if I didn't try? "Not at all," the executives smiled politely. "Go right ahead." They were sure there would be no problem.

I was touched by their prompt consent—and then realized they thought there would be no problem because I was sure to fail. It's true that the executive secretary himself had been one of the few Americans who had been admitted to China in recognition of the relief work Quakers had done during World War II. But it was preposterous that I would be admitted—I, who had done nothing for China. Worse than that, I was the child of a father who had been accused by the current government of being an imperialist and a spy and attempting to rob the People of their heritage. With China still in the throes of the Cultural Revolution, my proposal was, to put it kindly, laughable.

The discussion reverted to Dave's assignment. As the men talked on about Southeast Asia, I felt a trickle of renewed pride in my Hunan heritage. I was proud of Hunan's long history and its central place on the map of China. I was proud of Hunan's inelegant version of Mandarin and its hearty cuisine featuring hot peppers, fatback, and a local delicacy accurately called "stinking bean curd." I was proud of Hunan's fertile red soil and its hardworking people with their reputation for being bossy and opinionated, insular and independent. Now I felt a revitalized sense of kinship with them. The more I thought about them, the more I appreciated their invigorating obstinacy. Theirs was a tradition of stubborn rebellion against authority that stretched back for centuries, and centuries of China's rulers had considered Hunan to be one of the more bothersome areas of their domain. I shared a part, albeit a very small part, of this staunch tradition. *This* erstwhile citizen of Hunan, I decided, was not going to be daunted by a few doubts in Philadelphia.

As soon as we were settled in Hong Kong, I composed a letter to the China Travel Bureau in Beijing, applying for myself alone, as a nurse hoping to learn from the Chinese health care system and, incidentally, to visit the hospital where I was born.

Months passed with no response. I didn't mind. I relished being back in Hong Kong, where Dave and I had lived for five years in the '60s and had adopted our daughters as babies—one found by the police on a dimly lit landing of a tenement stairwell, the other in a ditch along a path leading down from a scabrous cluster of squatters' shacks clinging to a hillside. Renee was now ten years old and Jenny eleven. Since the mid-sixties, our home had been in the Germantown section of Philadelphia, where the girls had gone to Quaker schools. Here in Hong Kong, Renee attended a British primary school and Jenny had chosen a Catholic school for girls because the students were Chinese and classes were in English. Our girls were not enthusiastic about their respective school experiences. But Renee perfected a wicked imitation of her teacher's British accent, and Jenny's Quaker upbringing reportedly introduced some startling ideas in catechism class. Dave and I concluded they would survive. Meanwhile, we did all we could to enjoy Hong Kong again, visiting our old haunts, hiking and picnicking, and gorging on the local cuisine.

But now, only ten weeks before we are to return to the States, I still have not heard from Beijing. I am relieved. Well, I tried. The doubts of the head office in Philadelphia were justified, and now I can get on with my life undisturbed. Madame Liu, however, has other ideas. "You must go to the China Travel office here in *Hong Kong*!" she urges. Her face turns tragic, and her Mandarin becomes faintly reminiscent of Peking opera. "Say to them you want to see your *birthplace* before you leave, maybe never to return!" She pauses. I can almost hear Chinese violins wailing in the background. "You tell me next week what they say!" She looks at me fixedly until I promise to go.

A couple of days later I find myself standing in line at the China Travel Bureau. From what I can see, people in front of me are being turned away in regular succession. My mouth is dry. I stand behind a tall American carrying a briefcase, relaxed and assured, his shirt collar open. When he reaches the front of the line, he pulls out a sheaf of papers and starts talking in fluent Mandarin to the woman behind the counter. I hear him mention the name of an Ivy League university. *Why put myself through this?* I think, and half turn to leave, but stop at a sudden vision of Madame Liu's stern gaze. The woman behind the counter shakes her head and the tall American walks off, shoving his papers back in the briefcase.

I look at the woman behind the counter. From the expression on her face, I can tell this is not the time to smile. My heart thumps in my ears. Madame Liu glares at me from somewhere behind the woman's left ear. There is no escape. I step up to the counter and swallow, my refurbished Mandarin wiped out as though it had never been.

Speaking in English, I say I'd like to apply to visit China. The woman replies with the faint Oxbridge accent acquired by those who learned their impeccable English at the Foreign Language Institute in Beijing: "What is your reason?"

"I want to visit my birthplace before I have to return to the United States." I pause, but there is no response. "I'm very sorry to hurry, but my time here is limited, and I may not have another chance." Violins sob faintly.

"Where is your birthplace?"

"Changsha," I tell her, and add that while I am there I want very much to visit the birthplace of Chairman Mao as well.

"When do you want to go?"

I stand very still. "Pardon?"

"When do you want to go to Changsha?"

"In January," I reply. "Then I must return to the States with my family."

She reaches under the counter and brings out some papers. "You fill these out and send them to this address in Beijing," she says.

"You mean there's a chance I can go?"

She looks at me impassively. "You try. There is not much time." She beckons to the next person in line.

It is two days' work to complete the forms. Even though I am applying only for myself, I have to write biographies of my parents and Dave as well, describe our children, and explain our work. My hopes fade as I complete the application, for I suspect that no amount of yearning to visit the Chairman's birthplace and no amount of eagerness to learn about the "new China" will outweigh my father's history. But to satisfy Madame Liu, I mail the application.

Exactly four weeks later, when Dave is in Laos, I receive a letter from Beijing. On a single sheet of paper there is one paragraph. I, my husband, and my children have permission to enter China on January 3, 1974. I am to send a detailed itinerary immediately.

No one is around to hear my shriek of joy. I shake the letter in my disbelieving hand and the paper crackles reassuringly. It is real. We are going to Changsha. I've done it. I've *done* it! Unbidden, the polite skeptics in Philadelphia flash through my mind. This is me, if you please—little insignificant she-won't-cause-any-problem me! I see the tall American scholar at the China Travel Bureau with his sheaf of credentials. Credentials, ha! Mentally I toss my head. *We* are going to Changsha. That's what is wonderful—we are *all* going. I feel a wave of gratitude to the China Travel Bureau. That impassive, impersonal, impenetrable bureaucracy in Beijing has surpassed my vision and erased my fears by including the whole family. Whether it is the work of a sympathetic bureaucrat acting out of the deeply ingrained Chinese love of family or from a pragmatic calculation of the additional profit to be made from our augmented visit, it doesn't matter. My vision blurs with tears. Dave and the girls will come with me to visit my past, and somehow that removes all doubts and fears and makes things whole.

As I wait for the bus to the telegraph office in Kowloon, I try out several messages to send Dave. Telegrams are expensive and one should attempt to pack as much as possible into a few words. Moreover, relations between Laos and China are strained at this time, so I can't tell him outright about the letter from Beijing. Finally I settle on

"INVITATION RECEIVED FOR YOU AND GIRLS TO COME HOME WITH ME JANUARY THIRD STOP WILL YOU COME STOP BJ"

A few hours later, an equally circumspect telegram arrives from Laos:

"DELIGHTED TO TAKE SENTIMENTAL JOURNEY WITH YOU STOP LOVE STOP DAVE."

When the girls come home from school I tell them the exciting news. They know I've applied to go to China, but like everyone else (except Madame Liu), they have not taken it seriously. Besides, it is now late November; we have plane reservations to return to the States at the end of the year, and the girls are eager to be back with their friends in Germantown. Now we will be delayed at least two weeks. They look at me with no joy.

"You mean we're going to *China*?" Jenny asks, as though it were the South Pole.

"Do we *have* to?" echoes Renee.

A bucket of ice water over my head couldn't cool me more effectively. After a moment of shock, I am gripped by a cold rage, and I feel my eyebrows go up. "Oh, no," I reply with icy calm. "You don't have to go." I feel my eyebrows come down. "You can go back to Germantown and stay with the Fishers. That's a good idea. You can go straight back to school, and Dave and I will go to China and we'll have a *ball*."

There is a rather long pause. The girls exchange glances. "Well," Jenny says finally, "I guess we might go to China."

I consider the possibility. "No way." My voice begins to rise of its own accord. "This is *my* trip, and no one is going on *my* trip who just 'guesses' they're going! I'm not going to travel with anyone who just 'might' come along. Oh, no. If you go on this trip, you're going to *ENJOY* it!" I find myself pointing my finger at them, something I have never done before.

Taken aback, the girls look at me wide-eyed. "All right. Okay," they say. "We will."

"Well, if you go," I say, pressing my advantage, "you're going to keep journals and write in them every day,"

"Okay."

"*And* you're going to eat everything put in front of you."

"Okay, okay."

"Okay," I say, too, feeling wonderful. I hug them. "I'm so glad you're coming!"

THE TRAIN

Our train from Canton to Changsha rocks and clacks its way through the night. The girls are asleep on the upper bunks in our compartment and Dave slumbers on the lower one across from me. I lie awake and think about coming home.

For the first time in many years, I bring out my memories of Changsha and look through them. Here's one of the road that went past the hospital where I was born. The road was called the Ma Lou (pronounced "ma low", in the Hunan dialect), meaning "the Great Horse Road," but there were no horses. It served as a major thoroughfare for foot traffic, rickshaws, and carts moving in and out through the north gate of the city. The Yale-in-China hospital loomed on one side of the Ma Lou like a red brick cliff with roofs that curved out at the corners. On the other side, the long wall of Yali, the boys' school compound, was broken by the front gate, where the gate man lived in the gatehouse and kept track of who went in and out.

In the early morning on the Ma Lou, whiffs of incense from a wayside shrine vied with the passing stench of carts pulled by straining coolies hauling buckets of human sewage out of the city, to be dispensed as fertilizer in the rice paddies and vegetable patches that carpeted the countryside. Very soon traffic picked up as farmers took their produce into the city and stores opened to do business in the cool of the morning. There were no cars and very few bicycles. But in the city's web of narrow streets, rickshaws dodged in and out among coolies carrying loads which teetered high above their backs. Heavy carts creaked by, pulled by men hauling bricks, sand, bags of rice, and tubs of fish with water sloshing over the sides. Women jounced through the throng, carrying baskets of chickens and ducks and vegetables, slung from each end of a pole over the shoulder. Usually there was a wheelbarrow on its way to market with a pig strapped to it, squealing in duet with the wheelbarrow's screeching axle.

When I was very young, I rode on my mother's lap in a rickshaw or on the back of my parents' bicycles in a wicker seat made especially for me. In my early teens, I navigated the Ma Lou on my own bicycle, joining the flow into the city to weave in and out through the traffic, ringing my bicycle bell, which gave a musical *ding-dong* unlike the mechanized whir of bicycle bells in the States. Vendors called out their wares—handmade straw sandals, folding fans of varnished wood and black paper, mats of woven bamboo, stacks of "ghost money" to be burned at funerals, ensuring wealth for departed relatives in the afterlife. Other vendors sold snacks—everything from hot or cold noodles to twists of batter called *you tiao* dipped out of vats of bubbling oil. I always stopped to watch one particular man who sold miniature animals perched on bamboo wands—tiny exuberant dragons and delicate phoenixes with plumage of many colors, blown from hot melted sugar as if fashioned from molten glass. His artistry with the slender blowpipe was so sure that it looked accidental as he blew and twirled his fantastic little creatures into existence. I was allowed to buy *you tiao,* because they were hot, but not the animals, for they were likely to be contaminated with germs breathed from the tubercular lungs of the emaciated vendor.

To go out on the Ma Lou was to embark on an adventure, like taking a ride on a turbulent river. To come home from the Ma Lou was like being washed by the current into a safe and quiet harbor. But sometimes coming home did not feel safe. Occasionally there were beggars crouching against the wall near the Yali gate. They started to whine when I approached, and displayed their sores and deformities, some of which were self-induced or had been inflicted on them in childhood to make them more suitable as beggars. Whatever the reason for becoming a beggar, it was unwise to leave the profession, for then one would have to reckon with the secret societies and the beggars' guild, to which all beggars paid protection money.

If I saw beggars waiting, I approached the gate apprehensively, bracing myself against whatever they might invite me to behold. I did not give them money, because if I gave to one, the others would raise the volume of their supplications and come limping and crawling toward me, insisting on their share. Once, when I was thirteen, I was riding back to the compound and a beggar near the gate stepped in front of my bicycle. Her face was etched into a tragic mask as she held out a baby, silent and limp. Flies were clustered on its eyes. I jumped off my bicycle and stood looking at the ground between us while she murmured continuously—a soft, liquid, multisyllabic moan, as though willing me to look at the child again. But I didn't raise my eyes, for I knew if I looked once more, I'd never see anything else. And so the beggar and I stood, each in her place, as distant from each other as two planets. Then I heard the gate man open the gate behind her. Hurriedly I pushed the bicycle around her and through the gate, pausing on the other side until I stopped shaking and my heart stopped pounding in my ears. Then I got on my bicycle and pedaled slowly down the tree-lined path toward home.

The train slows down and my weight shifts forward, recalling me to the present. *What if that baby were Renee or Jenny?* For a moment I am washed by the passing edge of a huge sorrow, and I step back quickly. *Whatever kind of life people here are living today, it's got to be better than that.*

The train jerks to a stop. I sit up and look out the window onto a platform backed by a cement wall. In the light from a train window, I see two large characters painted on the wall—perhaps the name of the town. A couple of people walk away from the train, small clouds of their breath preceding them. One of them is pushing a bicycle. Light glints briefly on the moving spokes, and the platform starts to slide backward. I shine my flashlight on my watch. It is four in the morning. We are due to arrive in Changsha at 7:59. Four more hours.

I wrap myself in the blanket and sit by the window, looking out at the dark as the train picks up speed. I think of the time I rode my bicycle one moonless night on the Yali soccer field, making circles and figures-eight, round and round, faster and faster, as though I were flying, exhilarated by the speed and the breeze and the smoothness of the ride and not being able to see the ground, yet feeling safe.

I think of the kite we flew on that playing field when I was about four years old. It was as tall as I, a magnificent construction of paper and bamboo shaped and painted like a Chinese scholar in long robes. One windy afternoon my father and I, with my playmate Rosemary Ying, flew the kite so high that we could no longer see the color of the scholar's robes against the sky. We sent him letters—pieces of paper slit so as to slide up the string in the breeze—until a strong gust broke him loose. He went swooping out over the field, trailing the string of letters after him, and dived out of sight behind the school buildings. When we found where he'd landed, I didn't recognize him. He'd come to a soggy end in the school swimming pool, leaving a tangle of string with slivers of bamboo and shreds of colorless paper floating disconsolately on the murky water.

We fished the remains of the kite out of the water and carried them down the playing field toward home, where the faculty houses stood along paths bordered by tall trees native to south China. There were other trees as well—lacy gingkos, and ponderous camphors spreading their dark branches over the ground. In springtime fruit trees dressed themselves in blossoms and posed gracefully in pools of fragrance. Azalea flared with color in the spring, and in the summer jasmine and gardenia blossomed, their perfume heavy in the windless air.

Because there were few trees elsewhere, the compound was a sanctuary for birds. My mother often pointed out the iridescent flash of a flycatcher through the trees. And there was the oriole who came each year to nest in the camphor tree outside my bedroom window. I was never able to spot him or any member of his family, but we located his nest, a bag of twigs hanging up in the shadows of the tree. My father could whistle the notes of his song so perfectly that it fooled the oriole into answering him. I learned to approximate the oriole's notes, but I could not reproduce the sweet and fluid trills my father achieved. Throughout our days in China, the oriole's song was the signal my father used to let us know he was approaching home at the end of the day. Whenever I heard it, I knew the three of us would be together again and everything was all right.

Under the syncopated rhythm of the train's progress I whisper-whistle the oriole's song to myself, and I am engulfed by an unexpected wave of longing. Am I really returning to the place where I began? Will our house be there? Will it be as I remember? The sound of the train wheels fades, and through a break in the mist of decades I see our house as it had been the last time I was there, when I was fifteen—a gracious brick bungalow with gabled windows and tiled roofs dipping up at the corners. The brick walk was bordered by my mother's flower beds, and gardenia bushes hunched glossy green under the bay windows. The camphor tree loomed out back.

I remember how the screen door to the porch slammed behind me when I ran inside. In the living room with its low ceiling and black lacquered floors, the Peking rugs looked as though they were floating on dark water. Sometimes I sat on the window seat overlooking the garden to watch a bird in the pedestaled bird bath shaking water into the sunlight, or Ho Shi-fu, the gardener, pulling up buckets at the well in the curve of the path.

In the dining room I could look out the window to the back courtyard where Chen Shi-fu, our household helper, did the laundry. ("Shi-fu " is the honorific title implying skill, used for male servants and craftsmen). Using Chinese soap like amber jelly, he scrubbed the sheets on a wooden washboard in a wooden tub and swished each one around in the milky water until it formed a fat twist he wrung out and dropped in a basket nearby on the ground. He brought the sheets down crackling dry from the line and dampened them by spraying their folded surfaces with mouthfuls of water, then ironed them with flat irons heated on a charcoal brazier, the air above it warped and wavering from the heat. When he pressed the hot metal to the damp cloth, a sudden mist of steam rose past his face, taking with it the wrinkles from the fabric.

From the dining room I move to the hall and into my bedroom, the room that framed my days. In the mornings, I woke to the sharp smell of smoke from the kitchen, where the cook was burning the toast (he burned it every morning and then scraped it until it was the right color). If it was wintertime, I lingered in bed for a few minutes, watching my breath form plumes of vapor above my face, and then jumped from under the quilt, grabbed my clothes, and ran through the dining room, blue with toast smoke, to dress in front of the living room fire.

In the evenings after I was tucked in bed, I made up songs, playing the piano on my knees, and sang myself to sleep. Sometimes I listened to my parents playing trios in the living room with Auntie Bay, who taught music at the Presbyterian Girls' School, not far from our compound. Her piano created the setting for musical conversations between my mother's violin singing high and sweet and my father's answering cello, sonorous and sure. On other nights, when my father wasn't busy, he sat on the edge of my bed and recounted the next installment in the ongoing saga of Kibutch and his kayak. He always left the Eskimo boy in some kind of peril from which I knew the intrepid lad would escape in the next installment. But if several nights passed between installments, sometimes I'd have to remind my father what had happened.

"Well, let's see," he would say. "Where were we?"

"Don't you remember?" I'd say. "The kayak had turned over, and Kibutch was swimming under the ice with the polar bear after him"—or some equally unlikely scenario.

"Oh, yes," my father would reply. "That's right. Well . . ." and he'd go on to get Kibutch out of trouble only to head him toward the next misadventure, with interesting details in between about breathing the air just under the ice, or Kibutch's sled dogs, or the blubber he ate for a snack.

Thinking of snacks, I remember how, late on winter nights, I woke to the slow tapping of the noodle vendor's wooden gourd as he walked up the Ma Lou. The sound came crisp and hollow on the cold air. If it stopped abruptly, I knew that someone who couldn't sleep was having a soothing bowl of hot noodles. After a while, the vendor's tapping resumed and gradually diminished to stillness as he walked away and I drifted back to sleep.

I look out the train window, hoping for some signs of dawn. I don't want to do any more remembering. But it is still dark and there is nothing to look at but the moving pictures in my mind. Reluctantly I watch myself move up the hall to my parents' bedroom at the front of the house.

The room is as it was that day I first heard Beethoven's Violin Concerto, shortly after my tenth birthday. My father had borrowed a 78 rpm recording and was playing the records on our wind-up Victrola on the window seat. A hint of my mother's perfume lay on the air, and sunlight streamed in the bay window looking onto the garden. I stopped just inside the door, halted by the opening measures of music. The needle was dull, but I barely noticed the buzzes and scratches as the violin entered in leaping octaves, then picked up the orchestra's statement and spun it into the upper corners of the sunlit room. I stood, caught in my mother's scent and the violin's golden thread, until it broke off to give way to the hissing of the needle going round and round at the blank center of the record. The sound merges into the rhythm of metal wheels on the railroad tracks. Now, through the train window, I discern the outline of shapes steadily swinging past my view, and I imagine another silhouette—the outline of my father standing against the sunlight coming in the bedroom window. He is looking out at the birdbath. *Daddy.*

While Dave and the girls sleep on, I sit immobile at the window, journeying into the past, which is becoming the present. The darkness outside now is lighter. A black backdrop of ancient hills moves slowly past against the predawn sky. As light seeps into the moving scene, I look up steep valleys terraced with rice paddies and softened by giant fronds of bamboo. Here and there a farmhouse of mud and thatch crouches on a ledge overlooking a misty valley or huddles at the base of a cliff like a slumbering beast in the slow dawn. As the light increases, it reveals the rose-colored soil of Hunan. *Yes,* I say to myself with a thrill of recognition. *Yes. I am here. This is more than home. This is where the world was all the time. This is where I have always been.*

CHANGSHA

The train pulls in at precisely 7:59 A.M. While Dave and the girls gather our bags, I take one last look out the window, searching for something familiar, something known. The old railway station used to be a noisy, dirty, smelly, smoky, colorful, crowded place with people running here and there through clouds of steam and shouting to each other in earthy Hunan tones, last-minute passengers pushing onto already crowded cars, and vendors reaching up with a final snack to people who leaned out the windows to pay with banknotes so worn that they could have been mistaken for scraps of old rags.

But this station seems quite new. The walls are painted a light blue and white. The platform is a gray expanse of cement crowded with quiet and soft-spoken people who look neither happy nor unhappy, neither hurried nor idle. They are dressed in gray or dark blue trousers and dingy padded jackets—sturdy young women with two pigtails over their shoulders, older women of different shapes and sizes, all with bobbed hair, and gray-faced men wearing limp cotton caps with small visors like those seen on heroic peasants and workers in revolutionary posters. There are no vendors here or anyone hanging out the train windows. The only splashes of color I notice are the bright hair ribbons on a little girl holding her father's hand and a quotation from Chairman Mao on a wall, painted in gold on a red background.

Our attendant, a young woman with the inevitable pigtails, firmly ushers us out of our compartment, and the four of us pile onto the platform lugging our bags and suitcases. A man dressed in a well-cut Mao suit steps forward and introduces himself in faintly Oxbridge English as Mr. Zhang, our guide and interpreter. He looks to be in his thirties. He does not smile, but Dave and I smile politely and say we are very glad to meet him. The girls solemnly say hello. Mr. Zhang says hello back and smiles. A few people pause to look at us, but most go on about their business without seeming to pay attention.

Mr. Zhang introduces the young woman with him as Miss Wu. Her full cheeks are red from the cold and her braids lie glossy black down the front of her padded jacket. *"Huan-yin!"* she says, meaning "welcome"—a greeting I'd never heard in the old Hunan—and nods to us with a bright

Socialist Realist smile. Then, without warning, she wrests the heaviest suitcase from Dave's grasp and staggers off with it to the exit, heedless of our protests as we hurry after her through the crowd. I meant to look around, but there is no time. I wonder fleetingly if this is the new train station reportedly built shortly after the Communist government was established in Changsha over twenty years ago. But then I realize that this building is too new for that. This station has nothing to do with my father. He did not kneel on this cement.

When we get outside, Miss Wu is standing at the door of a van parked at the gate to the station. With a theatrical flourish she motions us in, and we climb into its plush interior with seats covered in red flowered velour. It pulls away from the gate and, with an irritating blat of the horn, turns into streets I have never seen before. They are wide and clean, lined with dingy shops and dusty trees and full of moving bicycles. The people look well fed and warmly clothed, but there isn't much talking and no gesticulating or yelling. All the noise is mechanical—the incessant whirring of bicycle bells, the derisive comments of our horn, the blaring of loud speakers declaiming something momentous in Beijing Mandarin or playing revolutionary music that consists of a succession of triumphant climaxes sung by exulting choruses. We pass signs in the middle of intersections with quotations from Chairman Mao and wall posters showing bright and smiling peasants, noble factory workers with well-developed pectorals, and heroic soldiers frowning determinedly as they step forward, shoulders back and fists raised. At last we turn onto a wider boulevard and into the grounds of the Hunan Guest House. Nothing we have seen so far has anything to do with the Changsha I remember—nothing familiar, nothing known.

It is in our hotel room—a high-ceilinged chamber off an echoing hall—that I first catch a whiff of familiarity. The walls are whitewashed and the floor is lacquered black. The scent of that particular varnish is overwhelmingly right. *Yes.* For a moment I am back in our living room with its black lacquered floors. *Yes. This is it after all. I have been here.*

Once we are settled, a white-coated attendant ushers us downstairs, where we are seated at a round table in a cold and cavernous dining room, empty except for ourselves. On the table is an elegant version of a typical Hunan breakfast—*shi fan,* a very hot, totally tasteless rice gruel to be eaten with bits of pickles, fermented bean curd, tiny dried fish, salted cabbage, and boiled peanuts served on plates in the center of the table.

On a scale of one to ten, my fondness for *shi fan* is about minus five. As I wait for my portion to cool, Jenny and Dave start to consume theirs with what looks like relish. Renee, however, eyes hers dubiously. With a flash of sympathetic insight, I know she is thinking of the term she and Jenny have previously applied only to the tapioca pudding served at summer camp: "elephant snot." I tend to agree with her assessment, but, mindful of setting a good example, I say cheerily, "Oh, *shi fan*. I never liked it much, but here goes!" and slurp up a spoonful. As its mucoid sliminess slides over my tongue, again I am surprised by that ephemeral rush of familiarity. *Yes. This is it. I've done this before.* No one seems to notice my moment of suspended animation. Renee, after a brief interval of contemplation, downs her *shi fan* without comment and polishes off the communal plate of peanuts.

And so it goes throughout the day—a preview of the rest of our days in Changsha. Preoccupied with absorbing the new and unfamiliar, I am now and then touched by a sudden shock of familiarity and nostalgia which, like déjà vu, passes almost before I recognize it. The unexpected shifting back and forth between the unfamiliar and familiar is tiring and confusing—how confusing I don't realize until one evening a couple of days later. The language around us doesn't seem quite right. One evening, as we are writing in our journals before going to bed, I say to Dave: "I wish people would go back to speaking *Hunan hua* like they used to," referring to the Hunan dialect. "Then I could really understand more." Dave, who learned his Mandarin at Yale and used it for two years in Taiwan, looks surprised. "But they *are* speaking *Hunan hua*," he says. "I can hardly understand a word they say. Or what you say, for that matter."

After a moment of surprised realization, I am enormously gratified that some subliminal part of me has remained Hunanese. Over the days we are in Changsha, my confidence with the language increases until on our last day Mr. Zhang remarks, "You speak pretty good *Hunan hua*." This is praise indeed from the dispassionate Mr. Zhang. "But," he adds, "you speak with a Beijing accent."

In the brief time we have in Changsha, Dave and I try to learn as much as we can about this "new China" and how it works. We visit Chairman Mao's birthplace, communes, factories, schools, a department store, clinics and pharmacies, and day care centers. Our hosts arrange a visit to a ping-pong ball factory for the girls, but, of all the sights, the girls are most taken by specimens gleaned in the operating room of a commune hospital—a double-headed fetus and an ovarian tumor the size of a basketball, floating in alcohol, with before and after photographs of the woman who had grown it.

The day comes when we have arranged to meet old friends—old friends, that is, of my parents. I have no idea where my own friends might be, but in the States I was able to prepare a list of my parents' friends and colleagues whom I thought would most likely to be in Changsha. I didn't plan to mention the list, however, unless it seemed appropriate. When we arrived in Changsha, Mr. Zhang had asked if there was anyone I would like to see, and so it seemed all right to give him my list.

The person I have been particularly anxious to see is Mr. Ying, who had been dean of Yali. (His daughter, Rosemary, had flown that kite with me when I was four.) I remember him coming to our house almost every day to discuss school affairs with my father, sometimes with other men from Yali and sometimes alone. I remember hearing my father and him through the open door of my father's study, their voices rising and falling, punctuated sometimes with laughter and sometimes with dry sniffs from Mr. Ying, who had the habit of briefly flaring his nostrils and breathing in through his nose when he was about to make a suggestion. He was taller than my father, very erect, with high cheekbones and narrow eyes. Unlike many Chinese, his handshake was firm; he had a ready smile and laughed low and easily, like my father. In fact, he and my father came to resemble each other in some subtle way I couldn't describe, for they looked very different. But now, over the past twenty years, we haven't even known if Mr. Ying is still alive.

After a couple of days, Mr. Zhang says he has found everyone on the list—yes, even Mr. Ying. He is retired now, Mr. Zhang says, and living on the grounds of the Second Middle School. Indeed, everyone on the list lives in Changsha. We invite them to dinner at our hotel on an evening near the end of our visit.

All six of our guests are waiting for us in the lobby when we come downstairs. I recognize Mr. Ying immediately. He is standing apart from the rest, dressed in a dull blue Mao suit that hangs loosely from his shoulders. He looks a little bewildered but otherwise much the same, a little older perhaps—after all, he is in his seventies, a little stooped; he has never been stooped before—and thinner, the skin pulled even more tightly over his cheekbones than I remember. I go up to him and take his hand in both of mine. His hand is thin and dry. "Mr. Ying," I say, my voice unsteady. "Are you well?" He looks at me for a moment and then his face breaks into a smile—his radiant warm and open smile, which I had forgotten. He says, "Yes, Betty Jean. I'm quite well. And you?" When he smiles his eyes crinkle at the corners like my father's. My eyes fill with sudden tears. I let go of his hand reluctantly and introduce Dave. Then I turn to our other guests.

We walk into a private dining room where there is one large round table laden with wineglasses and plates of appetizers. Dave and I, acting out our roles as hosts, gesture at the seats and jokingly say in Chinese, it being evident that everyone there speaks excellent English, "*Suibian zuo*—please sit wherever you'd like," trying to lighten the atmosphere and introduce a note of friendly informality. It doesn't work. Each person walks soberly to a chair and sits down, politely murmuring, "Thank you."

There is a pause. I look around the table. Except for Mr. Ying, who looks the same, most of these men bear only a vague resemblance to what I remember from long ago; one or two I don't recognize at all. But, incredibly, we are all here. For a moment I feel as though my mother and father were with us also. "This is wonderful," I say impulsively. "I'm so glad you could come! I never thought something like this could happen!" Then I wonder if this last remark might be construed as criticism of the ruling regime and hasten to repair the damage. "How fortunate I am that the Chinese government so generously gave us permission to come," I say, feeling as though I am following a script in a propaganda film. But they smile back, and one of them—I'll call him Dr. Chin—says with some warmth, "We are very happy to see you." He appears to act as their spokesman. I remember my mother had told me he had been one of the men who was most outspokenly anti-American during the final months before she left Changsha ahead of the Communists' arrival. With a chill, I wondered if Dr. Chin is being very brave to speak, or perhaps he is in the safest position to make welcoming remarks. Were their smiles real or just polite?

"Well, *qing, qing, qing!*" I invite enthusiastically, indicating the center of the table, laden with appetizers. "Please!" Dave and I begin putting food on their plates. From then on, dish after delicious dish is brought in, but our guests eat mostly what we serve them—token amounts only. In the old days everyone served themselves and their neighbors and consumed large amounts of whatever it was with gusto and laughter and loud conversation.

Tonight the conversation is measured and low-key, marked by periods of silence. Our guests, even Mr. Ying, ask nothing beyond inquiring about our health, and initiate no conversation with us or with each other. However, when we ask them questions, they respond easily enough, talking about their work and what they are doing. From what they say, I gather that although there were some problems in each of their professional fields, such as not having enough trained staff or equipment, things are improving or progressing rather well.

I look around the table again, this time with that haunting sense of not quite déjà vu. These people *look* familiar, as though at one time they were real, but now, somehow, they aren't really here. As time drags on, my joy at seeing them freezes to a numb charade of careful courtesy while I search for innocuous topics of conversation that I hope will carry us safely to the end of the meal. The air seems freighted with questions, and I try to answer some I think they are unable to ask, recounting briefly our experiences since we left China. They listen with what I take to be only polite interest. On my part, I cannot ask them about the one event they all have shared and which must be occupying all our thoughts during this interminable meal, the last event that connected us: the mass meeting or rally held to denounce my father twenty-three years ago. I will call it his "trial," for lack of a better word in English. The unacknowledged occurrence of this event lies over us like a blanket, muting all discourse and deadening all emotion. In this muffled atmosphere I cannot bring myself to commit the hypocrisy of proposing the obligatory toast to "friendship between the people of the United States and the People's Republic." Nor can I salute our past friendship or "the good old days," because that would suggest nostalgia for all the Communists have fought against. So the wine remains untasted.

When our guests finally leave, I feel depleted, as though I have spent the evening hauling an immense, surreal burden. Only years later will I learn something of the burdens our guests had brought with them this evening—monstrous loads of pain and fear and sorrow, unspoken questions, and frustration at their inability to tell what happened to them or to review shared memories. Baffled at their muted response to our visit, I think perhaps they have lost interest in us, but I'm not sure of this. I have no idea of what is going on under the smooth surface of life in China presented for the approval of "foreign friends." I only know that I feel self-conscious and wary, as though I am moving through these days in Changsha on tiptoe, unaccountably careful not to disturb . . . something.

On our last day in Changsha, we visit the old Yali compound, now the campus of the Hunan Medical University. For me, this is to be the high point of our entire trip. In addition to my house, I very much want to see the school gymnasium, although I didn't tell our hosts ahead of time for fear they would find some reason to cancel our visit. I have never seen the gymnasium, for it was built after my mother and I left China, but it is as important to me as our house. Shortly after the Communist government took control of Changsha, the school administration under the new regime asked my father to request money from Yale-in-China to replace the gymnasium destroyed by the Japanese. When the new building was completed, the first event to be held in it was my father's "trial."

This visit to the old Yali compound will remain in my mind with the vividness of a watershed event. It is a cold gray day. Through the morning tangle of bicycle traffic, our van makes way with its imperious horn down streets I still don't recognize. Suddenly I see the hospital where I was born, looming over the street like a moldering brick cliff. I feel a wave of familiarity and then nothing. We pull up to the gate of the Yali compound, just as I remember it. We get off the minibus and approach the gate. The gate man smiles and bows us in (in the old Hunan, that other gate man never bowed). "*Huan yin, huan yin,* welcome," he says, and we step into another unfamiliar place. Inside the entrance where once there were open spaces, tree-lined paths, and low brick buildings with graceful roofs, now there is an unfamiliar assemblage of massive brick or cement rectangles, though one or two buildings might have been here from before. A delegation of unsmiling men meet us inside the gate and introduce themselves as officials of the Hunan Medical University.

They usher us into a conference room for the usual meeting with introductions, presentations, and tea. Dave and I ask questions and carefully note the answers in our notebooks while the girls write and draw pictures in their journals at the far end of the table. After an hour of this, our hosts start us on a tour of the compound. They tell us that instead of accommodating a few hundred Yali boys, the present campus, somewhat enlarged, now houses twelve hundred medical students being prepared to serve the People, along with eight hundred teachers and staff. I express appreciation for this progress and look around with interest.

"Where is the gymnasium that was built after Liberation?" I ask casually as we stroll down a path leading toward the center of the complex. Our hosts look at me blankly and say nothing. "The gymnasium that was built with the money my father was asked to get from Yale," I say less casually, not believing they don't know what I'm talking about. I came to China for this, and if I have to commit the solecism of mentioning my father, so be it. I stop walking and wait politely for their answer.

Finally one of the men says, "It is now a temporary dining hall. When the new one is finished, it will be used again as a gymnasium."

"Oh," I say. "That is very interesting. I would very much like to see it."

They seem reluctant as they turn back along the way we just came and onto another path going off to one side. Soon we see a one-story brick structure in the gracious style of the old Yali buildings. It looks old and tired. I try to imagine what it looked like when it was newly built in 1951. I try to imagine what happened that day on this path where we now are walking. But my mind won't cooperate. The building stays old. The stone walk before us remains quiet and empty. There is no indication, no sign, no trace of what occurred that day, no echo of the harangues, the chanted slogans, the shouting crowd, no emanation, no change of air, no slight jarring of existence as I walk down the path toward the building. If I am passing through a remnant of my father's presence as he walked between the lines of his accusers, or through a residual aura of Mr. Lao, the principal of Yali, as he stepped out from among the jeering crowd, I don't feel it. I don't feel anything.

We stop at the closed door of the building. Our guides don't offer to show us inside, so I take one picture, and after a couple of silent moments we resume the tour. As we walk on I begin to feel heavy, as though I have overeaten. Nothing seems familiar until they point out one of the old faculty houses that used to be near ours. "Oh, yes!" I say, and paste an interested smile on my face. We turn a corner, and there, amid the rubble from the unfinished dining hall, is our house.

I recognize it as one recognizes a dear friend in a body now shriveled with age and twisted by paralysis. Dwarfed by the grim buildings around it, the house stands alone with shabby dignity in a bare dirt yard that looks recently swept. Its faded walls are pockmarked and grimy and the front porch has been cemented in, but the lines of the roof, the gables, and the bay windows hint of past graciousness and comfort. I look for the camphor tree, but it isn't there. Someone explains that the house now accommodates several families and single professors. Our hosts lead us around to the side and up a flight of steps into a hall where our bathroom used to be. We turn toward the front of the house to my parents' bedroom.

The door is open. Everyone steps back so that I can go in first, and our hosts, watching my face, gesture me through as though saying, "Open sesame". They have gone to so much trouble for this moment, I know I must not disappoint them. The cold gray light of winter pours through the room's bay window. I feel the surface of my face stretch in a delighted smile. We are introduced to Comrade Wang, a chemistry professor at the university. This room is her home. I shake her hand and say how pleased I am that she lives here. It is the right thing to say. Everyone seems to relax a bit, and I begin a reminiscent tour of this strange chamber with familiar walls enclosing alien space.

Dreamlike, I hear myself move into happy commentary: "Here's where my parents' bed was," I say, "and my mother's desk!" At last our hosts are smiling, sharing my moment of joyful rediscovery. I point to the spot where the window seat used to be. "This is where my mother read to me, and my father played music on our record player." I move to the bay window overlooking the empty yard. "From here," I say, "we could look out at the . . ." I turn to Mr. Zhang. "How do you say 'birdbath'?" and I explain in English what it is. He supplies the words in Mandarin and I hear my voice chatter on.

But inwardly I am silent, for this room is really empty. This room holds nothing I have known, nothing I remember. The room that I remember is not here. That room was in another time, another place, another life.

The Yali campus from the Ma-lou (early 1930s)

Xiang-ya, the Yale-in-China hospital, showing the entrance off the Ma-lou (1974)

With Rosemary Ying and my kite (1937)

Our house in Changsha, with Ho Shi-fu carrying water to the back (1943)

Our house in Changsha, (l to r) BJ, Renee, Jenny (1974)

My parent's bedroom (1974)

The dinner party in Changsha, Mr. Ying is on my right (1974)

The 'gymnasium', site of my father's 'trial' (1974)

Front of Mao Ze-dong's house in Shaoshan (1974)
Back (l to r) Mr. Zhang (our regular guide), Dave
Front (l to r) Renee, BJ, Jenny, our local guide for Shaoshan

PART II
1936–1951

BEGINNINGS

I am being carried feet first up a mountain. Although I am only four years old, four men are bearing my sedan chair up a rocky path so steep that my feet are higher than my head. The men have refused to carry my mother and me together, so I sit alone in an open seat slung between two poles. The men lift the chair over an inward bend in the path, and I am momentarily suspended over two thousand feet of empty space. I grip the arms of the chair, not daring to move, and when the path briefly levels off, I look ahead for my mother. There she is, in her sedan chair, her violin stowed safely beside her. I twist around and look over the chair back for my father. He is climbing up the path close behind me, his cello in its grimy canvas case under his arm. "Daddy," I say. He looks up briefly and smiles before looking down again. Shung-ma, my amah (the Chinese equivalent of a nanny), in a snowy white top with a high collar and loose black trousers, is in a sedan chair behind him. She is followed by several men carrying our suitcases and boxes suspended from poles over their shoulders.

The sun is hot on the mountainside. Eventually we stop to rest in a grove of pine trees ringing with a chorus of cicadas. The men unwind the rags around their foreheads and wipe their faces as they go off to a wayside stand for refreshment. Mother and I get up and walk on the pine needles in the shade until the men return and we climb back into our chairs to go on. It takes most of the day to reach our destination.

Our destination was a house in Guling, a village situated on Lushan, a long mountain with several peaks that rises more than four thousand feet out of the flood plain of the Yangtze River in Jiangsxi Province. Lushan was constantly changing with the weather. Sometimes the mountaintop was in the sunshine, and one looked down on a floor of clouds that parted now and then to reveal loops of the river far below, glittering like a piece of tinsel dropped on the featureless plain. At other times the whole mountain was in the clouds, its cliffs and crags draped with shawls and shreds of mist. Clouds poured down steep valleys in silent torrents, and billows of white vapor boiled up to collide with them in soundless explosions that alternately hid and unveiled the dark flanks of the mountain.

In bamboo forests, thousands of slender columns loomed dimly through the fog. Streams chuckled down wooded hollows and shouted over the rocky falls of dry ravines. Pavilions with curved roofs perched on lookouts over the plains, and temples nestled in the folds of the mountain. In some temples, redolent of ancient smoke, guardian gods grimaced fiercely in the gloom; in others, Buddha sat with downcast eyes, undisturbed by the single reverberation of a deep-throated gong. Higher on the mountain pine forests replaced the bamboo, and higher still the upper contours of the mountain soared against the sky.

The cook once said that tigers—*lao fu* in the Hunan dialect—roamed the remote reaches of Lushan. I thought of a scroll painting I'd seen of a tiger stretching down a mountainside, one great paw reaching forward for a foothold on a rock. Now I saw him pacing in the sunshine down Lushan's precipitous trails and lurking in the bamboo forests at night peering out with yellow eyes.

During the first half of the Twentieth century, Westerners and wealthy Chinese came to Guling to escape the summer heat of the plains for the cool nights and morning mists on the mountain. Their houses made up a large colony in Guling for summer vacationers, with a variety of activities to provide a change of pace from the rest of the year—tennis, swimming, and ping pong tournaments; a theater group, a choir, and an amateur orchestra; hiking and fishing and temples to visit. For children my age, there was a kindergarten taught by my mother to earn money to pay for our house on the mountain.

That summer we rented our house from friends with the Presbyterian Mission who were home on furlough. It was located at one end of the colony, set into the mountainside, two stories high, with a stone front porch and large, airy rooms—big enough to accommodate the many guests who, by my mother's account, came to visit that summer.

The only guest I remember was introduced to our household by the cook shortly after we had settled in. He was a scrawny kitten we named Blackie for obvious reasons. He quickly learned that whenever the cook made loud sucking noises, there would be a bowl of rice and fish just inside the kitchen door. On this diet Blackie soon filled out, but he didn't get fat, for when he wasn't sleeping off his last meal he was expending the extra calories on pestering the household. I quickly developed the habit of giving a wide berth to likely places from which he could ambush my unsuspecting ankles; at suppertime he caromed around the dining room like a billiard ball gone berserk, and when I got ready for bed at night, he lurked in the socks at the back of my drawer, peering out with yellow eyes.

One rainy afternoon my father wrapped a small stone in a wad of paper and suspended it on a string from the center of the living room ceiling, just above Blackie's reach. Then my father crumpled some paper to make a crinkling noise—a sound the kitten couldn't resist—and we waited to see what would happen. Blackie peeked around the door frame separating the living room from the hall and hunkered down, eyes wide, tail twitching as my father swung the wad in a circle. Equally absorbed, we held our breath. Blackie wiggled his rear and catapulted into the room after the flying paper, grazing it with his paw. We cheered. He sprawled on the floor. We moaned. Shung-ma and the cook came in to watch. My father kept the paper swinging in circles, and Blackie chased it round and round, staggered off on a tangent, came about, and tottered back into the fray, finally ending up on his hind legs, spinning around until he landed on his back, paws helplessly paddling the air.

We laughed so hard we collapsed. My father was doubled up on the couch, Mother was sobbing, and I couldn't breathe for the stitch in my side. Even Shung-ma and the cook were smiling. When the kitten finally righted himself, the cook called him into the kitchen for an extra serving of fish and rice, and while Blackie replenished his resources, I crouched by his bowl and stroked his glossy fur. I loved him very much that day. In the days that followed, I begged my father to do it again, but he never did. Perhaps he knew that such laughter occurs only once in a lifetime and that nothing thereafter would quite match it.

But when I think of Guling, it is not the tiger or Blackie that first comes to mind; it is my toe. Toward the end of the summer, my parents spent a whole day at the church down at the other end of the valley, rehearsing with the orchestra for the final concert of the season featuring the *Messiah*. Shung-ma and I stayed at the Brandauers' house for the day. Freddy Brandauer and I had frequently played at each other's houses, and in my mother's kindergarten we sat next to each other and nibbled salty watermelon seeds when we thought no one was looking.

That afternoon there was a prayer meeting at the Brandauers' house. Mrs. Brandauer, at the prayer meeting, must have thought Freddy and I were with Shung-ma and the Brandauers' amah. The amahs, engaged in a cozy chat behind the kitchen, must have thought Freddy and I were with Mrs. Brandauer at the prayer meeting. We were, however, in front of the house looking for something to do. We found a small pile of dirt with some ants going in and out of a hole in the center. Freddy poked it with a stick and more ants ran out. He poked it again and again, and soon hundreds of ants were dashing around in all directions. There was a little pond nearby, neatly bordered with rocks, and in a moment of inspiration I ran over to the pond, picked up a rock, and, running back, dropped it on an unoffending ant. Freddy followed suit. Meanwhile, the prayer meeting launched into a hymn, and the happy rhythm of the refrain fueled our zeal.

Freddy and I ran back and forth faster and faster, dropping rocks and hurrying back for more without waiting to see if we had scored. Then Freddy picked up a really big rock. I paused to watch with admiration. His face turned red as he lifted it above his head. "We will come rejoicing," caroled the prayer meeting, and with arms straight, Freddy hurled the rock down at an ant heading toward my sandaled foot.

I remember the noise I made. Not the pain. The noise scared me so much that I yelled even louder. Blood welled up sluggishly from my big toe. I looked at it and shrieked. Freddy looked at it and joined in with a sympathetic bellow. The prayer meeting stopped in midrefrain. By the time Mrs. Brandauer and the amahs got to us, Freddy and I were well launched into a duet of remorse and pain that reached operatic proportions.

Mrs. Brandauer took me to a missionary doctor vacationing on the mountain, and my toe eventually recovered without the complications more common in those days before tetanus shots and antibiotics. In the aftermath, I remember being puzzled, even a little miffed, that Freddy was given as much sympathy as I. But after a while my toe became very interesting as the nail loosened and turned black. No one else had a toenail like it. I offered to show it to anyone who might be interested until it finally dropped off and we returned to Changsha.

Changsha, the city of "Long Sand," sat flatly on the west bank of the Xiang River in south-central China. There were no sand bars, long or short, to be seen, but down the river's broad expanse stretched an island that perhaps in distant times was sandy enough to give the city its name. During the first half of this century, foreign businessmen used to live with their families on the island, in houses like Victorian mansions set amid gardens and groves of orange trees, which, in turn, gave the island its present name, Orange Island. But most of the city's inhabitants, including foreign missionaries of various persuasions, lived in a maze of stone streets slimy with ancient moisture and lined with shops and markets where many of life's activities were carried out in the open.

Changsha had been the capital of Hunan Province for over two thousand years—a center of government, commerce, culture, and literature. It was also the center of a large and fertile area where much of China's rice was grown. Considering the character of its people, it is not surprising that before the Boxer Rebellion in 1900—a failed attempt to rid China of all Western influence—only one or two Westerners had crossed into Hunan from less hostile provinces. When they were finally admitted to the province, Changsha was one of the last cities to accept them. It was Hunan's daunting reputation, and the fact that the province was known to produce strong leaders, that drew the attention of alumni from Yale University, whose Christian faith challenged them to work where the need was greatest and where the effects of education might most influence China's future course. And so Yale-in-China was started, with headquarters in New Haven and in Changsha a college, a teaching hospital, and a boys' junior and senior high school called Yali.

My parents came to work at Yali in 1931. Only my father had been given an appointment—to assist with the administration of the school and teach religion. Mother came along as his wife. She soon took on the job of music teacher for the school and conducted the Yali Glee Club, but she wasn't paid for it—a state of affairs she didn't approve of. She had earned her own way teaching kindergarten, both before and after her marriage, until she came to Changsha with my father. But for a middle-class married woman to earn a separate income was seen as unusual, perhaps even aberrant, by the powers that were, if they considered at all. She was expected to live off her husband's income, and any work she did was considered an adjunct to his position. But when a single woman came out to work in China, she received a salary. Mother did not understand why marriage disqualified her from doing the same. In spite of her objections, she threw herself into her teaching at Yali with dedication and enthusiasm. But she never did accept the idea, so prevalent in missionary circles at the time, that doing good was its own reward.

My mother grew up between the two parts of her name, Winifred. Her parents already had one daughter, Dorothy, and they hoped Mother would be a boy whom they could name Fred, after her grandfather. When Mother's arrival did away with this plan, they tacked Wini- on the front and told her about it when she was old enough to understand. Thereafter she lived between Wini, the ladylike, biddable, and proper daughter of a Presbyterian minister she was expected to be, and Fred, who harbored a more adventurous, contrary, and independent nature considered in those Victorian times to be typical of boys.

In Changsha I loved to hear my parents tell about growing up in California—because that's where I really came from, even though I wasn't born there and "remembered" it only from photographs and family stories. One of my favorite stories was about the Fred side of my mother's nature. When she was five years old, she was watering the front garden of their house in Oakland, California, happily spraying the flowers, when her father, my grandfather Wintler, walked out of the house, dressed to officiate at a fancy wedding in the church next door. Mother turned the hose full on him.

"Why'd you do it?" I'd ask, hovering between delight and horror at such a deed.

"I don't know," Mother usually said. "Instinct, I guess."

"And then what happened?" I'd say, hoping she would remember.

"I don't remember," Mother would reply. "Probably I got spanked and sent to bed without my supper."

I tried to imagine Grandfather Wintler sopping wet, but the only likeness I knew was a sepia photograph of him in his late thirties, leaning a little sideways in an armchair—an unsmiling man with rimless glasses on a thin nose, wearing a black suit and vest over a white shirt with a high collar and tie.

"I got spanked often," Mother continued. "Especially after my mother died." Here Mother looked very sad. "She died when I was five, you know. She was young and very beautiful, even though she was sick with heart trouble a long time. Aunt Dorothy and I were left poor little orphans."

I pictured her mother gliding around the house in a drooping white dress, pale and beautiful, with a cloud of light brown hair, like her wedding picture, until she lay down and died with Grandfather Wintler leaning sideways in a chair by her bed. But I knew that Aunt Dorothy and Mother weren't strictly orphans. They still had their father. Besides, the things they did while growing up in Los Gatos were too interesting for me to feel sorry for them.

Los Gatos was a small town dozing in the sunshine at the base of the Santa Cruz Mountains, amid prune and apricot orchards and surrounded by hillsides of dry grass dotted with gnarled oak trees. When Mother was eight years old, the family moved from Oakland to Los Gatos, where Grandfather Wintler took a job as pastor of the town's Presbyterian church. He had recently married again, this time the eighteen-year-old daughter of their landlady in Oakland. "He must have married Hazel because he thought she would be like an older sister for us." Mother said. "But she wasn't." Here Mother closed her lips tightly as though holding back words. After a pause, she continued: "I was always getting into trouble. Not like Aunt Dorothy. She was always good." Mother insisted that Aunt Dorothy was brighter and more gifted than she was. Mother said it so often, I believed her.

The sisters did all the housework and cooking; they made their own clothes, and crawled over clods of clay in prune orchards with horse pads on their knees, harvesting the ripe fallen fruit for what Mother called "pin money." She also played the piano, gave violin lessons, and, possessing a very nice soprano voice, took the part of the princess in the senior class operetta, in which my father, who had a pleasing tenor, played the prince. She finished high school in three years so she could graduate with Aunt Dorothy, and thereafter the sisters left home as soon as possible. They entered the only two professions open to women at the time—nursing and teaching. Aunt Dorothy went to nursing school in San Francisco and Mother to what was called "normal school" in Sunnyvale to become certified as a kindergarten teacher.

If the Fred part of Mother was independent and self-sufficient as a kindergarten teacher, the Wini part yearned to be "just a married lady." To Mother, being married meant being taken care of, and being a lady meant needing a lot of help. Her appearance supported the claim, for she grew up to be a slender five feet tall with blue eyes and light brown hair. Independence and helplessness sat uncomfortably side by side in Mother's soul. Her solution was to enter enthusiastically and efficiently into the endeavors she chose and to claim helplessness when confronted with activities she had not chosen—or for which she believed she had no ability.

To live in China during the first half of the century was to find oneself in unexpected and sometimes perilous situations. Mother's response was to expect the worst. She worried even if nothing was immediately apparent to warrant anxiety. Yet when forced by events to cope with difficult circumstances, she invariably managed with courage and skill, in spite of herself. Thus she lived in precarious balance between imminent panic and unintended competence. As I grew up I saw only the panic and took the competence for granted. But no matter what state Mother was in, she always paused for beauty, especially things of ephemeral beauty such as flowers and butterflies and melodies. And she possessed a spontaneous sympathy for her students, friends, and family, which laced their lives and ours with love.

My father's innate chivalry reinforced Mother's belief that she was unable to do those things she was convinced she couldn't do. Shortly before they were married, he started to teach her how to drive her Uncle Jack's Model T. The windscreen was down, and Mother was at the wheel and doing very well until they ran into a swarm of bees. "Dwight!" she screeched, and took her hands off the wheel to fight the bees. My father, also fighting bees, grabbed for the wheel too late. The car landed in a ditch. Thereafter Mother refused to drive, and for the rest of his life my father cheerfully drove her wherever she needed to go

Cheerfulness, in fact, was the hallmark of my father's life. Or rather, optimism. It showed in the deep laugh lines etched at the corners of his eyes and his ready smile. Perhaps he inherited his hopeful outlook from his father—an ebullient and progressive professor of education at the University of California at Berkeley. His mother had tuberculosis, so they built a ranch house on a hillside above Los Gatos, where the climate was considered especially salubrious for people with that malady. My father lived a storybook life on that hillside, with Granddaddy Rugh, who came home from Berkeley on weekends, Uncle Vin, my father's older brother, who fell out of the hayloft and broke his arm, Aunt Wini, his little sister, who came along later, Buttercup, the pony the children rode bareback over the golden flanks of the hills, Bingo, their dog, who would clean your plate for you if you held it under the dinner table, and the one-rope swing tied to the branch of a hillside oak, where you could run and jump on the stick at the end of the rope and twirl way out over the valley and back. After Vin left home, my father, while still in high school, took care of his sister and his mother, who was beginning to succumb to her disease. She died during his first year at the university in Berkeley.

My father was a short and sturdy man, with dark eyes and skin permanently tanned an olive brown from growing up in sunny Los Gatos and, later, surfboarding in Hawaii, where he was often mistaken for Hawaiian. For him the world was a safe place, no matter what happened. Although he spoke of it rarely, his faith in God's love informed his life. It made him sure of the ultimate rightness of things so that he greeted new ideas with interest and new revelations of science with curiosity. He saw changing circumstances as opportunities rather than threats, and, expecting things to turn out for the best, he was usually right. His unassertive good will and unspoken confidence, along with his ready sense of humor. laced my life, and the lives of many others with a sense of warm assurance and the security of laughter.

After their marriage in 1924, my parents lived for several years in Honolulu, where my father started the student YMCA at the university. He also helped establish the first multiracial church in the islands, the Church of the Crossroads, where later he was ordained as a Congregational minister. Meanwhile, Mother set up and directed a kindergarten for over a hundred children of Japanese laborers who came to work on the pineapple plantations. But in spite of what she accomplished, she felt inferior to my father. In China, many years later, her eyes would glaze over at dinner parties when the conversation turned to world events, science, religion, or politics.

"You can talk about those things so well," she'd say to my father after the guests had left. "But I'm just no good at it."

And my father would say, "But of course you are, dear."

"No, I'm not!" she'd reply, her blue eyes bright with indignation.

This exchange occurred so often that I came to believe her. In my teens, I wondered sometimes at the unaccountability of love, which had brought two such different people together. But in spite of their differences, or perhaps because of them, an aura of old-fashioned romance shimmered through their dealings with each other. Nine years after their marriage began, I was the long-awaited achievement of their mutual regard. With my arrival, our family was complete.

My parents decided to call me Betty Jean—potentially a big mistake. But, thanks to Uncle Fritz, I escaped growing up to be the timid and tearful, pale and puffy little individual dressed in ruffles whom anyone would become if she was always called Betty Jean. When I was still a baby, Uncle Fritz Schoyer decided to call me BJ. He wasn't my real uncle. He was a "Yale Bachelor"—one of a changing roster of recent graduates from Yale University who came to teach English at Yali for two years at a time.

Somehow my new name stuck, and as I grew older, it appealed to me more than "Betty Jean", which made me feel small and proper. Betty Jean was used by my relatives and teachers and for formal occasions, but my English-speaking playmates and friends called me BJ, which made me feel casual and confident

My Mandarin Chinese name, Bo-qin (sounds almost like "baw-chin"), was given to me by a distinguished scholar who taught Chinese literature at Yali. Bo-qin was considered a very clever and auspicious name, as close to sounding like Betty Jean as Mandarin could get, yet freighted with subliminal references to classic Chinese poetry, music, and undying friendship that I didn't fully understand. The Mandarin pronunciation of my name made me feel shy and speechless, like a proper Chinese child in the presence of her elders. Chinese grown-ups called me Bo-qin. But my Chinese playmates and friends called me by the sloppy Hunan version of my name, which sounded like "Buh-jin," and with them I felt confident and comfortable. With them I was myself.

Like Mother, I grew up between my names—not only between the formal and informal versions in each language, but between the languages as well. At first I wasn't aware that my Chinese and English names embodied different vantage points from which I would view the world. When I was very young, I stepped from one point to the other without thought and felt no discontinuity. I did not realize that each language carried with it realities for which there were no words in the other—just approximations. Only gradually did I become aware of the approximations and the different realities they represented. And only then did I begin a lifelong search for the understanding that would bring the two realities together, as a pair of binoculars, each eyepiece bearing separately, brings a distant object into close and perfect focus.

The Closet and the Bomb Shelter

I've heard that it's impossible to remember your days in kindergarten. Your neural pathways aren't yet set to record such early memories, or you don't have the context in which to place the memory. Whoever said that didn't know my first kindergarten teacher. I will call her Miss Ting.

It was in Changsha the year before we went to Guling. Among the faculty children in the front hall on the first day, I was the only non-Chinese. Miss Ting's bobbed hair hung over the top of her head like a black helmet, and she seemed very tall in her blue cotton gown with its stand-up collar as she introduced us to our surroundings. She had already shown us the hooks where we were to hang our aprons and the basin where we were to wash our hands. Now she pointed to a heavy wooden door just outside the entrance to the kindergarten room. "Do you know what this is?" she asked. The door was painted green, secured with a hasp and a thick stick through a heavy metal loop. I was about to tell her it was a door, but she went on without waiting for an answer. "This is the closet," she said, "with a tiger inside. *Lao fu*," she said again in the Hunan dialect. "Tiger."

We stared at the door in silence. Nothing stirred behind it. I imagined the tiger standing there, like the one in an animal book I'd seen, his eyes glowing yellow in the dark. I wondered how she fed him. "Anyone who doesn't pay attention," she said slowly, "anyone who doesn't obey, anyone who is bad"—she paused again—"will go in the closet with the tiger. Do you understand?" After a moment a few of us nodded. "Say 'Yes, Miss Ting,'" she ordered .

"Yes, Miss Ting," we echoed raggedly.

"Together, once more!" she said.

"Yes, Miss Ting!" we answered in unison.

"Louder." Her voice rang out with bell-like intonation. "Say 'Yes, Miss Ting.' Again!"

"Yes, Miss Ting," we shouted, our tones matching hers exactly.

"Good!" she exclaimed. "Now we start."

In our new white aprons we followed her, like a covey of juvenile pigeons, into the room and sat down where she told us. I settled myself firmly on my chair. This was *my* seat. I looked around. Everything looked grown-up and interesting. This was *my* school.

In the days that followed I didn't tell my parents about the tiger. None of my fellow kindergartners seemed to think it worth mentioning. Perhaps we thought it was standard equipment for kindergartens. In any case, I found it easy to get along in Miss Ting's kindergarten. Most of us did. All we had to do was to pay attention, do exactly as she said, and give wide berth to the green door in the hall.

I was enthusiastic about everything. We learned songs about the sun getting up in the morning and going to bed at night, and the moon hanging up in the sky—all with appropriate gestures. We learned dances featuring flowers and butterflies and rain, as one does in Chinese kindergartens. We played games like drop the handkerchief and blindman's buff. We pasted and folded paper. With our tablemates, we constructed towns of little wooden blocks painted like parts of buildings. And we yelled "Yes, Miss Ting!" in unison, several times a morning. Sometimes on the way to wash my hands in the hall, I stopped at a safe distance in front of the green door and listened for the tiger. But he was very quiet.

The cold weather came. The temperature rarely went down to freezing in Changsha, but the moisture in the air was bone-chilling and held the vapor of one's breath momentarily intact before it dissipated. All of us looked fatter, because we wore layers of sweaters and knitted leggings or padded cotton jackets and pants under our aprons. A coal stove heated one end of the room, but at my table our breath hung in front of our faces. We started to make decorations for Christmas, our chilled fingers fumbling with scissors, shiny paper colored on one side, and paste made of flour and water.

One day we were busily working with paper and paste when suddenly I heard Miss Ting shout. I looked up to see her grab the arm of a boy across the room. He screamed as she pulled him away from the table. Paralyzed, we watched them. Miss Ting dragged the boy to the hall with him shrieking and struggling, his face red and shiny with mucus and tears. She flung open the green door, pushed him into the closet, slammed the door shut, and with a flourish thrust the stick through the metal loop. Behind the door we heard thumps and banging and muffled cries of anguish.

The other children remained transfixed, but I screamed. And screamed again. People rushed into the hall to see what was happening. I continued to scream. I refused to look when they opened the green door to show me there was no tiger in the closet. I continued screaming when they tried to show me the boy was unhurt. Someone ran all the way to the music building to get my mother. When she arrived, she knelt on the floor and held me tightly, rocking back and forth. In the warmth of her familiar presence, I was finally able to calm down enough to hear her. "It's all right," she was saying. "There's no tiger, dear. No one is hurt. It's all right. There's only wood in the closet. Only wood. No tiger. It's all right; it's all right."

So far as I know, no one mentioned the tiger after that day. Considering the comparative composure of my fellow kindergartners, my behavior must have been considered an aberration—perhaps an *American* aberration? To some, my reaction might even have seemed funny. In the end, it was just one of those things that happens and then is past—a very Chinese point of view. Life—more specifically, kindergarten—must go on. And though the tiger in the closet was to come back to me at unexpected times in the future, I must have absorbed some of my playmates' equanimity, for I am told I returned to Miss Ting's kindergarten in the new year and, to all reports, enjoyed it. Perhaps my parents sent me back on the theory of getting back on the horse that threw you. Although I don't remember what it was like being back in Miss Ting's class, I suspect that, like my more practiced Chinese friends, I learned to forget (or was it suppress?) horror and found kindergarten without the tiger much the same as when he had been standard equipment.

We children in the Yali compound lived and played within the shelter of its walls, totally unaware of the impending chaos in the outside world. My playmates were a mixed group, and I played with each in whatever language was most useful. Among my non-Chinese playmates were Freddy Brandauer, of rock-dropping fame, and Peggy Greene, whose father was the physician who had officiated at my birth. She gave me a pair of white mice in a cage for my birthday, starting me on a long career of close association with an assortment of animals throughout my growing-up years—an assortment my parents may have thought would make up for the baby brother or sister I periodically requested but never got. Among these sibling substitutes were several cats, a dog, two lovebirds, an owl, several turtles, a tortoise, ducklings, rabbits, guppies, goldfish, and tadpoles. Peggy Greene's mice lived messily and multiplied mightily and left me with a lifelong fondness for their cozy mouse smell.

Teddy Heinrichsohn also came to play at my house from the mansion where he lived on Orange Island. He was always neatly dressed in shorts and shirt in summer and a suit with a vest and tie in the cooler months. With Teddy I spoke English, though he also spoke German and Chinese, his father being German and his mother Chinese. At the Shanghai American School, which we both attended ten years later, Teddy was tall and played football, but in those early years in Changsha, he was slight with straight black hair and brown almond eyes, and in spite of his clothes he was very agile on my jungle gym. I went to his house once, and saw the kennels, where his father bred German shepherds and cocker spaniels as a hobby.

On most days I played with faculty children who lived in nearby houses much like ours. The school carpenter had built a jungle gym in our front yard, and there we invented elaborate routes to the top, where we swung by our knees until the upside-down trees made us dizzy. We took turns riding and pulling a little rickshaw on the soccer field and held pretend tea parties with my set of china doll dishes. At one memorable tea party Rosemary Ying and I consumed an undetermined number of pebbles from my father's game of Go, which resulted in an outing to the hospital X-ray department.

Also among my playmates in those early days was Jiang You-qin, whose father was the principal of the Presbyterian Girls' School near the Yali campus. Half a century later, not far from where we once had climbed on the jungle gym, she and I were to stand together on a stage in the old gymnasium built with the funds my father had obtained from Yale-in-China, while she described to me what happened at my father's "trial." As a student at the girls' school, she had been required to attend and had stood among the hundreds who had shouted at him and applauded as his friends denounced him.

The year before we went to Guling, 1936, the Japanese tightened their hold on Manchuria. Their more moderate leaders in Japan had been assassinated, leaving unrestricted power in the hands of those intent on expanding over East Asia. Weakened by competing warlords and the conflict between Chiang Kai-shek's Nationalists and Mao Ze-dong's Communists, the Chinese struggled to resist the Japanese while trying to bring their vast and antique nation into the twentieth century.

The music building, where Mother taught her classes that autumn, was a one-room structure of brown timbers and white plaster beyond the camphor tree outside my window. At nap time I could hear the Yali Glee Club rehearsing for the fall concert. The students' voices sounded strong and full in happy harmony through the open windows of the little building:

> *Home, home on the range,*
> *where the deer and the antelope play . . .*

It may seem incongruous that young Chinese men in the heart of that ancient land were singing a nostalgic song celebrating the Old West in America when all the news was uniformly disheartening and threats of war and disaster loomed like thunderheads over the horizon. But they sang with a defiant gaiety and resonance that made the song their own. Perhaps in that darkening time the words had a special appeal:

> *Where seldom is heard*
> *a discouraging word,*
> *and the skies are not cloudy all day.*

With the onset of cold weather, the windows of the music building were closed and the Yali students started practicing Christmas carols. I don't know how many students were Christian, but a good proportion of them were not. They sang the Christmas songs anyway with enthusiasm and feeling. My first memory of Christmas is of Yali boys singing carols to the accompaniment of a portable pedal organ late on Christmas Eve. Bundled in a blanket, I sat in the bay window of the living room with my parents and looked out to the end of our walk, where the carolers stood around the organ and sang by the light of a lantern. Ours was the last house on their route. When they finished singing, they trooped up the steps and into our living room, where we had tea and cookies waiting for them. They loosened their jackets and warmed their hands at the fireplace. They admired our prickly Christmas tree decorated with my paper chains and the precious Christmas balls we had unpacked from a box stored in the attic. Mother played the piano and we sang more Christmas carols, ending with "Silent Night" sung softly in Mandarin. When they left, the students called back in Hunanese from our front walk, "*Sen-dan kuai-lo,* Happy Christmas!"

"*Sen-dan kuai-lo,*" we replied from the door. And so, for us in Changsha, the year ended peacefully—the last year before the war.

In July 1937, while we were in Guling, the Japanese fired on Chinese troops doing training maneuvers outside Peking. That was the beginning of all-out war between China and Japan. By the end of the month the Japanese had taken Peking, and in August they bombed Shanghai. When we returned to Changsha from Guling, they were bombing further and further south and west into China. At Yali, dugouts were tunneled into the sides of the hill on which the chapel stood. These were the bomb shelters for the students and staff and whoever was nearby when the air raid siren sounded. My father had a bomb shelter built in our basement—a reinforced room large enough to accommodate several families, with sandbags and extra-strong beams. I'd always loved our cool basement with its heavy damp smell, and now I waited eagerly for the siren to go off again so we could try out our new room.

The day soon came we heard the siren raise its warning voice in the distance. It was strange to drop what I was doing without putting it away and head straight for the basement stairs. The cook with his family went ahead of us, followed by Ho Shi-fu, the gardener, and Chen Shi-fu, the household helper. We had just picked up our stools to follow when our neighbors started to come into the house through the back and front doors—teachers, their wives and children, their servants and families, and whoever happened to be stopping by at the time. They nodded and smiled their thanks when we pointed the way into the shadowed basement, lit by a single kerosene lamp hung from the ceiling. They piled good-naturedly into the shelter, some sitting on stools they had brought and others standing. Finally we came down to join them, but we couldn't get in the room without causing a crisis of compression. Some neighbors offered to come out, but my mother and father wouldn't hear of it. After much polite protesting back and forth, we placed our stools just outside the door, planning to squeeze in at the last minute if necessary. The lamp was put out and we sat in the dark until the all-clear sounded. Then my father lit the lamp and we picked up our stools to stand aside for our neighbors to file out of the room and up the steps into daylight.

In November the Japanese committed the infamous "rape of Nanking" and bombed further inland while the Chinese forces crumbled in front of them. On November 24 the first bombs fell on Changsha, deep in the city, quite far from Yali. I don't remember that bombing. Neither do I remember ever getting to sit inside our bomb shelter.

The fighting spread across China so rapidly that by December the American consulate advised all American women and children to leave the country. Mother wanted to stay, but, feeling it would be safer for me, my parents decided we should go. Mother wouldn't leave without my father, so he came, too, planning to return to Changsha after Mother and I were settled somewhere outside China. We left Changsha the day before Christmas and eventually arrived in Honolulu, where we lived in a house up Manoa Valley with an avocado tree in the front yard. I attended another kindergarten, where I fell in love with the teacher, Mrs. Ford, and learned how to tie my shoelaces. After six months Mother and I sailed to California to stay with Aunt Dorothy and her family, and my father returned to China to help evacuate Yali from Changsha into the western mountains of Hunan, out of reach, we hoped, from the Japanese.

The night before Mother and I left Honolulu, I woke up to a moaning sound in the next room. As I came awake I realized it was Mother crying. Then I heard the murmur of my father's voice. I knew what he was saying, because I'd heard him say it before. "It will be all right. Dearest, please don't feel this way. We'll be fine. Sooner than you know, we'll be together again." But the moaning continued.

Perhaps it was then, with the magical logic of cavemen and children, I made a connection between my mother's worry and my father's reassurance. They always went together: Mother worried, then Daddy reassured, therefore things turned out all right. When I was old enough to disconnect the parts of this proposition, its essence had taken hold, and in times of uncertainty it became a magical technique for survival, a kind of mental bomb shelter: *If I could think ahead of the bad things that might happen, then they wouldn't occur and we'd be safe, just as Daddy promised.*

BACK HOME IN CALIFORNIA

Aunt Dorothy was a superb housekeeper. She had given up nursing when she married Uncle Ed because he didn't want her to work, even though she'd been in charge of five operating theaters at the University of California Hospital. Thereafter she exercised her formidable administrative talents and expended her nursing zeal on her house and her family—including Mother and me when we came from Honolulu to live with them.

Aunt Dorothy and Uncle Ed with my cousins, Phyllis and Bob, lived in a house on Fremont Street, a quiet suburban street lined with pepper trees in San Mateo, on the peninsula south of San Francisco. Things at their house seemed brand-new and at the same time inevitable, as if they had always been there, from the sprinklers in the lawn and orange poppies blooming against the stucco of the house to the bouncy beds with soft pillows and snowy sheets tucked in with folded corners and Sunday dinners with roast lamb and potatoes, mint jelly, green beans, hot rolls with butter, pear salad with mayonnaise on a crisp lettuce leaf, cake for dessert, and best of all, a glass of cold milk so rich I had to scrub it off my upper lip.

Mother always said it was Aunt Dorothy who wanted to travel and have adventures. "I was the one who wanted to settle down and be a housewife," Mother said. "And look what happened. I married Daddy and had to go *all* the way to China! Dorothy was the one who got to stay home and keep house!" Mother made it sound as though keeping house was much the preferable thing to do, and after seeing Aunt Dorothy work, I agreed. On weekdays she and I were the only ones at home; Mother was at San Francisco State working on her bachelor's degree, Uncle Ed was also in San Francisco working for the telephone company, and Phyllis and Bob were at school. While they were away, I trailed Aunt Dorothy around the house as she went about her daily tasks.

In her neat cotton dress covered by a freshly laundered apron, Aunt Dorothy did everything it took three servants to do at our house in Changsha. The results were the same as we had in Changsha, but she did everything differently. She kept everything very clean—but with a vacuum cleaner, not the fine grass broom and damp mop Chen Shi-fu used at our house, She cooked on a gas stove, where the heat came on at once, not like the wood-burning iron range that dominated our kitchen in Changsha. She sewed dresses and suits and coats herself on her electric sewing machine at home rather than having a tailor come from the Tailors' Street to measure and then bring back his creations for several fittings. She went shopping in a car to the grocery, instead of walking to the street market with a basket over her arm as our cook did, to bargain with vendors over the best buy for fruit, greens, fish, and slabs of meat from the butcher. She watered the garden with a hose, instead of doling the water out with a dipper from a bucket filled at the well, and she raised bantam chickens in the backyard for their eggs—small birds little resembling the "real" chickens strutting round our back courtyard until killed by our cook for dinner.

She did the laundry in an electric washing machine with a dasher that jerked back and forth until she stopped it with a lever on the side of the tub. Then she pulled out the dripping clothes one by one to be flattened through an electric wringer into a laundry basket placed strategically on the floor. When she brought in the laundry from the backyard, I buried my face in the folds of the sheets to inhale the sweet scent of sunshine deep into my chest. She sprinkled them with drops of water from her fingers and rolled them up to get damp while she did something else. I asked her why she didn't spray them with water from her mouth, like Chen Shi-fu, but she said she was used to doing it this way. Later, when she decided the sheets were ready, I watched her operate the clanking electric mangle Uncle Ed had bought for her. With a twist of her wrists she guided the folded edge of a wrinkled sheet into the mangle, and as the smooth cloth rolled out stiff and white from the bottom, clouds of steam hissed up past her face, taking the wrinkles from the fabric with them.

Phyllis was my playmate. Although she was three years older, she didn't seem to mind spending time with me when she got home from school. After a snack, we might hunt for eggs in the chicken coop or hold a tea party with painted tin doll dishes in a playhouse built by Uncle Ed in the backyard. For a while we managed a bug hospital on a shelf in the playhouse, where we lodged a baby snail in the center of a toy truck tire, tenderly deposited grasshoppers in mason jars stuffed with grass, and made worms comfortable in matchboxes filled with dirt.

I didn't see much of Bob, who was in high school. He was quiet like Uncle Ed and had a lopsided grin. When he came home from school, he went directly to an enclosed porch at the front of the house, where he worked on his model airplanes. On the few occasions I saw him work, I stood on my toes at his worktable and watched him carefully cut and glue pieces of balsa wood together and hold them in place until they stayed on their own. While he waited, I sniffed the sharp fragrance of the glue, gazed up at his aircraft, asked him what they were, and immediately forgot their names, full of letters and numbers—delicate replicas of biplanes and the new single-wing fighters and bombers, built to scale from kits and precisely painted with colored enamels. They floated below the ceiling on almost invisible threads, a miniature squadron heading for an unknown destination.

After supper Aunt Dorothy and Phyllis and I did the dishes. Mother went to her room to do schoolwork, and Uncle Ed sat in the living room to read the paper. Sometimes he went to his workshop if he was refinishing a bureau or building more shelves for the garage or fixing a broken chair or bicycle. His workshop was as neat and clean as Aunt Dorothy's kitchen. Uncle Ed didn't say much, even when there were guests for dinner. His most frequent remark was "Is that so?" delivered so quietly that only many years later did I catch the irony with which he underlined it. But when he gave an opinion, everyone listened, and when he fixed something, you knew it would work forever.

On weekends we went on day trips in Uncle Ed's Ford, down to Los Gatos, where Mother and Daddy grew up, and further south to Pacific Grove on the coast near Monterey, where Aunt Wini, my father's sister, lived with my cousins Jean, younger than I, and Jerry, who was my age. Uncle Oxy, their father, usually wasn't home because he was in the navy. Their life was so different—not only from ours in Changsha, but also from how we lived on Fremont Street—that it was like being in another country. They lived on a narrow dirt street with the fairy-tale name of Mermaid Avenue, near the waterfront on Monterey Bay. Aunt Wini smoked and didn't seem to mind if the breakfast dishes piled up in the sink or if Jean and Jerry ran around in bare feet. They had smooth skin brown from the sun and large brown eyes like Aunt Wini and Daddy; Jean wore sunsuits, and Jerry didn't wear a shirt at all and could swim like a fish.

One weekend we drove to Mount Hermon in the Santa Cruz Mountains, where Mother and Aunt Dorothy used to go camping on summer vacations when they were girls. Their father and stepmother both liked to fish, so they camped by streams where the sunlight slanted down through the redwoods like shafts of light in a cathedral. Aunt Dorothy didn't fish; she much preferred reading a book. But Mother became expert at casting a fly. She learned to know where a hungry fish would most likely be lurking in an eddy, and, flicking her line in a soaring arc over the water, she could land her fly ever so gently just above his nose. Fishing, Mother admitted, was one of the few things she could do better than Daddy.

It was at Mount Hermon where the events took place that I always thought of as "the fish story" after my parents first told it to me in Changsha. It was a story of mythic dimensions resonating with themes peculiar to our immediate family and also to our place in the wider family constellation in America, separated as we were in China. When I was five, I didn't recognize that this was its true appeal. I never tired of hearing it because each time I hoped that, magically, the ending would change.

My mother and father spent their honeymoon at Mount Hermon, and the story always opened with the information that they fished for their supper every evening, when the trout were rising. On the last day they were there, they went out for a walk without their fishing gear and found themselves strolling along the bank of a stream.

"We came to a place where there was a little pool," my father said, "with the bank hanging over it right near where we were walking—just the place for a fish to wait for a bug to drop in the water. So we looked very carefully, and you know what?" Here his voice dropped to a whisper, and I would hunch my shoulders in an expectant crouch. "Right there in the shadow of the bank was the biggest fish you ever saw, just resting in the water nice and easy, waiting for a bug, his tail going back and forth, back and forth like that," and my father waved his hand slowly back and forth. I could see the fish just as he described it.

Mother took up her side of the story "I said, 'Look, Dwight!'" she said softly, then, in her regular voice, "and the next thing I knew, Daddy had jumped in the pool with a huge splash and came out again with that fish in his bare hands. He still had his camera around his neck." Here she usually smiled, but I didn't, because that was the most significant part of the story.

My father shook his head in happy wonder. "That fish was the granddaddy of all trout, too smart to be fooled by anyone's cast and fly. Which is why he grew so big. We knew the family back in Los Gatos would never believe us, so we took a picture of Mother standing on a rock holding the fish in her hand. Then we went back to our cabin and ate it for supper."

I could see Mother standing on a rock in the middle of the stream, the granddaddy of all trout hanging from her hand, and Daddy on the bank, looking down into his reflex camera, its strap still looped around his neck.

Mother was right. The next day when they returned to Los Gatos, the family didn't believe them. When Uncle Vin heard the story he said, "Oh, yeah?"

"Just you wait," my mother and father said. "We have the picture to prove it!" And when the photograph was developed, sure enough, Mother was there on the rock with her arm held out. But where the fish was supposed to be was just a spot where water had splashed on the lens.

Each time they came to this part, I couldn't believe they'd had such bad luck. If only they'd taken the fish home the next day instead of eating it!

"Was the spot *exactly* where the fish was?" I'd ask.

"Exactly," my father would say.

"And what did Uncle Vin say?"

"He said, 'A likely story!'" and my father would laugh. But I knew the story was true, and my face got hot with suppressed fury. I wanted to shake Uncle Vin until he said he was sorry and of course it was true.

On our visit to Mount Hermon with Aunt Dorothy and Uncle Ed, I asked to see the famous place where Daddy caught the fish with his bare hands, but Mother didn't think she could find it. I stood on a footbridge and looked down at the sun-dappled stream, remembering as though I'd been there how it had happened. The stream felt familiar, just as I'd imagined it in Changsha, and I looked for a pool in the shadow of the bank. But here I didn't see any pool. I wanted very much to see it. For if I could have seen it, Changsha and California would come together, like two parts of a whole, connected at last by a story that was true in both places.

Sometimes on Saturdays we drove across the Bay Bridge to Berkeley, where Granddaddy Rugh, Daddy's father, who was a professor at the university, lived with his second wife, Sarah, in a stucco bungalow, damp-smelling and dark with wood-paneled walls and lots of books. After the World's Fair opened, we visited Treasure Island several times and wandered through a surfeit of wonders—but later I remembered only a very tall tower and billowing tufts of cotton candy that magically diminished to just a taste in my mouth. More memorable were shopping trips to the most magnificent department store in San Francisco, the Emporium, where we glided up and down through warm perfumed air on clacking escalators with wooden treads, and looked down on glittering glass counters amid acres of aisles populated with women wearing hats and gloves and high heels.

Once, when we were in San Francisco, we drove past the Mission District, where Aunt Dorothy and Mother had lived with relatives on a hill near Twin Peaks. Their mother had just died, and with no one at home to take care of them, they stayed in San Francisco while Grandfather Wintler remained with his church in Oakland, across the bay. Mother was just my age, five going on six. I tried to imagine what it was like that April morning when she and Aunt Dorothy were awakened by a monstrous roaring noise like a hundred freight trains rushing toward the house.

Their bed started to jiggle. The noise grew louder and louder and the bed jerked back and forth, harder and harder, until it ended up in the middle of the room under the gaslight fixture, which was twisting around like a snake dangling from the ceiling. The walls shivered, and cracks spread over the plaster like giant spiderwebs. They heard crashes and tinkles all through the house and thumps on the roof as the chimney fell down and bricks showered past the window. Then the freight trains roared away and the shaking slowed to a stop. "And then," Mother said, "it was very, very quiet."

"Did you cry?" I wanted to know.

"I don't remember," Mother said. "Aunt Dorothy and I just hung on to each other till Uncle Fred came and told us to get dressed and go outside, because there might be another quake. He didn't know if the house would be safe."

The family camped outside in the yard for three days, sleeping on mattresses under an acacia tree near the street. For meals they cooked canned food saved from the larder on a stove they built with bricks from the chimney. Over the iron fence, they watched the fires start down in the city and grow into one huge conflagration. Every day Mother and Aunt Dorothy were sent to the top of the street to watch the fire's progress and warn the grown-ups if it got to a certain point.

On the morning of the third day, the wind had shifted and the fires slowed down. From their station the girls just made out a tall man a block away, climbing the steep street toward them. As he came closer, they saw through the smoke that it was Grandfather Wintler.

"What did you do?" I asked, finding it hard to swallow.

"We ran down the street as fast as we could, and he hugged us both off our feet."

Grandfather Wintler had come as soon as he could; he had taken one of the first ferries across the bay and walked all the way up from the end of Market Street, around burning sections of the city, to their neighborhood.

For the hike back to the ferry, the girls were given two oranges from the family's meager food supply, and they set out. Block after block they trudged down Market Street, taking turns riding on Grandfather Wintler's shoulders, past smoldering ruins and people poking about in the rubble. After a while they got thirsty, but Grandfather Wintler told them to save their oranges for later. When Mother told me the story in Changsha, I saw her orange as the only bit of color in an otherwise gray and colorless scene. I felt it in the palm of my hand, its smooth pebbled skin pushing against my fingers, as if ready to burst with sweet, tangy juice.

After a long time they came to a woman sitting on the curb with two little girls. They had nothing with them but the clothes they were wearing. Grandfather Wintler stopped. "Daughters," he said, "don't you think it would be good to give them your oranges? It looks like they need them more than you do." So Mother and Aunt Dorothy, each already well equipped with a Presbyterian conscience, handed over their precious fruit. "But not very happily, I'm afraid," Mother always said. "That was the hardest thing I've ever done. There was nothing I wanted more than that orange!" and she would end the story leaving me with my hand empty and the lifelong impression that although it may be better to give than to receive, it is also likely to be unrewarding.

In November the news came that Changsha had been burned by Chinese troops in advance of the invading Japanese. Unwarned, thousands of people were burned to death, but the word from the head office in New Haven was that all the Yale-in-China property escaped the fire. There was no news of my father, but at the beginning of December Mother received a telegram from a friend in Honolulu who had heard a message on his shortwave radio that my father was safe and well, and sent his love. Fortunately, Yali with its students and faculty had already moved into the western mountains of Hunan. I'd heard mention of a fire in Changsha, but nobody seemed to make much of it and it never occurred to me that my father might be in danger. I'd been oblivious to Mother's anxiety. Christmas was coming, and I could think of little else.

One weekend before Christmas we drove to the Emporium in San Francisco to see Santa Claus. I sat speechless on his knee while he talked into my face, his breath smelling like cough medicine. A week or so later, I developed a fever and cough. Aunt Dorothy put me to bed and made a mustard plaster out of a piece of old sheet smeared with a warm mush of hot cooked mustard that looked like yellow vomit and smelled worse. She put it on my chest, secured it with a towel and a large safety pin, and said it would "loosen my chest." Mother sat by my bed, stroking my hair and giving me water to sip through a bent glass straw. After a while Aunt Dorothy removed the plaster, but for the rest of that Christmas Eve, its harsh smell lingered, scouring my sinuses and reaming out my breathing tubes. On Christmas morning the cough was gone, but on my chest where the plaster had been was a patch of measles. I spent Christmas day in the darkened room, dozing fitfully and sipping fruit juice while the measles spread. Aunt Dorothy said I'd caught them from Santa Claus, who had looked a little red in the face, she thought. Now, with the benefit of wider experience than Aunt Dorothy, I think I must have caught the measles from someone else, because it was not measles that made Santa Claus' nose bright red nor was it cough medicine that had left its signature on his breath.

By New Year's Eve I felt much better and took an interest again in what was going on. It was then that I faced for the first time the shock of time's passage. It occurred to me that if the new year was going to be 1939, 1938 would be unaccounted for. What happened to it? I wondered. Mother said that 1938 would just be gone. Where did it go? Nowhere, she said. It just went. When would it come back? It wouldn't, she said.

"You mean it'll be gone forever?"

"That's right, dear. Each year is new. That's what 'New Year' means."

The idea was like a bombshell. This last precious year with everything in it would be gone forever. Things would never be the same. I'd assumed that years returned like my playmates in Changsha, who came back after they'd been away, or like us, always returning to our house at Yali, like closing a circle. But now everything seemed slippery. Here and now were sliding away, and ahead loomed a yawning vacancy where nothing was familiar or known. Yet everyone seemed very calm about it. No one else seemed to share my sense of loss or to be afraid of the coming unknown. Perhaps it was so terrible that no one talked about it—a secret everyone knew and no one mentioned. Or perhaps it was so ordinary that it wasn't worth talking about. In any case, I felt sorry for 1938; it would just go away and be forgotten. All that I'd done in it would go away, too, and I would never be the same again or do the same things.

In the morning it was 1939; nothing was different, and neither was I. But things did change. On June 30 Mother and I left on the *President Coolidge* for Hong Kong. From there we would go to Shanghai. With the fighting in China getting worse, Mother wanted to be closer to my father, and Shanghai was considered safe, since large parts of that city were controlled by Western powers, which were officially neutral in the conflict between China and Japan. Mother was to teach kindergarten at the Shanghai American School, and I was to enter first grade and learn, at last, how to read.

Mother and I leaned on the rail of the second-class deck of the *President Coolidge* and looked down at Aunt Dorothy and Uncle Ed, with Phyllis and Bob on the dock far below. I held one end of a colored paper streamer, which sagged down to where Phyllis held the other end. Now and then we waved to each other. Between the ship and the dock grew a web of colored streamers with people holding on to the ends and shouting last-minute comments and messages. Suddenly the air vibrated with an enormous dark sound as the ship's horn bellowed once and again. Everyone waved faster, the web of streamers grew tighter, and the people on the dock gradually changed position without moving. We were pulling away, imperceptibly at first, then faster, until the last streamers snapped and the web slumped in a tangled mass of color onto the widening strip of water. Aunt Dorothy, Uncle Ed, Phyllis, and Bob were four small figures at the edge of the pier. Then they slipped out of sight and out of reality. But I knew they would come to life once more when I came back home to California.

THE EAST RIVER

We returned to Hunan in the summer of 1940, when I was seven years old. For part of the way, we journeyed up the East River in a cargo junk. Through a flat landscape under an immense sky, the boat moved imperceptibly up the back of the river, occasionally passing a walled town perched on the distant bank. It took eighteen days to travel two hundred miles. The trip stands alone as a time unrelated to the rest of my life, complete in itself, a world apart. Years have gone by without my thinking of it, yet I recall it with the clarity of a scene suspended in a glass paperweight.

My mother and I had spent the last year at the Shanghai American School, where I was in first grade and Mother taught kindergarten. My father had been in Hunan two years, helping Yali and part of the hospital move from Changsha to the town of Yuanling, at the base of the mountains in western Hunan, out of the way of the Japanese. Now my parents decided the three of us should be together again despite the spreading blight of war.

Except for the precipitous Burma Road over the southern extension of the Himalayas—a passage bombed constantly by the Japanese—the only open route into China was up the East River. More direct routes to Hunan were blocked by fighting, and Japanese troops occupied the major cities on the way to Changsha. Transportation was uncertain, and bandits in the countryside preyed on everyone, except perhaps the Japanese. But if we traveled on the East River, we would stay in what was called "Free China," avoiding the Japanese and, with luck, the bandits as well.

When school ended, my father joined us in Shanghai to buy supplies for Yali and the hospital while Mother stocked up on provisions for our family to last the two years we planned to be in Yuanling. To reach our destination, we were to go up the East River about two hundred miles to a town called Longchuan, from which point we hoped to travel by truck over three mountain ranges to Shaoguan, near the Hunan border, then by train to Henyang, and finally another boat to Changsha. After staying in Changsha a few weeks, we were to go up the Xiang River to the great Dong Ting Lake, and thence up the Yuan River to Yuanling—about five hundred miles in all.

We left Shanghai in late August. I had a new straw hat with a broad brim, a new wicker suitcase, and my books. I also had Little Bear, a toy koala that had been given me the year before by an Australian nurse on the ship going to Shanghai. Little Bear had kangaroo fur; his legs were movable and his head turned; he had a flat black nose, beady eyes, and round upright ears. He was my constant companion.

We were not the only passengers on the junk. Miss Ling, a nurse, was going to Changsha to marry a doctor in our hospital. She was very quiet. Two missionaries were on board as well—Mr. Aldecott and Mr. Beamer, I will call them. Mr. Aldecott owned a pair of bushy eyebrows and disapproved of things in general. Mr. Beamer, a rotund young man, was the more memorable of the two because one night, while boarding the boat, he fell into the water with a mammoth splash. In addition, he was the proud possessor of an air mattress—something I had never seen before. Mr. Aldecott and Mr. Beamer espoused a version of Christianity much stricter than ours. Two Yale Bachelors, on their way to teach English at Yali, made up the rest of our contingent. Their version of Christianity was not at all strict. They joked a lot and didn't seem to disapprove of anything. A mountain of crates and boxes went with us—fifty-eight in all, for the school and hospital. Finally, there were our own suitcases, boxes, and trunks.

From Shanghai we took a ship to Hong Kong and from there a launch that deposited us on a beach on the China coast north of Hong Kong. According to my mother, it was a two-and-a-half-hour walk from the beach to the nearest town, where we were to spend the night. Sweating men with rags tied around their heads carried our baggage, some hauling carts piled with the bigger boxes and trunks, others with smaller boxes and suitcases suspended from either end of a pole over the shoulder. With my new hat low on my forehead for shade, I trudged between my parents, clutching Little Bear with one arm and waving away the bloated flies that tried to land on my face to sip the sweat. Sometimes my father carried me on his shoulders. Every now and then we stopped for a swallow of warm water from his canteen. Mother told me years later that she and my father managed to distract me whenever we passed a dead coolie lying by the roadside. Each lay with the load he'd been carrying when he dropped, untouched by passersby, for it was the beginning of the cholera season. Thanks to their distraction, I never saw what cholera did to people. I only knew it as the reason for the unwelcome vaccinations I had to have each year—"cholera shots," we called them.

The following day Miss Ling and Mother and I were carried almost twenty miles in sedan chairs to Dan Shui, a town on a tributary of the East River. The next task was to engage a junk to take us up the river. No one knew how long it would take to procure the boat or how long it would take to go upriver to the point where we were to hire the trucks. As junks had no motors in those days, the timing of a trip depended on the size of the boat, the cargo, the wind, the condition of the river, and what happened along the way. In that place and time there were no deadlines.

We were at Dan Shui for a week, in a temple outside the town, our room dark and smelling of old smoke. As I remember, Dan Shui was festooned with sausages. They hung in shiny loops in front of shops and houses and in the market. They even hung under the temple roof outside our room. They were delicious—smoky, meaty, and sweet, with crackling skin that popped when you bit into it, releasing juices fragrant with garlic, anise, and hot peppers—the best sausages I've ever eaten.

But the most memorable feature of our stay in that town is indelibly impressed upon my psyche. It was there that my parents started me on Klim. I was so traumatized by Klim itself that it was years before I realized that the brand name, Klim, is *milk* spelled backward. It was, I believe, the first attempt at powdered milk. It was whole milk, fat and all. As there were no Western cows in the interior, Mother conscientiously stocked up with a two-year supply, calculating my consumption at one cup a day. Either my father or mother would put the requisite amount of clumped yellow powder in a cup and stir in tepid boiled water. After several minutes of vigorous beating with a spoon, the result was a pale yellow fluid with bubbles clustered around the edges such as one sees in stagnant ponds. Clots floated sluggishly on the surface, like globs of pus, and when I put the cup to my mouth, I felt its sweet rotten smell on my face. My parents sympathized but insisted. To make it fun, my father decided to time how long it took me to drink it up, so I could try to beat my previous record. Somewhere in the fifty-eight boxes he found a stopwatch intended for track meets at Yali. Every morning after breakfast I held the cup to my lips, my eyes on his thumb crooked over the watch, and at his signal, "Ready, set, go!" he'd punch the watch and I'd start to swallow and gag. I believe my record was fourteen seconds.

My father finally found a *chuan lao ban,* or boat master, who agreed to take us with a cargo of lime to Longchuan. The *lao ban* promised that the boat, now on its way to Dan-shui to load the lime, was brand-new. A price for our passage was agreed on. When the boat arrived, however, it turned out to be old and battered. The *lao ban* regretted his mistake but was unable to change the agreement. As it was the only junk of sufficient size going in our direction, we had no choice but to take it—unless we wanted to wait in Dan Shui indefinitely and hope the Japanese would not take over the town in one of their periodic occupations.

The craft was a large junk with a crew of several men. Dirty gray sails lay in accordion piles at the bottom of the mast, and the wooden decks shone with a rich sheen from the feet of the boatmen. The stern slanted up gently, and on either side of the bow was a large eye. For thousands of years river people had painted eyes on their boats to aid them in making their way over the sometimes turbulent and dangerous waterways of China. I later discovered that if I lay on my stomach and reached over the side, with my father holding my feet, I could just touch one of the eyes.

Behind the mast was a long, tunnel-like shelter made of bamboo matting, worn and broken in places, where we slept and ate for the next eighteen days. A horizontal space between the bottom edge of the matting and the deck provided ventilation. Along the outside of the shelter ran two narrow runways where the boatmen walked as they poled the boat through shallows or rapids. From inside the shelter we sometimes saw their feet through the ventilation slit, slapping along the runway as they pushed the boat up the river. A square wooden well was built into the deck toward the front of the shelter, where we sat to eat, our legs dangling into the well. At night the well accommodated two collapsible army cots on which Miss Ling and I slept. The lime was stored beneath the deck, and on hot nights its acrid sting filled the shelter.

In front of the mast were the oarlocks, with huge oars stored alongside, and at the stern, the heavy handle of the rudder stretched forward over the deck. The cooking was done over a charcoal fire in a brazier on the front deck. Toward the back of the boat, a wooden cubicle perched partway over the water. It had a hole in the floor, opening onto the water below. At first my mother accompanied me when I visited the cubicle. But soon I mastered the trick of dealing with my underwear and squatting over the hole to aim accurately, one hand holding a wad of gray paper the consistency of crepe paper, while the other hand held shut the grimy curtain at the door.

We boarded the boat one evening for an early departure in the morning. It was dark when our baggage was finally stowed away, and by the light of a flashlight we teetered on board over a plank that bounced as we stepped on it. The space under the shelter was lit by a small and smoky oil lamp, so we were engulfed by moving shadows as we prepared to bed down for the night. One by one, the members of our party lay down, accommodating as best they could to the unyielding wood beneath them. My mother and father used all their blankets to pad the deck where they slept next to my cot. Mr. Beamer blew up his air mattress and groaned with fatigued ecstasy as his body sank into its voluptuous resilience. Gradually silence settled in, accentuated by the sleepy sound of water against the boat. I felt comfortable and expectant, cozy and safe in the tunnel made by the bamboo matting. With Little Bear beside me, I watched the shadows move over the matting until the lamp went out and the lapping water lulled me to sleep.

Our days quickly settled into a routine. I usually awakened before dawn to the crowing of roosters in the towns where we had tied up the night before. Charcoal fumes crept into the shelter as someone started the fire to prepare the morning rice. Soon I heard the boatmen hawking and spitting as they cleared the night's accumulation of phlegm into the river and rinsed their mouths before eating. Through the tunnel opening I watched the sky turn pale and the mist lift off the river until sounds in the shelter signaled it was time to get dressed. By the time I was dressed and Mother had braided my hair, the bedding and cots were folded away, and it was light enough for us to gather for morning worship—a hymn, Scripture reading, and prayer for the day. It was also light enough for people from other boats and from the town to see us and to come watch the foreign devils go through their strange rituals. I had become accustomed to the stares of people who had never seen blue eyes or light curly hair, but I was relieved when the boatmen took to pushing off from shore before our morning worship. Perhaps my father suggested it.

The boatmen cooked their own food and ate before us, rinsing their bowls and chopsticks over the side when they were finished. We were careful to rinse ours with boiling water before we used them. Evidently our precautions were effective, as none of us got sick. Miss Ling and one of the Yale Bachelors did our cooking. Breakfast was always *shi fan*, the watery rice gruel endemic in south China's breakfasts, with bok choy, well stewed to kill germs, and perhaps some salt fish. While everyone else had tea, I had Klim. On that boat, breakfast was not my favorite meal. The other meals were much better. They were simple, but the food was fresh and well flavored, served with fragrant rice, each grain light and fluffy.

Our boat tied up for the night in the late afternoon, because the walled towns along the river closed their gates at sunset. People started to follow us as our group walked into the town to look around and buy food for the next twenty-four hours. Inside the walls it was much hotter than on the river, but it felt good to walk around after sitting in the boat all day. We always stopped first to buy cookies. It seemed that in every town, the bakeries made cookies at about that time in the afternoon. To be safe, we bought them only when they were hot out of the oven. They were wonderful—rich, flaky almond or anise cookies that melted in one's mouth, the only sweets we had during the trip.

It was Miss Ling who bargained for food in the marketplace, because she was more likely to get a good price than we foreigners: tea leaves pressed into blocks, tea oil for cooking, soy sauce, black vinegar, leafy greens, scallions, ginger, fermented black beans, thin green beans a foot long, cakes of freshly made doufu or bean curd (pronounced "dough-fu" in Chinese), a scrawny live chicken with matted feathers, or a river fish dipped from a wooden tub of water to gasp out its life in our market basket. No one sold prepared poultry or bought dead fish. The Chinese ate them as fresh as possible, with good reason. In the market stalls there were pieces of pork hanging from hooks, covered with moving carpets of flies. We rarely ate meat.

Flies were everywhere. They multiplied in the open latrines, which we smelled as we entered the town, and in the collection pits of night soil outside the walls. Flies lit on our hair and clothing; they crawled in the perspiration on our necks, and we constantly waved them away from our faces. They lit on the heads of the children who swarmed around us, and moved unheeded over the faces of babies carried by the women who gathered to touch my braids, feel my skin, and stare into my face. My blue eyes looked colorless to them. "How can she see?" they asked each other.

"She's blind!" Others disagreed: "No, she's not! Look how she walks. See how she looks at you!" They stared, jostled by their neighbors, and laughed, calling to their friends, "*Lai kan! Lai kan!* Come see!" I didn't like them touching me, but I pretended not to care, for I'd learned they would laugh even more if I pulled away.

The crowds around us became so thick that people had to stand sideways, and when we asked them to move, they gave way slowly because of the pressure of people from behind. The men in our group pushed ahead to ease our way through the narrow streets so that we could complete our shopping before the gates were shut for the night. In every town it was the same. After a few days of going into the towns, the group decided it would be best if I remained on the boat with Mother.

On the river there was nothing to tell us what century we were in. The days would have been the same if we had been on that boat a hundred or two hundred years before. Our watches had no meaning, for our activities were determined by the light on the river. Sometimes there was nothing by which to measure our progress, because the river was so broad that the flat banks were barely visible. If there was a landmark on the horizon, it stayed the same size for hours. The sail stood taut in the wind like the gigantic wing of a moth, and the water flowed slowly under the boat like brown syrup. Sometimes the breeze failed and the boatmen got out the oars, one on each side. They faced ahead, standing two to an oar, stepping in rhythm as they pushed forward, hands high, and pulled back, hands low. The boat moved ahead in small surges, and between surges the water lapped back and forth against the sides as though we weren't moving at all.

One day we were jolted back into the twentieth century, a day when ours was the only boat on that part of the river. Suddenly we heard a shout, and one of the boatmen pointed toward the horizon. Far away in the sky there was something glinting in the sunlight. The boatmen talked excitedly among themselves, hauled down the sail, and pulled out the oars as the head boatman swung over the tiller and we headed for the nearest shore. It was a single airplane, droning high above the river in the distance. Before we left Hong Kong, we'd heard that a plane such as this had tried to bomb a boat carrying some Catholic sisters up the East River, and had strafed them when they'd made it to shore and were running for shelter. Fortunately, the bombs missed the boat and no one was hurt—that time.

Now our boatmen pulled frantically on the oars. As soon as we got to the bank, the *lao ban* threw an anchor over the side and the crew leaped to the bank and ran off through the rice paddies. We followed them, plunging through water and mud, squashing the green rice plants into the muck. Finally we crouched against a mud bank between paddies while the airplane traced lazy circles high above the river. It never came near us. Perhaps it didn't see our boat huddled against the bank. Perhaps we weren't the target it was looking for. Or perhaps it was lost. After a while the sound faded and the sky was empty. We waited, but the plane didn't return. Then, wet, muddy, and tired, we made our way back to the boat, our shoes heavy with clay from the paddies. When we got back to the boat, I found Little Bear lying unharmed on the deck where I'd left him.

I was dazed with fatigue as we prepared for bed and was dozing off when I vaguely heard Mr. Beamer blow up his air mattress as usual. Each time he took a breath, he sucked in a long lungful of air, paused, then blew it into the mattress with a hollow resonance that vibrated through the shelter. At last he stopped, and I heard him start his usual groan of relief as he lay down on the mattress. But this time the groan was interrupted by a loud pop. My eyes opened. A prolonged hissing sound followed, and when it finally died out, there was silence. My father put his arm over Mother's shoulders, which were shaking. Next to me, Miss Ling turned over. I hugged Little Bear and waited. After a few moments, I heard Mr. Beamer muttering and moving about, but no one else moved. Evidently they were all asleep.

Mr. Beamer never got his mattress fixed. Maybe he didn't have a repair kit. Someone on the boat must have brought along a tire repair kit, because all of them would be using bicycles when they reached their destinations. But nobody offered him one, and for the rest of the trip he slept on the deck, padded with what was left of his mattress.

Most of the days were uneventful, but I wasn't bored. Occasionally my father let me use his Underwood portable typewriter, and I typed out pages of nonsense words that he then read back to me with great drama, ending the peroration with knotted brow, puffed cheeks, and raised fist. Then he and I would roll on the deck with hilarity, while Mother would exclaim in mock exasperation, "Honestly—you two!"

Sometimes we sang rounds—"Row, Row, Row Your Boat" and "White Coral Bells"—and played card games with the Yale Bachelors, such as Pit, Flinch, and Old Maid (my favorite in those days, long before feminist consciousness-raising would make it unacceptable). The Bachelors taught me how to play solitaire with regular playing cards, although we knew that Mr. Aldecott and Mr. Beamer didn't approve of those kinds of cards. Once my father used my watercolors to show me how to wash a piece of paper with faint color to make the sky and the river, on which I drew a boat with a gray moth wing. My mother read to me every day, and by the end of the trip we had finished *The Secret Garden* and *The Wind in the Willows*. On my own, I made my way with increasing facility through several of the Burgess animal storybooks. Lost in the world of those stories, I felt a tiny mental jolt when I looked up from my book and found myself back on the river. Sometimes I didn't feel like doing anything at all and just sat with Little Bear in the wind and sunlight, mesmerized by the creaking of the rigging and the slow surge of the boat moving upriver.

Sometimes we ran aground in the middle of the waterway, shallow with silt, and the boatmen had to push us free with long poles. Once we got stuck on a sandbar, and we had to get off the boat onto the sand while the men unloaded our baggage and pushed the boat off. All the men helped, except for Mr. Beamer, who had developed a bad back. After the baggage was stowed on board again, we decided to rest and eat lunch before going on. With the junk tugging at anchor in the middle of the river, my father asked me if I wanted to go swimming. I knew how to dogpaddle, but I didn't consider that to be real swimming, like the crawl, which he could keep up indefinitely. He secured a towel around my waist, tied a rope to it, and dumped me, squealing with delicious alarm, into the river. Then he pulled me through the water, walking along the runway on the side of the boat. It was glorious fun to go from the hot sun into the cool water and splash along, moving as though I were doing the crawl. At the end of the runway he pulled me out and walked back. "Again, Daddy!" I yelled, running after him. "Do it again!" And so he did, again and again. Now, half a century later, I wonder what the boatmen thought of us.

The boatmen believed the river god was a jealous god. Since the beginning of remembered time, the river people of China had known that any living creature that fell into a river belonged to him. No one was to rescue any person or animal from drowning, or even attempt to do so, for fear of angering him. He could wreak havoc throughout the countryside with floods that were followed inevitably by famine and plague that spread far beyond his purview. Thus, anyone who denied the river god's claim might be responsible for the death of thousands, if not millions, of people. We must have appeared very ignorant to the boatmen as we tempted the anger of the river god, or else very irresponsible.

One day the Yale Bachelors decided to play cards. It was a windy day on the river, and the water was swift and choppy, the banks far away. The heavy junk bobbed up and down and rocked back and forth in the waves as we plowed our way under full sail up the river. The Bachelors sat under the bamboo matting to shelter from the wind; grabbing the nearest suitcase, they balanced it on edge against the matting to block the breeze blowing through the ventilation slit. The bamboo matting was rotten. The suitcase belonged to my parents. It was heavy. In addition to clothes, it held our family's valuable papers and my mother's diamond engagement ring. Our passports were there, our visas, our permission to move through the country, the money with which to buy our food, pay our passage, and hire the trucks to take us overland. It held our first-aid supplies and the ephedrine tablets my father and I took when we had asthma attacks.

My mother and I were on the front deck when the boat lurched over on one side and we heard a shout. As the boat rolled back again, someone pointed over the side and we saw the suitcase bobbing in the swift current, already quite distant. Suddenly I noticed my father standing on the runway at the side of the junk. He kicked off his shoes and dived into the water after the suitcase. Quickly his head became just a dot against the brown reaches of the river far behind us, and I saw his tiny arms flailing rhythmically in the crawl before he disappeared .

The head boatman refused to turn around to go after him, but after much exhortation by our fellow passengers, he did shorten sail so that we barely made headway through the water. There was nothing more we could do. Mother and I clung to each other. "Dwight," she moaned, "Dwight." I couldn't swallow. *Daddy*, I thought. And then I thought, *This is just another story*. But it wasn't.

I don't know how long we waited on the deck. After a while we saw a smaller junk moving over the choppy water toward us. It was a funny-looking boat with clothes hanging from the rigging, blowing in the breeze, and draped over the sides of its bamboo shelter. I couldn't understand why everyone suddenly started to cheer as the boat came closer. Then I saw my father standing on the front deck with the suitcase open beside him. He waved and turned to gather up the clothes. Mother and I clung to each other again and started to cry. When his boat bumped against ours, he jumped on board and gathered us into a big hug. "Dear heart," he said to Mother. "Don't cry. Of course I'm all right!"

The suitcase had caught on a sandbar in the middle of the river. My father had climbed up beside it and waited for a passing boat. But when one came by, it wouldn't stop. So, holding the sodden suitcase in one hand, he went back into the water after it. When he got to the boat, the people in it wouldn't help him and kept on going. Finally someone took the suitcase but wouldn't pull him out of the water. At last he managed to haul himself onto the boat, and once he was on board, the boat people agreed to catch up to our junk—for a consideration.

In the Western universe, time moves inexorably in one direction, opposites can never meet, and a journey starts in one place, ending in another. On the East River we sailed into a Chinese universe where time stood still and opposites like yin and yang were intertwined, each dependent on the other—safety and danger, laughter and terror, love and loss—and the most important thing about our journey was that it ended where it began, with us together. It must have been on the East River that I first sensed the ancient and cyclical endurance that was China, and began to form an attachment so deep that it exists below thought, like the irresistible attraction one might have for music first heard in the womb and thereafter hauntingly familiar, perhaps forgotten but never lost.

HOME TO CHANGSHA

Our days on the East River evaporated behind us, forgotten in the bone-shaking din of our overland trip over three mountain ranges to Shaoguan, a town in northern Guandong Province where we were to get the train into Hunan. The three of us now were wedged next to the driver in the cab of a truck carrying the supplies destined for the school and hospital. Hour after hour, the truck leaped and crashed over the rocks and ruts of what was supposed to be a road. My father, on one side, braced himself against the door and clamped me to his side with his free arm. Mother, on my other side, held on to a rope coming out of a black hole in the dashboard and pushed her feet against the floor as if riding a bucking bronco.

We tried to shout over the roar of the engine and grinding gears, the crunch of depleted shock absorbers, and the deafening clatter of loose parts connected to the truck more by habit than by any visible means of attachment. But our voices jiggled and shook so much that we couldn't understand what we said. I started to sing "White Coral Bells" and my father joined in as the second voice in the round, but we got to laughing too hard to sing. Between bounces, my mother said, "Silly!" which made us laugh all the harder.

The truck bounded over some especially rough spots, and soon we stopped laughing to concentrate on keeping our seats. In spite of the narrowness of the road and frequent curves—or perhaps because of them—the driver propelled his vehicle with panache. When we came to a bend, he leaned on the horn and put his foot to the floor so that the truck careened around the corner, tipping first toward one side and then the other while the three of us held on for dear life, dipping and swaying like synchronized ballet dancers. The few oncoming trucks that we met were driven with the same verve as ours, and I now realize that for our driver to slow down would have been an admission of cowardice. There were several near misses but no collisions. By the end of the trip, Mother's rope had been replaced more than once because it had frayed against the sharp edges of the hole in the dashboard.

Despite the discomfort, there were things I liked about the truck. Its horn recalled the motor traffic of Shanghai, where a myriad horns echoed in the chasms between department stores and office buildings and movie theaters. The truck's horn brought back the excitement and delicious terror I'd felt in Shanghai, where we saw the movie *Snow White and the Seven Dwarfs*. Now in the truck I thought of Snow White's long dress and black hair.

"I wish I had hair like Snow White's," I said.

"What made you think of that?" my father asked, looking down at me braced against the curve of his shoulder.

"I don't know; I just like her hair."

My father smiled and returned to looking at the road.

Mother glanced at my braids reaching halfway to my waist with curls below the rubber bands and wisps plastered to the edge of my moist forehead. "You have very nice hair, dear," she said, and clutched harder on the rope as we leaned toward the driver.

I also liked to sniff the truck's exhaust each time we slowed down and the smoke from the tailpipe drifted forward. It made me think of riding in the double-decker buses in Hong Kong, where the acrid fragrance from motor vehicles in the street below rose to the upper deck and reminded me of California, while underneath lurked the more organic smells of China— hot peanut oil, incense, and sewage. West met East in the perfume of the truck's exhaust, and for a magic moment I was connected to both.

By the end of the first day in the truck, my mind and bottom were numb. We had left the river valley and were winding through higher country. It was past nightfall when we came to the small town where we were to spend the night. The low shapes of houses loomed blacker than the surrounding dark. Here and there was a dim square of warm yellow light where a lamp glowed through the oiled paper covering a window. The moving beam of our headlights momentarily illuminated a few families sitting in the cool dark outside their houses.

The truck turned into the courtyard of an inn and gave a final shudder as the driver turned off the engine. Suddenly it was very quiet. A man with a lamp came to the door and called to the driver. We piled stiffly out of the truck, and after a prolonged discussion with my father about the price, the man ushered us into a room at the front of the courtyard. In the middle of the room, he put the lamp on a table with a high stool on each side. The room was in shadows beyond the meager circle of lamplight. On the street side of the room, I could dimly see a large window, divided into smaller rectangles by a lattice covered with oiled paper. A wooden platform on legs stood indistinctly against the opposite wall, with a mosquito net of indeterminate age tied in a huge knot above it. My eyes were drawn to the one vivid spot in the room—a ceramic chamber pot of generous proportions, sitting under the platform. It was decorated with red and orange peonies painted on a white background. As I gazed at it, the pot swelled larger and larger, its lustrous sides brighter and brighter, gathering most of the light in the room. I blinked and it went back to its original size.

My father ordered supper with tea, and rice wine with an empty bowl. When the food came, we sat on the stools around the table. Mother rinsed the tea cups, rice bowls, and china spoons with some of the hot tea and wiped them with a clean handkerchief while my father poured the wine in the bowl and lit it with a match. As he ran the wooden chopsticks through the flames, I stared at the blue light flickering over the surface of the liquid, and my parents' voices receded to a faint murmur. After a while the flames went out and a bowl of rice appeared on the table in front of me, steaming and fragrant. I leaned forward and inhaled. "Have some *doufu*," my father said, and piled some fried bean curd with chives and fermented black beans onto my rice. I picked up my bowl and chopsticks and shoveled in a warm, comforting mouthful. Suddenly I was awake and hungry. The food was wonderful.

Preoccupied with eating, we didn't react to the first soft pop. After a while there was another one, followed by an irregular series. We looked around and saw that the paper covering the window was now perforated with little round holes. Even as we looked, a couple of fingers poked through the paper, and in each of the other holes an eye glittered at us in the lamplight. It took us a moment to absorb this surreal scene. Mother dropped her chopsticks and waved her hands at the window as though shooing chickens, her consonants explosive with exasperation: "*Chu, chu, chu!* Go, go, go!" The eyes didn't move. Like many people who rarely saw foreigners, the spectators probably couldn't believe that she was speaking an understandable language or that her gestures meant anything within rational comprehension. My father got up and started talking as he walked to where our blankets were stacked on top of a suitcase. "*Nimen zuo shenme?*" he asked sternly. "What are you doing?" Perhaps his Chinese was more persuasive than Mother's or his dark hair and eyes made it more believable. The eyes started to disappear. He picked up a blanket and draped it over the window, blocking out the remaining eyes and ending what must have had been the best show in town for some time.

When supper was cleared away, we sponged off with water in an enamel basin and put on our nightclothes. The bed was made of boards covered by a thin matting. On the matting were piled a couple of quilts that at one time had been bright with many colors but now had faded to variations of gray covered with grime. My mother and father gingerly lifted them off the platform and draped them over the table. Then my father took out a can of yellow powder—"bug powder," we called it—and poured it in a line around the wooden border of the bed. That done, we carefully spread out our own blankets within the area outlined by the powder.

I thought of the bedbugs and fleas gathering in the shadows, waiting for us to lie down. I always reacted strongly to insect bites. Fleas left fiery hills of insatiable itching larger than the ones left by mosquitoes, bedbugs left flat welts on my skin—mesas of concentrated misery that took days to subside—and sand flies left dusky volcanoes of pain. All were exacerbated by the heat and sweat through which the bites were delivered. I found it almost impossible not to scratch when I was awake and completely impossible when I was asleep. My fingernails were cut short to prevent infection, but regularly in the summers to come, my bites were to become infected and blossom into the crusted sores of impetigo, which spread in patches over my lower legs, sometimes with a spot or two on my arms. In those days before penicillin, Mother read to us in the hot evenings from books by Haliburton and Dickens while my father soaked the stained bandages off my legs with boiled water. Then he gently pulled off the softened scabs and dead tissue with a pair of tweezers. I sucked in my breath and flinched and tried to concentrate on the story as tiny rivulets of blood ran down my legs. Sometimes I cried, and my father would pause. "Brave girl," he'd say. "I'm almost done." And Mother would stop reading for a moment and say, "Betty Jean, dearest, I'm so sorry." She never looked at my legs. When all the sores were picked clean, my father applied a black ointment that smelled of sulfur, then wrapped clean bandages around my legs. I sat limp with relief while Mother finished the chapter.

But that was in the years ahead. On this night we climbed onto the platform, being careful not to disturb the bug powder, and tucked the mosquito net under the edges of the blankets. With Little Bear in the curve of my shoulder, I settled down between my parents and imagined hordes of bedbugs coming to a sudden halt at the line of bug powder, where they milled around in frustration before retreating in disorder and going home hungry. I went to sleep, secure in the certainty that we were safe within our magic perimeter. In the morning we woke up, unbitten.

After the inevitable breakfast of *shi fan,* my father asked to have our thermos filled with *kai shui,* boiling water, and we packed up. The last thing we did was to take down the blanket from the window. Although my father paid the agreed price for our food and lodging, the innkeeper was unhappy. The price of oiled paper was exorbitantly high, he said, and he expressed his disappointment at my father's refusal to pay the cost of replacing the paper on the window of our room.

"It wasn't we who tore your paper," my father pointed out. "You should ask the people who did it."

"Ask the people who did it?" echoed the innkeeper incredulously. "How can I do that?"

"How can you ask us when we *didn't* do it?"

The innkeeper looked at my father and changed his tone. "Please," he said. "You can spare a little toward the cost."

My father shook his head, and we walked out to the courtyard, where the driver had slept with the truck.

"*Zau!*" we said. "Good morning!"

"*Zau,*" answered the driver, and added in reply to our query that, yes, he had eaten. An interested crowd had gathered, undoubtedly enlarged by reports of the previous evening's entertainment. People at the back stood on tiptoe, and everyone watched as we climbed aboard. The driver swung into his seat, called farewell to someone in the crowd, and turned on the ignition. Mother grabbed her rope and we braced ourselves. I pulled Little Bear to my chest, and my father pulled me against his shoulder. The truck hesitated. It coughed, sputtered, shook, and cleared its throat. Finally making up its mind, it roared into life, hesitated once more, and then lurched out of the courtyard, leaving our audience engulfed in a cloud of fragrant exhaust.

Coming home to Changsha was like the healing of a surgical incision—quiet, unseen, mysteriously complete. One day you notice you can move once more without effort, without the care that had become almost automatic. When we left three years before, I had cut Changsha out of my reality. Each new place we lived in—Honolulu, San Mateo, and Shanghai—became my total world to the exclusion of all others. Aside from momentary—almost theoretical—recollections, it would have been disorienting to think about Changsha. So I shied away from remembering, as though I might not learn to manage each new present if I recalled the past. I forgot how to speak Chinese.

Now, back in Changsha, the past and the present were safely together, and suddenly I was whole. I stepped onto the walk leading up to our house and recognized home, not with my mind but with something composed of my eyes, my nose, and my skin that went directly to the back of my throat, where it burst and blossomed into fireworks. This was *our* walk, this *our* birdbath, this *our* porch, *our* living room and dining room; this was *my* bedroom, *my* camphor tree, and this—this was me again. No matter that someone else had been living here, that some of the furnishings were different. This place *knew* me. The smells, the light, the feel were the same, and *I* was the same. My Chinese came back without my noticing, and from then on I used, without thinking, whichever language I needed to communicate.

During the years I'd been away, the children I'd known had left Changsha because of the approaching war. Yali was now in Yuanling, and part of the hospital was as well. During the few weeks we were in Changsha, my parents sent furnishings and supplies ahead to Yuanling and Mother gathered materials for my schooling. The Greenes and other Yale-in-China families had left books and manuals for home schooling provided as a correspondence course from the Calvert School in Baltimore. Because of the war, we would not be able to correspond with Calvert for my lessons, but the materials on hand were all we needed. Although the plan was for us to stay in Yuanling two years, Mother must have suspected we would be there longer, for she packed up three years' worth of materials. My Calvert education was to stand me in good stead, for when we returned to the States four years later, I was a year ahead of my grade level.

A few days before we left for Yuanling, Mother sent Chen Shi-fu to deliver a note to Mr. Heinrichsohn, the German businessman on Orange Island and the father of Teddy, my former playmate. The first I knew of the note was when Mother called me to the living room. "Betty Jean!" She sounded excited. "Come see what Mr. Heinrichsohn has given you!" When I arrived in the living room, Chen Shi-fu was taking a covered basket off his arm and placing it on the floor. I lifted the lid. Curled up inside, just waking up, was a puppy—a black cocker spaniel with floppy ears, liquid brown eyes, a pink tongue, and a stubby tail.

I couldn't believe it. Carefully I lifted her out of the basket and sat cross-legged on the floor to hold her on my lap. A rush of love surged through me, so strong that I couldn't speak. Her fur felt silky when I stroked her. She licked my ear, then wiggled out of my hold and scurried off to explore the living room. I sat on the floor watching while Mother read Mr. Heinrichsohn's note. "'Dear Mrs. Rugh,'" she read. "'Here is Molly. She is from my latest litter. You asked for an ordinary puppy or one we didn't want, but I think Betty Jean should have Molly to keep her company in Yuanling. I am overjoyed to have the opportunity to do this. With warmest regards and best wishes for . . .' Oh, dear." Mother stopped. "You'd better take Molly outside." She pointed to an expanding puddle under the suddenly motionless puppy, dangerously close to a rug. And so Molly entered our lives and made a place in my heart that, I have since found, is empty unless occupied by the presence of a dog. Each dog is different, but it exactly fills the space Molly made.

I was excited when it came time to leave Changsha for Yuanling. For one thing, this time I had Molly with me when we went to yet another new place, so I wasn't going alone. But beyond that, something important had happened in Changsha, although I wasn't aware of it at the time. Only now do I realize that I could leave Changsha and look forward to Yuanling because I had already touched base. I had been home.

YUANLING

We came upon Yuanling slowly on a gray December day as the boatmen rowed up the broad curve of the river flowing like liquid pewter between the hills. A few houses appeared on the right bank, then more, growing closer together until they formed a tumbled mass of gray-tiled roofs silhouetted against the hazy hills. Behind the hills the sky hung like an unwashed sheet. It seemed to take forever to row past the long line of houses that were strung for over two miles along Yuanling's only street, squeezed between the hills and the river. On a hillside across the river from the town, a pagoda stood like an elderly sentinel, with tufts of grass and small bushes growing from the cracks in its walls. Down on the water, sampans sculled through the current, and a few junks, their sterns curved up like fish tails, moved almost imperceptibly over the opaque surface as though pinned to their reflections. We paused briefly to accommodate the passage of a bargelike boat in front of us, crowded with people carrying pigs and poultry and produce. Gradually I became conscious of a constant low murmur from the town. The sound was almost indistinguishable from the brown-gray tones of the hills and river, houses and sky—a monotone, monochrome world. I felt flat and excited at the same time. Here was a new place.

Over a thousand years before, the city of Yuanling had been the flourishing capital of western Hunan, a center for commerce and culture and connection to other parts of the province. But after a century or so, the town sank into obscurity and remained there. In 1940 its most salient feature was its insignificance, which made it a highly desirable place to be. As Japanese forces spread into the larger eastern cities of China, whole institutions—schools and factories, hospitals and universities, with their staff and families and equipment—picked up and moved inland in search of places where they could continue their work without interference from the Japanese. The less significant the place, the less likely the Japanese would pay attention to it. That is why Yali and several other institutions, as well as thousands of refugees, chose Yuanling in which to settle, not knowing if and when they would have to move again. The city was thought to be out of the way of Japanese interests. But in the years just before we arrived, the Japanese had bombed it several times, perhaps because of its growing size and the new electric plant at the lower end of town—or perhaps because sometimes they were unable to reach their intended targets and had to unload their bombs before returning to base.

At last we came around the curve of the river toward the bank—so high it was almost a cliff—at the upper end of town. On the shingle below the bank, some sampans had been pulled up in a row like fish laid out to dry. With the boatman's wife at the tiller, the crewmen poled us onto the pebbly ground, where the boat scraped up until it stopped. We had arrived.

"Here we are!" my father said enthusiastically. Mother leaned back to look up at the wall of wooden houses perched high on the bank above us. "Oh, Dwight," she replied with no enthusiasm at all. Down at the water's edge, a group of women were squatting on a cluster of flat rocks and chatting loudly as they pounded wet clothes on the stones with wooden paddles. One looked up and pointed at me. The others stopped their conversation, looked, and laughed as though surprised. My father nodded to them. "Let's go, dear," he said, and walked down a plank to lead the way. The women watched as he carried our suitcase and his briefcase in one hand and with the other steadied Mother as she walked down the plank from the boat to the bottom of a flight of stone steps winding up the bank to end between some houses at the top. The steps were steep and worn, slippery with water and mud.

At the top we emerged from between two houses and looked down a dark and narrow street lined with single-story buildings whose tiled roofs almost met overhead. The street was noisy and crowded. Along one side someone was making string, which stretched in front of several shops. People moved up and down the street, shopping, bargaining, arguing, while others sat or stood in their doorways and surveyed the scene. Toddlers in split pants held on to their mothers' pants legs, and a woman held her baby out over the gutter, hissing suggestively to encourage performance. We heard an exclamation, and hastily stepped out of the way as a man came up the final steps behind us. He was carrying two wooden buckets of water slung on ropes from each end of the pole over his shoulder, his face dripping with sweat in spite of the cold. He paused at the top to change pace and shift direction, reaching behind with one hand to steady the ropes of the rear bucket. Despite his precautions, some water spilled out, splashing my shoes and socks. He didn't notice, but started out again with a smooth bouncing gait over the wet paving stones and disappeared down the street.

Across the street was a wall with a double wooden door in the middle. It was open, and as we stepped in, the gate man came out of the gatehouse beaming. "You've come back!" he said to my father, including Mother and me in his smile. He reached for my father's suitcase, but my father swung it out of his reach.

"Bu yau ke qi," my father protested. "Don't take the trouble!"

"Bu ke qi, bu ke qi!," the gate man replied heartily. "Not at all!" Giving up on the suitcase, he hurried off to spread the news of our arrival while Mother and I looked up the longest, steepest flight of stone steps I had ever seen. It led straight up from the gate. I couldn't see the top steps from where we stood. "We're up there," my father said, taking Molly's basket from Mother. Up we started again. I thought my legs would give out halfway up, and Mother stopped to rest several times, while people going down the steps paused to greet us or nod as they went by. We finally got to the top and looked up at a row of four large, square houses on the other side of the path from where we stood.

"That's ours," my father said, pointing to the last house on the right, and led us to the back of the house and up some outside steps onto a back porch on the second floor. Half of the porch had been closed off to make a small kitchen. "Here we are!" he announced, opening a door leading off the porch into the house, and we stepped into the rooms that would be our home for the next four years.

Our piano, trunks, and boxes had arrived ahead of us and stood in the middle of the floor with some pieces of furniture around the edges of the room. Mother looked around and caught her breath. Her eyes got red and tears ran down her cheeks. My father put Molly's basket down and said, "Oh, Kitty, dearest, please." He put an arm around her shoulders. "It will be *fine*. Let me show you. There's a brave girl." I took Molly out of her basket and walked into the front room. "You can fix it up any way you want," I heard my father say as I moved onto the screened porch off the front room. Mother said something, her voice muffled. I was trembling as I leaned on the porch railing. I hated it when Mother cried. I pushed my face against Molly's silky back, and she wiggled out of my arms. I let her go and pressed my nose against the screen. It smelled dusty. From here I could hear the murmur from the street at the bottom of the staircase. I looked over the treetops, down over the roofs of the town, and across the river to the hazy hills on the other side and the distant mountains. I was *never* going to cry like that when I grew up.

❧

Yuanling probably owed its existence to its location at the confluence of two rivers, making it accessible to two separate areas of the province. Just upstream from our end of town, the You River joined the Yuan. Below the point where they joined, the doubled flow swept past so smooth and swift that after a rain in the mountains, the different colors of the two rivers were kept intact for several miles—one half an opaque green, the other a murky brown. In times of flood, the swollen river carried debris on its back—trees and bushes, the bodies of dead goats and dogs and water buffalo, and parts of houses. Once I caught a glimpse of a man as he flashed by, sitting naked astride a thatched roof in the middle of the river, traveling too fast to be rescued, if anyone had tried.

The compound where Yali settled had been donated by the Evangelical Mission for as long as the school needed it. Enclosed within a brick wall, the campus was almost vertical. There was not enough level land even for a small playing field. The wooden buildings for the school had been erected in a hurry, their downhill sides supported by stilts. Several flights of steps connected the terraced levels of the compound, but the longest stretch was the stone staircase we had climbed from the gate to our house, 150 steps in all.

Mother recovered from her initial disappointment with characteristic speed and plunged into the business of getting settled. Chen Shi-fu had come from our house in Changsha to do our cleaning and laundry, and we had a new cook, Tou (pronounced "toe") Shi-fu. With their help and Mother's efficiency, we were soon established in our new home. Mother started me on my second-grade lessons, courtesy of the Calvert School, and began to prepare for the English and music classes she would teach the next term. My father resumed his work as liaison with the headquarters in New Haven, as helper to the school administrators, as chaplain and counselor for the Christian students, and filling in when an English teacher was needed.

Years later Mother admitted that she came to love our life in Yuanling, including our crowded living quarters. "Our rooms were *so* cozy," she would say wistfully, looking back through the softening mist of five decades. Entering from the back porch, the first room was our dining room. Because it had no windows, in summer it was the hottest room in the house, and the pewter candlesticks on the sideboard drooped in the heat like wilted tulips. During the school year Mother rehearsed the Yali Glee Club in our dining room, and the boys crowded in, standing room only. They watched her intently as she gave them their pitch, tooting on a little pitch pipe, and when she signaled the downbeat, they launched enthusiastically into song, singing a cappella. The whole house resonated with their singing. "Watch your quality, boys," Mother admonished when they got too enthusiastic, and their tone softened obediently as they blended their voices into chords of sound, unfolding in crescendo and back again in diminuendo, ending soft and full.

Beyond the dining room was our living room, at the front of the house. There we had our piano, desks, and books, and a washstand. During the day, light came in from a bay window opening onto the screened porch at the front of the house, where we slept. At night the room was lit by a light bulb hanging from the middle of the ceiling. We had electricity eighteen hours a day, as it was used to power the air raid siren at the other end of the city, but sometimes the light bulb faded to a glow, and then we used a pressure lamp fueled with kerosene, much brighter than the electric light.

On Saturday nights Chen Shi-fu brought in a wooden tub about four feet long and placed it on a piece of pungent waterproof canvas called *you bu,* permeated with tung oil. Then he poured in hot water from a couple of large galvanized tin containers shaped like watering cans. I took the first bath, soaping myself and lying back in three inches of deliciously hot water to stare dreamily at the light bulb receding through fragrant clouds of steam. When the water became tepid, I reluctantly got out of the tub, and another can was brought and emptied into the tub for my mother. When she finished, a final can was added to the water, now blue with soap scum, and my father took his bath. Then he called Chen Shi-fu and they ladled the precious water into buckets for the vegetable garden, and the tub and the *you bu* were put away for another week. We learned very quickly to conserve water, as we paid for it by the bucketful, carried up all the way from the river.

We slept on the screened porch at the front of the house. In warm weather my bed was placed alongside the railing, where I looked out over the dark city and river and sometimes saw the stars if the sky was clear. Not long after dark the city and the compound became quiet, leaving the night to the lonely song of a cicada or the patient comments of a cricket. Up there at the top of the hill, I could hear very clearly any noise from the cottages on the terraces below our house. One night I heard a woman die in the house below ours. She was the wife of a Yali teacher and had been sick a long time with tuberculosis. For weeks I'd awakened to her bouts of hollow coughs reverberating over the hillside. That night a particularly strident attack of coughing suddenly ceased in the sound of spattering liquid, and the next morning we learned she had died of a hemorrhage.

&

During our first weeks in Yuanling, Molly was my closest companion. She was always ready to play, and whenever I came into the house she went into transports of delight, as though I'd been away for a month. She slept on the back porch in a wooden box with a door cut in one side. If she wasn't in the house, she was usually tied up on the back porch, because now and then she took it in her head to wander. When that happened, I walked all over the compound calling her name, terrified that she'd never come back, but she always did.

When we first came to Yuanling, Molly was not thought to be a dog. A pedigreed cocker spaniel with glossy black fur, long fringed ears, stubby tail, and a loving disposition, she bore no resemblance to the street dogs of Yuanling—"wonks," we called them—which were mangy, lean, and mean, with tattered ears, festering sores, and ratty tails. I took Molly on the street by myself only once, when, under the watchful eye of the gate man, I went across the street to buy a pencil. Variations of that occasion, however, were played out over the first year we were in Yuanling whenever we took Molly out of the compound.

"What's that?" asked the man from whom I bought the pencil, pointing with his chin to Molly, who was pulling on her end of the rope. I tugged her to a stop and said she was my dog.

"That's a *dog*?" He looked skeptical. "Really? It doesn't look like a dog."

"It's a dog. An American dog," I explained a little defensively, mentally crossing my fingers because she'd been a gift from Mr.

Heinrichsohn, who was German. The shopkeeper slid each hand into the opposite sleeve and looked amused.

By this time a crowd was gathering, and Molly was making for various feet, sniffing interestedly. The feet shuffled back nervously. *"Ai-ya, ai-ya!"* exclaimed the crowd, and I tugged on her rope again. There was uneasy laughter as she sat down and simultaneously wiggled her rear, a habit she had. "What is it?" the crowd asked, and more people gathered in back, standing on tiptoe to see.

I pulled Molly to my side. "It's a foreign dog," the shopkeeper said knowledgeably, his hands still in his sleeves. When people laughed incredulously, he added, "Anyway, that's what she says."

I turned to leave, wondering how I'd get through the wall of onlookers. I couldn't see the gate man through the crowd. But the way opened as Molly and I approached. "That's not a dog," I heard someone say. "It's a baby lion."

"A lion? *That's* not a lion," someone else retorted. "It's more like a goat. A foreign goat!"

Some children took up the refrain and followed us as we walked the short distance to our gate. "Foreign goat, foreign goat," they chanted. "Foreign goat!"

Molly paid no attention, but I was furious. *Stupid!* I thought. *They're stupid. She does* not *look like a goat!* When she lingered to sniff the gate post, I said, "Come *on,* Molly!" and pulled her through, past the watching gate man. Preoccupied, I did not notice then that during the whole episode, while Molly had been the object of derision, no one had ridiculed me.

After a while, people seemed to get used to Molly, and she drew little attention beyond an occasional comment. Sometimes someone even held out a tentative hand to her as though wanting to make her acquaintance. Although the street children of Yuanling sometimes called after me, they never did make it a habit to call me names as they had in Changsha and in the towns along the East River. Perhaps that was because, compared to Molly, I did not seem so unusual. Or perhaps they even grew to like her, and by association accepted me as well. In any case, with Molly's presence, Yuanling felt like a friendly place.

Freud was wrong. The years between little-girlhood and the uncertainties of adolescence were not "latent." Those were the years when I owned my body completely. It did what I wanted—jumped and ran and sang and shouted and hopped, danced and twirled and climbed trees and hills, ran up and down steps, pumped swings, hung upside down, and stood on its head. I learned to embroider and knit, and on the piano how to shape the curve of a melody. Starting under the tutelage of Auntie Bay from the Presbyterian Mission at the other end of town, I progressed to the solid harmony of hymns and eventually to the contrapuntal colloquies of Bach Inventions.

In those years reading became almost an addiction. I had about two hundred books, British and American, my own supply augmented by those we found in the house when we moved in. It was an eclectic selection: Louisa May Alcott (my favorite), Mark Twain, Dickens, Edgar Allan Poe, *Lamb's Tales from Shakespeare, Grimm's Fairy Tales, Winnie the Pooh, The Five Little Peppers and How They Grew, Hans Brinker, Alice in Wonderland, Heidi, The Secret Garden, Treasure Island, The Little Princess, The Jungle Book, Anne of Green Gables*, and more. For four years I devoured them over and over again, living in their worlds and soaking up their language—the rhythms of English, the sound and feel of its words, and the tensile strength of its syntax. I also developed the habit of forgetting the content of what I'd just read, so that when I read it again it was fresh.

Outside our home, I heard very little English. As the only non-Chinese child in the city, I mostly heard and spoke Hunanese. For four years I had the same playmates—long enough for us to form friendships, to grow together, to fashion our own culture, and to share our absorption in the interests of the moment. Xi-xi (pronounced "shee-shee") was my best friend. She lived next door with her older sister and her mother and father, Reverend OuYang, pastor of the Evangelical Church, at the bottom of the staircase just inside the gate. Xi-xi had a round face, a shy smile, and a retiring manner when she was among adults but not when the two of us were together by ourselves. We were together as much as possible, and every day one of us would call the other out to play. Our voices carried well across the echoing space between our houses. I could hear Xi-xi from inside our house with all the doors closed: *"Buh-jin, lai lo!* Buh-jin, come!" I would run to the front porch and holler back, *"Lai da!* I'm coming!" and we'd meet on the ground between the houses. There my father had the school carpenter build a gymnastic bar, where we hung by our knees like two possums dangling from a limb, Xi-xi's bob hanging down like a black brush and my braids like yellow plumb lines. Or we just sat on the bar and talked. In front of the bar, the carpenter built a lofty wooden swing on which we took turns pumping so high that the ropes went slack and we swept above the level of the lower branches of a tall old "toon tree," we called it, across the path.

My other best friend was Tou Yuan-mei, our cook's eldest daughter. She was a little younger than Xi-xi and I, and although she, too, was quiet and proper when grown-ups were around, she showed her feelings more readily and was noisier than Xi-xi. Her mother often wanted her home to help out with housework or the younger children, but whatever free time she had, she was with us. When school was out, I usually met Xi-xi and Yuan-mei by the swing and the three of us walked around the compound, talking and knitting like Mrs. Tou and Mrs. OuYang. Those ladies were always knitting sweaters and leggings for their families, and when the clothes were finally outgrown by the youngest child in the family, they were unraveled to make something else. They gave us the yarn that had been used too often to make an acceptable garment, and we busily practiced different stitches, knitting squares and strips until our supply was used up. Then we unraveled the knitting and started over again. After some time we tired of having nothing to show for our diligence and started to knit in earnest. I knit my first sweater when I was nine, made with black yarn unraveled from an old sweater Mother and I found in the attic.

In hot weather we carried small teapots on our perambulations and sucked boiled water from the spouts, or munched on raw *liang shu,* a large root like a turnip, the juice of which was cool and fresh. We kicked a shuttlecock straight up in the air with the sides of our feet, seeing who could kick it the most times before missing. We bounced a rubber ball, competing in fancy moves between bounces. With other children on the compound we played hide-and-seek in the bushes on the various terraces bordering the stone steps. We jumped rope, intoning Chinese jump rope chants. We played hopscotch Chinese style, where you could *never* have two feet on the ground at once and had to hop over the square where the stone had fallen before you picked it up.

We made a graveyard behind my house. There we interred the dead mice from the traps in our houses, if their bodies were intact. For as long as it was interesting (a matter of a couple of weeks) we buried the mice in matchboxes while we sang "God Be with You till We Meet Again" in Chinese, and prayed long-winded prayers like the ones we endured in church.

We would have liked to give decent burials to the rats who held nightly track meets in the attics of our houses. But when they were trapped we were not allowed to have anything to do with them. They were disposed of by the servants—very carefully, for rats were known to carry bubonic plague. There had been only a few cases of plague in Yuanling, but in Changde, 150 miles downriver, the Japanese had dropped wheat with infected fleas, and a raging epidemic was prevented from spreading beyond the city only by the superhuman efforts of the mission hospitals working with the unprepared and underfunded health authorities.

Our days were punctuated by *jin bao*—air raid alerts. The year before we came to Yuanling the city had been severely bombed twice. Now Japanese planes passed near the city almost daily on their way to other targets. Occasionally the bombers were accompanied by fighter planes that strafed people trying to escape the bombs. It was generally believed that someday soon the Japanese would bomb Yuanling again. Thanks to the new electric plant, a very loud siren had been installed to alert the populace of approaching planes, and its urgent warning could be heard for miles wailing up and down over the town and river.

One summer day there had been a *jin bao* that lasted all day, and several people died from the heat, having stayed out without water on the bare hillsides in the merciless sun. Since then a system had been arranged so that people could judge when they should flee. After the siren's first warning, it sounded again when the planes came within what was considered a dangerous range—a fast, short wail that set everyone hurrying out of the city. Usually there was half an hour or more before this urgent warning sounded, and some days there was none at all. But in the closing months of 1940 urgent signals were more frequent and sometimes sounded only a few minutes after the first. The governor of Yuanling ruled that all shops should close at eight o'clock in the morning and open again at four in the afternoon so that people could evacuate quickly during those hours when *jin bao* were most likely.

On several hilltops behind the city, scaffolds were erected on which huge colored lanterns were hoisted—black for one plane, white for several, and red for many. When the siren went off, we paused in whatever we were doing, and I or one of the servants ran out to look at the distant scaffold, squinting to determine the color of the lantern, a dot against the bright sky. People would consult and confirm with each other—"Yes, yes. It's black!" or "It's white!" or "Red!"—and yell to others what they saw, then stroll off or hurry away, depending on the color. If it was black, we knew there was only one plane and went about our usual business. But when the ball was white or red, my father picked up a rug and a bag packed especially for air raids and we started out to a ravine behind the hill on which our compound was located. There, at the bottom of the ravine, the Yali boys attended classes in open sheds furnished with benches and portable blackboards. If the planes came within hearing distance, a soldier on a nearby hilltop blew his bugle and the entire school filed into a very large dugout that had been tunneled into the wall of the ravine. With all the school inside, the dugout was very crowded, so sometimes, if the weather permitted, the three of us walked back into the hills instead of staying in the ravine. Usually we hadn't gone far before the siren sounded the all clear, sliding up to a long, joyful hoot of release.

The first time we had a *jin bao* I was excited and scared, and held Mother's hand as we joined the line of people from the compound walking out the back way, past a Buddhist temple and down into the ravine. On the brow of the hill, we looked back and saw the townspeople scattered over the countryside, toiling up the hills with large bundles on their backs. Tears ran down Mother's cheeks as she watched them. "Poor, poor people," she said.

We followed the students down into the ravine and sat on a bench in one of the sheds. I wondered what was going to happen, and tried to listen for the bugle over the murmur of many voices, but nothing more happened that day. While we were waiting, my father took me to explore the dugout. Made in roughly in the shape of an M with three entrances, it was large enough to shelter the entire population of the compound, about seven hundred in all. Inside there was a wooden floor and double rows of benches along the walls, which dripped with moisture. It was colder in there than outside, but in summer it would be a relief from the sweltering heat of the ravine.

Mother said she never got used to the *jin bao*. But as days, weeks, and then months passed without a bombing, I did get used to them. In fact, I looked forward to them because they usually meant a break in schoolwork and I could play with Xi-Xi and Yuan-mei until the all clear sounded. But once in our first year, the earliest *jin bao* of the day sounded at half past six in the morning, and another time we had four in one day. Even for me that was too much.

There was a *jin bao* on our first Christmas morning in Yuanling. The urgent alert sounded soon after the first siren, then the bugle's warning, so we left our presents unopened and hurried out to the ravine. It was a cold, overcast day of bone-chilling damp, with rain in the air. When we reached the dugout, students were already seated along the walls. The mist of their breath hung like smoke in the dim light filtering in from the entrance. They sat tightly together in their padded jackets, hunched over in the cold, their chilblained fingers thrust up the opposite sleeve. As we stepped into the entrance, they shifted to make room for us. We sat there waiting for what seemed like a long time. Nothing happened. Someone further along the tunnel started to sing. The song spread rapidly, resonant and strong, along the benches until the whole tunnel reverberated with joyful harmony, some singing in Chinese, others in English:

> *Hark the herald angels sing.*
> *"Glory to the newborn king;*
> *Peace on earth, and mercy mild,*
> *God and sinners reconciled."*
> *Joyful all ye nations rise,*
> *Join the triumph of the skies;*
> *With the angelic host proclaim,*
> *"Christ is born in Bethlehem."*

And so we spent Christmas morning singing carols until the all clear sounded. We learned later that Japanese planes had spent the morning in the skies over Changde, bombing the town and strafing the inhabitants as they tried to flee.

༄

In the gray days of late winter, the city started to prepare for the most important festival of all, the lunar new year. Houses were cleaned, stoops were swept, special food was cooked, and new clothes were made for those who could afford them. Everyone seemed happier. It was a five-day holiday for everyone—a time for families. Shops were closed. People visited the houses of relatives and friends, ate special cakes and fruit, and looked forward to the culminating event of the season: the visit of the dragon for good fortune for the year.

On the night of our first lunar new year in Yuanling, most of the families in the compound walked down into town, mingling with the massed people packed along the sides of the street. I sat on my father's shoulders above everybody's head and thrilled to the exciting rhythm of the Lion Dance. In ancient times the Chinese hadn't seen many lions, and so the lion that dances at the lunar new year looks more like a giant pug dog than a lion. No matter. On that night he shook his head in fine style as he made his way down the street, pausing every few yards to twirl and lunge to the accelerated clashing of cymbals before they slowed down again and he went on his way.

After the lion moved on, the crowd pushed forward in anticipation of the dragon, who was snaking his way around the long curve of Yuanling's main street. In China, the dragon is an auspicious monster who brings good luck if one treats him right. People in the crowd readied strings of firecrackers to throw at the feet of the men who carried the dragon's painted cloth back draped over wicker baskets on poles. The men swooped the poles up and down and sideways in synchronized waves to simulate the progress of a giant snake. At the end of the dragon a painted paper tail arced up toward the sky.

We waited. Then we sensed rather than heard the distant thunder of the dragon's gigantic drum throbbing under the continuous fusillade of exploding firecrackers way back down the street. As the dragon approached, we heard the high shrilling of a flute playing a jaunty little tune over the deliberate cadence of the drum and the slow clash of cymbals. Now and then the dragon paused to dance and twirl in front of some shop that had paid for his visit, and the flute stopped while the drum accelerated to a roar and the cymbals vibrated into one continuous sound. Then they slowed to their marching rhythm again and the flute resumed its cheerful whistle, and we knew the dragon was on his way.

"Lai da! Lai da!" the crowd murmured. "He's coming, he's coming!" Slowly the dragon advanced up the street, emerging from the smoke of

thousands of firecrackers. The drum and cymbals grew louder, the flute more piercing. People around us started throwing strings of firecrackers in the street, and the noise expanded into a stupendous crescendo as the dragon approached. In the flaring light of continuous explosions, his magnificent head with bulging eyes lunged back and forth through the smoke in time to the ponderous pulse of the drum. I felt the power of his awesome beneficence throbbing against the sides of my head and through my face to my back teeth. The noise from the crowd, the shrill of the flute, the unspeakable din of the drum, the cymbals, and the firecrackers made it impossible to hear oneself shout, or even to think. It was wonderful.

The dragon passed, his head and swirling back fading into the smoke up the street. Soon the drum slowed down, then ceased. My ears were ringing when my father put me down. The chatter of the dispersing crowd seemed muted as we shuffled up the street through a carpet of red paper shredded from the firecrackers. Smoke drifted up past the overhanging roofs, and drafts of fresh air washed away the acrid smell of gunpowder. A stray firecracker popped like a period at the end of a sentence. As we walked home, I felt complete, filled with light, benevolence, and echoes of joyful pandemonium. I was embedded in Yuanling. I belonged here.

TOU SHI-FU AND THE ETHICS OF EATING

Our new cook, Tou Shi-fu, lived with his wife and two children in a three-room cottage near our house. Of medium build, with a shaved head, oval face, and direct eyes, he started out the day in a starched white apron that became increasingly wilted and stained as the day progressed. He was a scrupulously honest and sometimes uncomfortably upright man of uncompromising principles. A strict and conscientious father, he spoke little and seldom smiled. Mrs. Tou, who had been a primary-school teacher before she married Tou Shi-fu, smiled frequently. A quiet and pleasant woman, she kept their house very clean and their children very neat in clothes and cloth shoes she made herself. The Tous were faithful members of the Evangelical church at the bottom of the hill—dedicated Christians of a more fundamentalist persuasion than we liberal Congregationalists. A few months after we arrived in Yuanling, Mrs. Tou became pregnant with their third child.

In accordance with custom, after their surname, Tou, the children's given names consisted of two words, the first word being the same for all the children in the family — Yuan for Yuanling. The second part of their given names was individual. Thus the oldest child, a son, was named Tou Yuan-fu, *fu* meaning "prosperity." Tou Yuan-mei was their second child, *mei* connoting "beauty." Their third child, a daughter, was Tou Yuan-an, *an* meaning "peace." Perhaps Tou Shi-fu chose that name because she was born shortly before Christmas, at the start of our second year in Yuanling.

For that Christmas, Xi-xi, Yuan-mei, and I decided to put on a nativity play. With the help of our parents, we organized and assembled a cast heavily weighted with members of the Tou family and costumed mostly by the Rugh family. Eleven-year-old Tou Yuan-fu, in my father's bathrobe and with a dish towel fastened around his head, was Joseph. Yuan-mei, in a blue housecoat of my mother's and another dish towel for a veil, was Mary. Children of other servants and faculty, wearing various items of our clothing, were shepherds and wise men. We had planned to place a doll in the manger, but the baby, Tou Yuan-an, was born in time to star as the Christ child. The cast briefly included Molly, who represented the animals in the stable until she was relegated to the back porch for being too interested in the audience. Xi-xi and I made up the remainder of the cast.

94

We were both garbed in sheets cinched at the waist with belts of tinsel and with tinsel circlets around our foreheads. Xi-xi served as the heavenly host, and I, feeling very angelic with my hair flowing loose down my back, was Gabriel.

The production was presented in our living room. Our desks were pushed back against the bay window to make room for the performance, and a couple of sheets draped over a wire served as a curtain. When the adults in the audience were seated on chairs borrowed for the occasion and the children were settled on the floor, Mother started up on the piano with "O Come All Ye Faithful." Everyone sang while the sheets were pulled aside to reveal the Virgin Mary on a stool, knitting. Reverend OuYang, Xi-xi's father, started his reading of the Annunciation in mellifluous Mandarin measures, and I hoisted myself through the window from the sleeping porch onto Mother's desk, where I stood with arms spread wide as Gabriel announcing to Mary that she was going to have a baby. Mary, in turn, looked worried, put down her knitting, and stood up while Reverend OuYang read the Magnificat. A couple of scenes later, Mrs. Tou put Yuan-an in the manger, which otherwise served as a washtub, and the play progressed, with one unplanned intermission when the Christ child turned fretful. We sang Christmas carols accompanied by Mother at the piano while Mrs. Tou nursed the baby, who then reeled off to sleep. With the Christ child restored to the manger, events unfolded as foretold and ended with tea and Christmas cookies for everyone.

By our third Christmas in Yuanling, inflation had soared out of control. My weekly allowance was one million Chinese dollars, and I had to save for six weeks to buy a pencil in the shop across the street. When Tou Shi-fu did the daily marketing, he carried a small suitcase full of paper money. Neither the school's income nor ours could keep up with the inflation without drastic cutting of expenditures. Servants' salaries, however, were paid partly in a fixed portion of rice for each member of the family, and that remained unchanged.

Mrs. Tou's fourth baby, a boy named Tou Yuan-lo, arrived shortly before Christmas. It was hard to keep up support of this ever-growing family. After the holiday, my father invited Tou Shi-fu to his study to discuss the problem, telling him that he would be unable to provide for another child should they have one. In reply, Tou Shi-fu apologized for causing trouble and returned to the kitchen.

The next summer it became evident that another little Tou was on the way. My father invited Tou Shi-fu to his study and reminded him of their previous conversation. Tou Shi-fu again apologized for causing trouble. But, he explained, he and Mrs. Tou had prayed about it and God had promised them that Reverend Rugh would find a way to support the baby. "I can only have faith—faith in God," Tou Shi-fu said, and, perhaps by inference, faith in Reverend Rugh as well.

The fifth baby was born in time for Christmas. They named him Tou Yuan-li, in honor of Yali—also in honor of Reverend Rugh, who represented Yali and who indeed had found a place in our budget to accommodate the latest arrival. And so it came to pass that God's promise to the Tous was fulfilled.

Tou Shi-fu devoted as much energy and dedication to his profession as he did to his expanding family. He was an outstanding cook. His previous employers had been Danish missionaries who had left Yuanling before we came. From them he learned to make pastries, and he was so good at it that when they departed they gave him an antique springerle board that had been in their family. The board was a work of art—dark smooth wood with a subtle grain, finely carved with Scandinavian designs, smelling faintly of anise and quietly gleaming from the butter of generations of springerle cookies. For me, Christmastime in Yuanling is synonymous with Tou Shi-fu's springerle cookies impressed with designs from the board. They were, simply put, fit for the Christ child Himself. All other Christmas cookies I have known are but pitiful attempts at counterfeit, and as a result, Christmas for me has never again carried the flavor of the holy celebration it had then.

Mother had brought a few pounds of white flour and refined sugar from Hong Kong, meant for Christmases, Thanksgivings, and birthdays over the next two years, as originally planned. But we stayed four years instead of two, and the supplies ran out. I hardly noticed. From the ingredients available in Yuanling, Tou Shi-fu cooked a variety of food, both Chinese and Western. The local flour looked as though it had been swept up from the street—which was a possibility. He sifted it for pebbles and bits of trash and weevils and then spread it out in the sun for the final weevils to crawl out to where he could pick them off. The local sugar, called *bien tan* in Hunanese, was unrefined and came in hard brown slabs. Undoubtedly it was healthier than the white sugar we kept for special occasions, if one discounted the bits of straw and pebbles mixed into the local product. They were disposed of by melting the sugar to syrup so that the straw went to the top and the pebbles to the bottom.

The local dairy product was water buffalo milk, never drunk by the Chinese, who considered it unfit for human consumption. Indeed, in those days, if you should ask the average Hunanese about drinking milk, she would look as though you were suggesting a cup of cow saliva. Although I felt the same way, my parents didn't, and so I was presented every day with a cup of water buffalo milk at breakfast.

Water buffalo milk is high in butterfat and has a peculiar smell. We bought three cups daily from a farmer who had established a monopoly catering to the perverted milk-drinking habits of the foreigners in town. Like his brethren in other cities, he had tried adding water to his product to make it go further, possibly in the belief that, it being *water* buffalo milk, extra water would be acceptable and/or undetectable. But Tou Shi-fu possessed a hydrometer left him by his Danish mentors and had been able to demonstrate to the farmer that he was mistaken. Thereafter, each morning the farmer would come up the back steps and say to Tou Shi-fu, "*Lai da,* I've come," and ladle out three cups (smaller than the American measure) into the pan Tou Shi-fu wordlessly held out to him. Still saying nothing, Tou Shi-fu, whose silences were frequently fraught with unspoken feeling, would get out the hydrometer, put it in the pan, and watch the upright glass tube until it became still. While Tou Shi-fu checked the markings on the tube to make sure it was floating at the right level, the farmer was the picture of unconcern, carefully repositioning his milk can with total concentration or wiping his face with a rag while looking around absentmindedly. Finally, when Tou Shi-fu grunted and got out the money for three cups of milk, the farmer pocketed the payment, picked up the can, and thumped down the steps, saying with a hint of injured virtue, "*Zou-da,*"—"I'm going." Meanwhile Tou Shi-fu returned wordlessly to the kitchen with his 100 percent water buffalo milk and put it on the stove to boil.

Some of the milk was used for butter, which Tou Shi-fu made by shaking the milk in a mason jar until he got a knob of pure white grease. As there was no refrigeration, he had to make butter every day. Some of the milk was used for our cereal, and one cup was inevitably reserved for me. It came to the table warm with a white skin floating on the surface. Milk in this form was very slightly better than Klim. Given the option, I chose to pick off the wrinkled skin, which drooped off the edge of my spoon like a little rag, and drank the milk down without breathing, leaving Klim to the weevils.

But breakfast à la Tou Shi-fu was infinitely better than what we'd had with our previous cook in Changsha. Gone were the days of burnt toast scraped to approximate the right color. The grayness of Tou Shi-fu's bread, made from the local flour, was hidden by the golden perfection to which it was toasted. He made pancakes and waffles served with water buffalo butter and *bien-tan* syrup. We had whole-wheat cereal that he ground on a grindstone on the back porch from roasted kernels of wheat, out of which he also made a beverage like Postum as a substitute for coffee. His orange marmalade and his jams made from kumquats, pears, or peaches were ambrosial. His peanut butter, made from roasted peanuts repeatedly put through a meat grinder and tinged with sesame oil, was rich and nutty — the perfect complement for toast with kumquat jam. He owned a gadget for making sausages, and I spent hours watching him stuff the translucent casings with ground pork and spices. He also made our bacon, and smoked both the sausage and bacon in a smoke room under the back porch.

At noon we ate Chinese food, my absolute favorite, unless it included chestnuts, which I abhorred. I also didn't care for peas, lima beans, or liver, which all had the same pasty consistency as chestnuts; in fact, their very names *meant* bland, mealy pastiness. But I reluctantly tolerated them. They were usually served with Western meals, for which I had low expectations anyway. Chestnuts, however, either as a hot snack on a cold day or in Chinese food as part of a dish, were the worst. They were deceitful, purporting to be nuts and showing some promise of crispness when one's teeth popped through the skin, only to become soft and mealy inside with no hint of nuttiness whatsoever. My parents respected my antipathy for chestnuts because they were the only food that I absolutely refused to allow past my lips.

I stuffed myself on Chinese food at noon. If it was a day when Xi-xi had no school, I shoveled down my first bowl of rice and *cai* (pronounced "tsai")—the food in serving bowls at the middle of the table, such as bean curd with chilies, fermented black beans, and scallions; fresh river fish steamed with ginger and chives; or bok choy, which we called *"buh-tsai"* in Hunan, stir-fried in oil with garlic and a touch of salt. Then I'd pile my second bowl of rice with *cai* and hurry outside to the swing and call for Xi-xi. When she appeared with her bowl and chopsticks, we set out to stroll around the compound, consuming our rice at leisure and catching up with whatever was important since we had separated for lunch. Sometimes a servant or a student was passing by when we started out, and we asked him to hold our rice bowls while we climbed up onto the bar and finished our meal sitting balanced six feet off the ground. I have no recollection of what we talked about, but the food eaten in Xi-xi's company was the best I've ever had.

The evening meal was another matter. Dinner was always Western style. Grown-ups held the view that Tou Shi-fu's Western meals were as superb as his Scandinavian pastries, but I considered that opinion to be unenlightened hyperbole. As far as I was concerned, Western meals at best were to be politely tolerated. Consequently, I often ate dinner with a minimum of chewing, gulping it down with lots of water, impatient to go outside for a final hour in the twilight before bedtime.

In spite of my lack of enthusiasm for Western food, the rule at home was that I had to eat something of everything and clean my plate—a feat I accomplished when necessary by swallowing whole the single pea or lima bean served me as a result of negotiation with one or the other parent. But when we ate Western meals as guests at someone else's house, it was assumed that I would eat everything I was served, politely and without question—a trial for which I received little sympathy.

Chinese feasts were a different matter. One of the many advantages of Chinese over Western food was the practice of leaving food on your plate to signal that you'd had enough. Hapless foreigners unacquainted with this civilized custom gorged themselves cross-eyed, trying to empty their plates, at which point their hosts generously piled them high again. And when the foreign guest frantically tried to stop them, the hospitable hosts took this as the usual polite hint for more.

But whether food was Chinese or Western, I somehow became convinced it should be taken seriously and treated with respect. This attitude was reinforced by the Chinese world around us—a world in which anything edible could be made delicious (except chestnuts) and where taste, texture, and contrast were important, set off on a background of perfectly cooked rice. It was a world in which eating was literally a celebration of life, for starvation lurked on the other side of the compound wall. It was a world in which people memorialized everything from friendship to weddings with a feast, for eating together was a confirmation of their mutual humanity and the bonds that held them to each other. Over time I had acquired the opinion that to refuse food, even Western food, was like refusing friendship or declining a gift—despicably rude and uncivilized. In fact, this attitude became so ingrained that I came to believe, to my own discomfort, that to refuse food was unethical, almost a sin.

My views on the ethics of eating were put to the ultimate test by Miss Granner. She was an American nurse with the Evangelical Mission and lived on the ground floor of our house, where she employed a cook, Li Shi-fu, with his wife as household help. Miss Granner was a stocky woman with short gray hair and no-nonsense shoes, who spoke both English and Hunanese with a midwestern twang, always directly and to the point. She didn't approve of Mother. Late one fall she came to see me in our living room, where I was propped up on an army cot, coughing and wheezing with one of my periodic bouts of asthma and bronchitis, which lingered long in those days before antibiotics. She looked at me appraisingly and slid her hand under the blankets to feel my feet. Then, turning to my mother, she said, "Her feet are cold! Don't you have a hot-water bottle?" Mother, a bit surprised, said, "Why, yes, I do, but Betty Jean has a fever."

"Don't you know that she can get pneumonia if you don't keep her warm?" Miss Granner said. She stumped out through our dining room and told Tou Shi-fu to bring some hot water, which he did, making it necessary for Mother to produce the hot-water bottle. Miss Granner filled it, pressed out the air, twisted in the stopper, grabbed a towel from the washstand, wrapped it around the hot-water bottle, and put it against the bottom of my feet. It felt good. "This is how you do it," she said. "Now, you call me *immediately* if she gets worse!" and she clumped out of the room. Mother's eyes had turned more blue than usual and her lips were tight as she brushed back the hair from my forehead. After each whistling exhalation I pulled up my shoulders to suck in more air, miserable and confused, scared of Miss Granner, hurt for Mother, guilty for having cold feet, and wondering if I'd get pneumonia.

Later that year, on a crisp and sunny December day, Mother and I were walking outside toward the back of the house when Miss Granner came out on her front porch. She looked down at me. "Betty Jean," she said without preamble, "would you like to eat lunch with me tomorrow?" I stood absolutely still. Never had I contemplated such an eventuality. I looked up at Mother, who looked back questioningly. Then I looked at Miss Granner.

"Thank you very much," I heard myself reply, and wondered how I would spend a whole lunch alone with her.

"Good!" she exclaimed. "Li Shi-fu is planning a chestnut lunch— chestnut soup, chestnut *cai,* and chestnut dessert!" She beamed. "Isn't that wonderful?" She looked strange smiling.

My ears started to ring. I felt light-headed, my chest empty and my knees loose. I don't know what shocked me more—Miss Granner's happy enthusiasm, so out of character, or the prospect of not just one chestnut, not just one dish of chestnuts, but a whole *meal* of chestnuts.

"Yes, it's wonderful," I said faintly. "Thank you," and felt my lips stretch in a mendacious smile.

Mother squeezed my hand and we went home. "Oh, Betty Jean," she said, looking as though she was going to laugh and cry at the same time, "I'm so proud of you!"

At the dinner table that evening, she told my father the news. "Dwight," she said, "Betty Jean is going to have lunch with Miss Granner tomorrow."

My father looked a little surprised. Then he smiled at me. "Well, that was nice of her to ask you."

I didn't reply. He glanced at Mother and then back at me. I looked down at my plate, my eyes stinging. Mother spoke. "It's a lunch of chestnuts,*"* she told him, her voice flat. "All chestnuts."

"Even the *soup,*" I finally got out, still looking at my plate. There was a moment of silence.

"No!" my father exclaimed. "Really?"

I nodded. There was another moment of silence.

"And you're going." It was a statement.

I nodded again.

"Brave girl!" he said.

With those words I thought of a book about Joan of Arc I'd recently finished reading in a flood of tears. Remembering how bravely she had gone to the stake, I sensed the bonds of sisterhood stretching down through the centuries and felt a little better. *But,* I thought as I returned to my dinner, *she didn't have to eat chestnuts.*

The next morning at eleven-thirty I went downstairs by myself to eat lunch with Miss Granner. She and I sat across from each other at her dining room table. We shut our eyes and bowed our heads while she thanked God in the name of Jesus for what we were about to receive. "Amen," I said. (Joan of Arc, too, had prayed while the English soldiers tied her to the stake.)

Li Shi-fu brought in the soup. It consisted of ground chestnuts in a broth—a murky brown pool in the soup bowl in front of me. As I spooned it to my mouth, the receding liquid revealed two boiled chestnuts lying on the bottom of the bowl like dead snails. With my chopsticks I picked one up, pulled back my lips so they wouldn't touch it, and bit it in half. While Miss Granner concentrated on consuming the last drop in her bowl, I swallowed each half unchewed, gagging slightly. She helped herself to more. Politely I declined a second helping and left the remaining chestnut rolling around in my bowl—inconspicuously, I hoped—as it was taken away.

I had quickly grasped the fact that Miss Granner's cook was not in Tou Shi-fu's league. I also realized that Miss Granner had no appreciation for serving a proper Chinese meal. If she had, we could have had the soup last, which would have put it off for a while and obviated the need for dessert.

Fortunately Miss Granner did not pile my bowl with generous helpings of *cai,* which she should have done if she'd been a proper Chinese host. Instead she said, "Help yourself!" as though granting me a treat, and dug in. I do not remember our conversation during the meal. I believe we did very little talking. My attention was devoted to eating the non-chestnut part of each dish without appearing to neglect the chestnuts.

There were three dishes of *cai.* One was chestnuts protruding like little tumors from a dull green mound of steamed string beans flavored with soy sauce. Another was chicken and onions with sliced chestnuts that looked like water chestnuts but didn't *feel* like them when my teeth sagged into their substance. The third was chunks of pork with limp bamboo shoots among which the chestnuts lurked—little nodules of pastiness that dripped with coagulating gravy when I lifted them with my chopsticks. Unfortunately, Miss Granner didn't like spicy food, so there were none of the usual Hunan chilies with which to numb my mouth. But, blessedly, there was plenty of flaky hot rice to shovel in around the chestnuts, which made them less noticeable. I had three bowls of rice, but in spite of my efforts to avoid them, I consumed enough chestnuts to reforest a hillside. Miss Granner looked pleased.

After a very long time the meal ended with dessert—candied chestnuts in syrup. It was surprising. By that time, I didn't notice anything except the sweet slipperiness of the syrup.

At last I laid down my spoon and thanked Miss Granner. "I'd better go home," I said. She smiled and looked understanding, thinking, perhaps, that with all I had eaten, I had to go to the bathroom. When I arrived upstairs, my parents were working at their desks.

"Hello!" my father said.

"How was it, dear?" asked Mother.

They had recently finished a delicious Chinese meal cooked to perfection by Tou Shi-fu.

"It was all right," I replied with brave nonchalance.

"That's good," Mother said, and went back to correcting papers.

"Good girl," echoed my father, and resumed his typing.

I thought of Joan of Arc dying alone and unappreciated. "I'm going to call Xi-xi," I announced.

"Fine, dear," said Mother, not looking up from her papers. Evidently my father didn't hear, for he just kept on typing.

I loosened my belt and headed for the back porch. Raising my voice above the chattering typewriter, I spoke over my shoulder. "I still don't like chestnuts," I said, and walked out the door.

CHILD'S PLAY

Life in Yuanling was pretty ordinary, flowing smoothly from one season into the next. At least that's the way it seemed to me and my friends. True, there was talk of bandits in the hills not far from town, and there was always the war. But while the grown-ups tried to distinguish between true and false rumors that flickered over the city like summer lightning, for us children the war was only a muttering of distant thunder, and most of the time we paid little attention. Now and then we noticed it, as when there was a jin bao. But as the months passed without a single Japanese airplane coming within hearing distance, my friends and I looked forward to the next *jin bao*, secretly hoping that it would end too late for us to resume our lessons.

Yuanling was basically defenseless except for a contingent of pitifully underfed Nationalist troops—some of them armed with rifles—and their better-fed officers. We paid them little notice until one bright day in late winter. Xi-xi, Yuan-mei, and I were kicking our shuttlecocks on the path in front of my house when we heard Yuan-fu, Yuan-mei's older brother, calling us softly. There was something about his voice that made us pocket our shuttlecocks quickly and run to where he was standing by the wall at the side of the compound. *"Si ren lai da,!"* he whispered, "the dead men have come!" and he squeezed into the space between the houses and the wall, shuffling sideways. We followed until we reached a wider space at the base of an ancient *mei hua* or flowering plum tree overlooking the wall that separated our compound from an old temple on the other side. At that time the temple was being used as a hospital for sick and injured Nationalist soldiers. Quietly we swarmed into the tree's sturdy branches, shielded by clouds of fragile *mei hua* flowers.

From our vantage point we looked down onto a stretch of packed earth in the courtyard of the temple. On down the hill beyond the temple were piles of garbage and trash. I had never seen anyone who looked like a doctor or a nurse, but once when I was climbing the tree, I had seen a very thin soldier, his uniform hanging from his shoulders and hips as if from wire hangers, leaning on a stick and picking through the garbage. He moved very slowly. After one look I had backed down the tree, feeling shaky.

Afterward I'd avoided the tree, even though it was a good one to climb. But this day my attention was riveted to the courtyard.

A naked man lay in the middle of the open space. His eyes were closed. Some long boxes of raw pine were stacked next to a door opening into the side of the temple. In contrast to the glaring sunlight on the ground, the shadowed interior of the building looked black. Two men emerged from the dark rectangle of the door carrying another naked man by his arms and legs and laid him next to the first. The men on the ground looked alike. Their skin, draped loosely over their bones, seemed unnaturally yellow, their arms and legs like sticks. *Those are dead men,* I thought, but it didn't really sink in.

I held on to my perch and watched the proceedings through the mist of delicate blossoms. The carriers went in and out through the door until several naked men lay on the ground. Then the carriers took a box from the pile by the door and dropped two dead men into it, one on top of the other. That done, they pushed a lid down on the box and carried it off, slung between two poles, out the back door of the courtyard toward the hills. Other carriers did the same until there was one man left on the ground. He was too stiff to fit in a box with another man. When they had carried him off, we began to back down the tree, but just then the first carriers returned with empty boxes, which they stacked back against the wall. After the men finally left, we finished climbing down the tree and ran home for lunch

At the table my mother said, "You look a little hot, dear. Where have you been?"

"Playing shuttlecock with Xi-xi and Yuan-mei," I replied, shoveling down my first bowl of rice and *cai*.

"That's nice, dear," Mother observed, and started to tell my father about preparations she was making for one of her classes. While they talked, I refilled my bowl with rice and *cai* and escaped to meet Xi-xi for the rest of the meal.

"Didn't it sound . . . loud when they dropped them in the coffins?" I said, sitting down on the top step of the porch.

"Mmm," Xi-xi responded, her mouth full of rice.

We knew that every day those who had died in the previous twenty-four hours were taken into the treeless hills to be buried in shallow unmarked graves. But we only watched one more time, when we were sure our parents were occupied elsewhere. It wasn't so interesting the second time, and we didn't go again. After a while the hospital either moved or conditions improved, for there were no more skeletal soldiers picking through the garbage or skeletal corpses carried out to be buried.

The dead men weren't real. Real people had nothing to do with those inert stick figures clattering into those wooden boxes. But there was a madwoman in Yuanling whose reality came uncomfortably close to mine. She was a strong-looking woman of indeterminate age, whose dirt-streaked face was framed by hanks of dull black hair topped by a rag twisted around her forehead. She carried several bags and bundles, and her clothing hung in tatters with skin showing through in places. Once when I was on the street, I caught a glimpse of her sitting against a wall, surrounded by bags and smiling fiercely at the empty air. Sometimes she stood in the middle of the street and pranced and jigged on her bare feet in a wild dance. When the street children teased her or pretended to grab one of her bags, she went on a rampage and tore down the street, waving the bags and lunging at the children. "Crazy woman!" they chanted. "Crazy woman! Come along, come along, come along!" They stayed just out of reach and shrieked as she darted after them. We could hear them all the way up to my house, and when that happened, some of the children in the compound raced down to the gatehouse door to peek at her through the cracks. I didn't join them, feeling a kind of reluctance tinged with embarrassment that I couldn't explain.

One day Yuan-mei and I were starting up the stone staircase when we heard the shrieking again. There was a crash and the volume of screams suddenly increased. We turned and saw that the gatehouse door was open and the woman was dancing her jig *inside* the gate. From where we stood I saw the top of her turbaned head twirling and bouncing and her rags flapping, while the gatekeeper stood by helplessly. People from the street started pushing in at the gate. There was a lot of yelling. The woman jigged away from the people toward the bottom of the stone staircase. The top of her head tipped back, and she glared up the steps at Yuan-mei and me standing above her.

I couldn't move. The woman lifted a foot toward the steps and thrust her arms up at us. Released by Yuan-mei's scream, I turned and raced past the houses on either side, up the 150 steps after Yuan-mei. I heard the woman panting behind us. When we reached the top and turned onto the path, I glanced over my shoulder to see how far ahead we were.

No one was there. We stopped. My whole body was heaving, and I started to shake. *"Ai ya,!"* I panted, *"pa si da!"*—I was scared to death!" Yuan-mei was crying and didn't respond. We walked around to the back of my house, and she went home sobbing. My legs were weak, and I had to pull myself up the stairs to our back porch. No one was home but Molly, who greeted me with barks, wiggles, and a wet tongue. I hugged her, and after a while I went to the front porch, where I lay down on my bed by the railing and looked down at the stone staircase. The noise had stopped. People were walking on the paths and going up and down the steps as usual, as though it hadn't happened, as though no one like the madwoman existed.

In the days that followed we invented a new kind of tag. The game started with "it" hiding somewhere on a terrace by the stone staircase while the rest of us nervously went up and down the whole length until "it" came roaring or sneaking out to try to catch one of us. Then we scattered, screaming, along the terraces and up the staircase until someone was caught. That person, in turn, became "it" and the game started over again.

After a day or so we had to move our game because of the traffic and the noise. Grown-ups toiling up and down the stone staircase shook their heads and clucked as we ran shrieking past. We shifted our venue to the topmost level of the compound, but soon we stopped. It was enough—at least for me. When I was "it," I felt something uncomfortably familiar that made me want to cry and make sure no one could find me. Soon we went on to other games and forgot about the madwoman.

One day I heard the familiar shrieking in the street below and knew the madwoman was at our end of town again. This time, in the taunts and shrieks of the street children, I heard echoes of what I hadn't thought of for a long time. Now I remembered how the street children of Changsha and the East River used to call out "Big nose! Big nose!" and "Foreign devil kid, foreign devil!" I hadn't felt anything then. Now my face turned hot and a lump burned in my throat as though I was ashamed of myself, as though there was something wrong with me. But I didn't know what it was, and after a while I didn't think about it anymore.

IN SEARCH OF QI

Except for Sundays, every morning around eight o'clock a cheerful cacophony of children's voices burst over the hillside. The noise came from one of the three other square houses along the path from ours, where there was a small primary school for the children who lived in the compound. Soon another chorus would join the first, chanting different words in different tones, then another, as each class tackled its lesson for the day. Xi-xi and Yuan-mei were there in second grade, and as I sat at home working my way through second grade with the Calvert home study system, I thought it would be a lot more fun to learn by shouting.

The next fall, when I was to start third grade at home, my parents agreed I could attend Chinese school an hour or so a day to learn how to read and write. I was eager to start. I loved the look of Chinese characters, and I wanted to be able to read like Xi-xi and Yuan-mei. Although they would be in third grade and I in first, I knew I'd catch up to them. After all, when I finished first grade at the Shanghai American School, I was reading third- and fourth-grade books, and I fully expected the same thing to happen again. I had heard grown-ups say that reading Chinese was so hard that it took several years of dedicated study before one could read even a newspaper. But I suspected they were exaggerating, as they did about other things that were quite ordinary, such as speaking Chinese or climbing the 150 steps up to our house.

At the opening of Chinese school that fall, I sat expectantly in a line of first-graders on a bench in the second row, our primers on the table in front of us. The teacher—I'll call her Miss Ju—held a piece of chalk and a primer in her hands and stood in front of the blackboard (literally boards painted black) waiting for us to settle down. She was a small, straight woman of indeterminate age, her jet black hair in the usual bob, her face stern. She reminded me of Miss Ting, my kindergarten teacher in Changsha. I resolved to do exactly as Miss Ju said.

Miss Ju held up her book and showed us how to open ours to the first page. The page was decorated with beautiful black characters written in the brush-writing style. They descended vertically in three stately rows down the right-hand side of the page. I could hardly wait to find out what they said. In the lower left-hand corner was a picture of a kitten jumping after a ball of yarn. Miss Ju wrote each character on the blackboard, announcing its sound in a penetrating voice, and the class chorused after her. Then we put the sounds together:

> *Xiao xiao mau,*
> *Xiao xiao mau,*
> *Tiao tiao tiao!*

"Tiny little cat," we chanted in two-two time, our voices dropping, with Hunanese intonation, a major third on the scale with the word for "cat." "Tiny little cat, jump, jump, jump!" On the word for "jump" we shouted on the highest tone triumphantly, "*Tiao, tiao, tiao!*" Then we started over again as loudly as we could, our forefingers moving down each row. My tones blended with those of the children around me as I discovered a shrill timbre to my voice I hadn't known I possessed. I was well into the swing of it when Miss Ju told us to move to the next page, decorated with more characters and a picture of a puppy chasing a ball. She wrote the new characters on the blackboard. "Little dog bark. Bark, bark, bark!" Her voice rang out in precise tones, and we started a new chant. After a while we chanted both pages in succession.

Eventually Miss Ju told us to stop and take out our slates and chalk to practice writing. She wrote the first character on the blackboard, the one meaning "little." It was only three strokes—a vertical line with a hook on the bottom and an elongated dot on each side. Simple. We copied it on our slates and waited. She walked back and forth between the rows to see what we'd done, pausing now and then to make a correction. Then she returned to the blackboard to introduce the remaining characters in turn: those for "cat," "jump," "dog," and "bark." They weren't so simple. Each consisted of several strokes that had to be put down in the right order and in proportion to the other strokes. She wrote each one slowly on the blackboard, showing us the succession of strokes while we followed her on our slates. The quiet in the room was broken only by the occasional squeak of chalk in midstroke. When our slates were full, we wiped them with a damp cloth and started over.

Although it had been fun to chant the lesson, I was a little puzzled. Chinese characters had always seemed mysterious to me, but I assumed that once in school, I would quickly learn how to unlock their secrets. In English, if I saw a new word, I could usually figure out what it was. But this wasn't like reading English. In the character for "dog" there was nothing that looked like a dog, and the character for "cat" had nothing feline about it that I could see. So I waited for Miss Ju to explain how we were to know what the characters meant. Meanwhile, I tried to memorize the configurations for "cat," "dog," "jump," and "bark" in the hope that soon I would understand how to decipher the new ones to come.

Days passed with no enlightenment. Each new lesson was the same— we chanted it until we knew it by heart and then Miss Ju showed us how to write the characters and we practiced writing them. My mind became jumbled with characters that looked vaguely familiar, but when I scrabbled for their meaning, it slipped away. It occurred to me that I didn't really care about reading a Chinese newspaper. For that matter, I wasn't sure that I wanted to go to the trouble of learning to read Chinese at all when I could read all I wanted in English. Doubt grew as my expectations shrank. But I still enjoyed chanting the lessons and trying to make characters with a special flair like the ones in the book At the end of each lesson, I consigned the new characters to short-term memory, not so much with the long-term hope of reading as with the more immediate goal of staying out of trouble with Miss Ju.

Chinese characters are symbols that began thousands of years ago as pictograms that have become so stylized that their original configuration is usually unrecognizable. However, there is a logic to the construction of many characters that gives a clue to their meaning. Moreover, there are specific rules for the order in which the strokes of a character are written. But in that first-grade classroom we were told none of this. If someone set down strokes in the wrong order, Miss Ju wiped them off the slate and said, "No. Write it like *this*." With the pupil holding the chalk, she firmly guided the child's hand under hers as she traced the strokes on the slate. Teaching was by demonstration without explanation. And mastery was achieved by the pressure of sheer repetition as the entire character, its sound, its shape, and the succession of its strokes, soaked into the muscles and larynx and slowly moved up the brain stem by osmosis, only last, if ever, reaching the higher learning centers where its meaning connected with the rest. My classmates seemed to catch on, but learning by osmosis did not come easily to me, and over the weeks the joys of becoming literate in Chinese grew very thin indeed. Frankly, I was bored in Chinese school and each morning trudged off to class with diminishing enthusiasm.

One day Mother asked me what I thought about taking Chinese lessons at home with Jeffrey Li, a student in her eleventh-grade English class. He came twice a week to work with my father on reading a thick book with tissue-thin pages covered with closely packed downward lines of black characters. When I asked what the book was, my father said he was reading Mencius. "What's that?" I asked, not realizing that reading Mencius in Chinese was comparable to reading Plato in Greek. He replied that Mencius had been a disciple of Confucius, who had lived long before Christ but had some of the same ideas. "Like what?" I asked absently, thinking about whether or not I really wanted to continue Chinese lessons. "Like the Golden Rule," my father answered. That brought me up short. What? Confucius thought of the Golden Rule before Jesus?

I remembered a picture at Sunday school in California showing Jesus preaching the Sermon on the Mount. I'd had the distinct impression that the Golden Rule started with him. Obviously they hadn't known about Confucius and Mencius in Sunday school, and for the first time I wondered, just a little, what else they hadn't known. I felt proud that a really good idea had come from China first and a little resentful that Sunday school had given Jesus all the credit. Evidently there were some advantages to reading Chinese. I decided to take Chinese lessons twice a week with Jeffrey.

Jeffrey was a typical Yali student with his head shaved to minimize care and infestation and dressed in black trousers and jacket done up to the neck. He must have been an excellent teacher for my father, but I was a student of very different caliber.

At our first session, Jeffrey asked me to read in the primer as far as I could. I opened it and launched into the first lesson, reading it perfectly. Gaining confidence, I went on to the second and the third. A few minutes later I successfully completed the last lesson I'd learned in Miss Ju's class, and looked up from the book. My performance had been flawless. Thanks to the hours I spent staying out of trouble with Miss Ju, I had absorbed enough by the osmosis method to declaim all the lessons by heart, using the pictures on the pages, rather than the characters, to confirm that I was saying the right words. To tell the truth, I could have recited all the lessons in succession without opening the book at all.

"Hao," said Jeffrey. "Good." Shutting the book, he went on, "Now, please write the first lesson." My attempts at writing were less successful, because I'd only learned the lessons by sound—I couldn't remember how to write the individual characters. So we started from the beginning. As the weeks passed, I made very little progress. I could memorize characters with a few strokes, but the more complicated ones slipped from my grasp almost overnight. To me they had no rhyme or reason, and no relation to what they were supposed to mean. My interest declined. With the onset of summer vacation, the lessons stopped and were not resumed the next fall. Jeffrey must have been as thankful as I.

It was six years later in Changsha that I decided to try again. Ever since I had been in Miss Ju's first grade I'd found something indescribable, something unaccountably attractive, about characters written with brush and ink. They marched boldly down the pages of my primer with an air of much greater significance than the mundane meanings Miss Ju assigned to them. Each one looked solid and immovable, yet together they looked full of vitality and potential motion. I wanted to make characters like that.

In China, calligraphy was considered the highest expression of art and culture. The brushwork with which a poem was written was an integral part of the poem, adding ineffable nuances and subtleties to the words and meaning of the whole. The art of painting grew out of calligraphy, and the quality of a painting was closely related to the quality of the painter's calligraphy. Many of China's famous painters were scholars and bureaucrats admired for their calligraphy. Although I didn't know these facts when I started out in Changsha, I did know that I was about to embark on something quintessentially Chinese.

I will call this tutor Teacher Wong—an elderly gentleman in a gray gown, permanently surrounded by the smell of cigarette smoke. He had a wispy beard and a mole on his cheek with a long hair coming out of it. His teeth and fingers were stained yellow with tobacco, and he had one pointed fingernail so long that it curved inward—the true mark of a scholar, who, by definition, did no manual labor.

At my first lesson, Teacher Wong opened a package wrapped in newspaper and handed me my new writing implements. First he took out a small ceramic bowl and asked me to fill it with water, a little over half full— he indicated the desired level with a rather dirty fingernail. I filled it and brought it back to the table. Next he brought out a bamboo brush about the size of a pencil, laying it on the table, and an inkstone—a rectangle of heavy black stone, about three by four inches, with a shallow raised rim precisely and finely tooled. When I hefted it in my hand, it felt cool and silky smooth. Finally he handed me a block of dried black ink shaped like a long domino. It had been pressed out of soot and water and some other substance that held it together when it dried and made it smooth and shiny. I ran my fingers over it and from them sniffed a delicate sooty aroma. A line of raised characters ran gracefully down one side of the ink block, with a gold outline of tiny leaves incised into the ink above the characters.

Teacher Wong arranged the implements carefully on the table and sat still for a moment. Then, moving very deliberately, he stretched his arms out in front of him and slowly folded back the cuffs of his sleeves. That done, he poured a few drops of water onto the ink slab. Holding his right sleeve out of the way with his left hand, he picked up the ink block and rubbed the end slowly round and round in the water on the stone until there was a fine slurry of rich black liquid pooled on the slab. He tapped the last drop of liquid off the ink block into the pool of ink and laid the block down on the table, its wet end resting up on the slab. Next he pulled a sheet of paper in front of him. Then he picked up the writing brush, carefully removing the cap from a soft tuft of very fine hair which he twirled slowly in the ink, drawing it repeatedly across the surface of the inkstone until the hairs were evenly saturated, but not too wet, and tapered to a fine point. He showed me how he held the brush in his right hand (in China using the left hand to write was unthinkable—like eating with your feet—so it was fortunate that I was right-handed). He demonstrated how to rest the forearm on the edge of the table, the wrist level and hand cocked up so that the vertical brush pointed directly down at the paper.

Slowly he let his hand fall forward, lowering the brush so that the end sank gently onto the page. It stayed there for a fraction of a second, and then he pulled it down diagonally in a slightly inward curve and with one smooth motion lifted his hand with a tiny flourish at the end. On the pristine expanse of paper glistened a perfect stroke, jet black, gently curving from its initial hint of emphasis and tapering precisely and yet naturally down to the thickness of one hair in a final slightly upward flourish. No extra spot or splatter detracted from the authority of its presence, self-evident and serene, brought to life by the elegant suggestion of upward flight at the very end. Teacher Wong and I looked at it silently for a moment. Then he said, "*Ni zo.* You do it." He twirled the brush carefully in the ink, put it in my hand, and showed me how to shape my fingers around it, and position my arm. Now I was ready to put brush to paper—the moment of truth.

I held my hand steady. It felt strange in this unaccustomed position. All my attention centered on the point of the brush. Slowly and smoothly I let my hand tip forward.

Splat.

Not to be deterred, I kept my hand down for what I judged to be a fraction of a second, then pulled it down in a curve, until, suddenly, I lifted the brush up and off the paper. There it was—a heavy curve of indecisive width with a dribble of ink wandering off the splat and an upward jerk at the end, as though the brush suddenly changed its mind. *"Hao!"* Teacher Wong said. "Good! Try again."

And so I did. Repeatedly. My assignment for the next lesson was to do pages and pages of this basic stroke in search of the perfect one. I'm not sure I achieved that, but I thought some were pretty good. For subsequent lessons I did pages of other strokes, some shaped like raindrops, others of various sizes, shapes, and directions. Then I graduated to putting strokes together in one smooth motion without removing the brush from the paper.

After a few weeks we got to characters, starting with "little" and "cat" and working our way through the lessons I'd done with Miss Ju. Teacher Wong wrote pages of large characters and gave me pieces of rice paper, thin like tracing paper, to lay over his pages so that I could write on top of his characters, matching my brush strokes to his. Sometimes I almost succeeded. But in trying to make my characters just like his, I usually forgot their meaning.

The next challenge was to write freehand. Teacher Wong supplied paper divided by a grid into boxes so that I could keep the characters the same size. But they still looked ungainly. Instead of being balanced, my versions were top-heavy or listed to one side. If I made one with a hook sticking out too far, I'd tuck it in on the next try, only to have a raindrop fall too far out from the other side or a flourish end with a dribble. My characters evinced no sign of hidden significance or hint of mysterious energy. They did not march confidently down the page. They just lay misshapen on the paper like dead insects.

Although I have since tried several times to learn to read and write Chinese, each character soon evaporates from my brain and muscles, leaving me only with the memory of its elegance and, if I'm lucky, a hint of its sound. A character's sound is considered the least important part of the written word, because it changes with the dialect in which the word is spoken. But the meaning of a character remains the same wherever it is used. The people of China speak hundreds of dialects, some so different that there are linguists who consider them to be different languages. But for thousands of years China has been held together by its written language, regardless of how it is spoken. Each character, by its configuration alone, carries with it the burden of China's civilization, culture, and longevity.

Long after my first encounter with Chinese characters, I learned that, according to Chinese tradition, there is something called *qi* (pronounced "chi") that is part of all existence There is no word for it in English. It is often translated as "breath" but is also described as "spirit," "energy," "vital force," or "substance." It is ephemeral like air and substantive like matter. Although *qi* is present throughout creation, each thing has its unique *qi*. Perhaps it was the paradoxical attributes of *qi* that caught my attention when I was first intrigued by the flowing solidity, the static vigor, and the asymmetrical balance of the characters on the pages of my Chinese primer. Even now, when I first glimpse a downward line of Chinese characters, their antique vitality brushes my consciousness like a breath of unexpected air, and I feel a tinge of anticipation like the excitement I felt when we first opened our primers in Miss Ju's class.

Today I remember how to write only a handful of characters. But I recall well each detail of the preliminaries—the elegant and focused series of precise movements that prepare the calligrapher for that moment when creation hangs in the balance and all awareness gathers at the point of the brush poised above the waiting paper to culminate in that most unaccountable of entities—an idea made visible. I cannot avoid the suspicion that if only I had persisted, if only I hadn't wanted quick results, if only I had endured the mind-numbing process of learning by osmosis, I would finally have acquired the art of writing characters, which expressed a hint of that mysterious quality that is *qi*. If I had, today I would be—in some small part at least—quintessentially Chinese.

FOX FAIRIES AND INDIANS

By the time I was ten, a staple source of entertainment for my friends and me was telling scary stories—not quite on a par with the dead men or the madwoman for offering excitement, but more reliable. Oblivious to the fact that we were following the centuries-old custom of *jiang gushi*, or telling stories to an audience, we gathered after supper on warm evenings, sitting outside on our stools in front of my portable blackboard. There we told our stories, made up as we went along. Sometimes a story was so successful that we had to keep each other company on the way to our separate houses in the dusk, leaving the person at the end to be safely escorted home by a servant or a parent.

Fox fairies figured largely in our narratives. Of all spooky beings, they were the most interesting and the most versatile. From the Tang Dynasty, more than fifteen centuries ago, fox fairies have been featured in the folklore of China—*fuli jin,* they are called in Hunanese. They were foxes who, having lived a very long time, could change at will into beautiful women who came out at night and lured unsuspecting men to their lairs for some kind of activity involving a bed that I didn't fully understand.

Our fox fairy stories always opened with a young man traveling to the provincial capital to take examinations. At the time we were telling these stories, I didn't know that a system of graduated civil service examinations had been the foundation of China's government for almost two thousand years, up to the early years of the twentieth century. If a student passed the examinations, he became a member of the gentry or a government official, his rank depending on the level of examination he had passed. Any boy whose family could afford to forgo his labor was eligible to take the tests, but he had to study for years and commit to memory the classic writings of the ancient sages. Those taking the tests sat sealed in their individual cells for three consecutive days, writing essays in a rigidly dictated style on assigned subjects. The system was democratic in that a son of any class could compete, and it was a chief factor in contributing to China's long history of stable government by bureaucracy, on one hand, and, on the other hand, to its almost fanatical dedication to the status quo. The examination system was also a basic element in the deep respect the

117

Chinese have for education, for it was by passing the examinations that a son could set his family on the road to fortune and power.

As storytellers, however, we were not interested in how our protagonists fared in the examinations. Oblivious to their profound influence on Chinese civilization, we only thought of the examinations as the best way to begin a fox fairy story. Xi-xi was very good at it. On a summer evening she might be the one to stand at the blackboard, the rest of us sitting around on our stools. . .

With a piece of chalk, she traces the outline of a mountain. The chalk clicks authoritatively on the board. "Here is Fuli-shan," she says. "Fox Mountain—known to be inhabited by foxes who have lived in its hundred caves for a thousand years." This, we collectively think, is a bold beginning. Quite unusual. We've never heard of a Fox Mountain. Until now, the convention has been not to use the word "fox" until the end of the narrative. Our interest is piqued, but we're not sure we approve of this innovation, and we follow her introduction critically.

"Down here," Xi-xi goes on, shading the lower half of the blackboard with the side of her chalk, "is a forest. And here"—she draws some winding parallel lines over the shaded part—"is the main road through the forest. It meets a road *here* that goes to Fox Mountain." The scene is set.

We settle back on our stools, and Xi-xi launches into her story. "The student, Fu-ren, was on his way to the capital to take the examinations. He had walked a long way from his home village and he still had a long way to go." She places the point of her chalk at the edge of the picture. "By the time he reached the forest it was almost dark." The chalk moves into the picture along the forest road. "Once in the forest, he sat under a tree by the side of the road to eat and rest until the moon came up so he could see his way." She draws a tree. "He fell asleep."

"Wait," I say. "What did he eat?"

"You-tiao," she replies promptly, referring to a deliciously crisp twist of deep-fried batter. She responds with the encouraging air of a professor answering an intelligent question from a promising student. "He got it in the last town before entering the forest. He has a peach, too," she adds, "but he doesn't eat it." She waits and then asks, *"Hao ba?* All right?"

"Hao da, all right!" I reply, impressed. The peach is a nice touch. I've heard it stands for long life and wards off evil spirits.

"He fell asleep," Xi-xi resumes, "and when he woke up, the moon was high in the sky." She draws the moon at the top of the blackboard. "He got up and walked along the road again." The chalk moves slowly. Her voice drops. "Far ahead, he thought he saw something moving down the road in front of him. Maybe some kind of animal? Or just a shadow in the moonlight?" The chalk hesitates. "No! It was nothing!" she exclaims, and the chalk moves on. We let out our breath. The twilight deepens and a couple of fireflies signal briefly in the gathering gloom.

"After a long time," Xi-xi says, back in her low voice, "he saw another road ahead. In the moonlight it looked like something was standing there." The chalk moves to a corner of the crossroads. "A person, perhaps? Yes! When he got to the crossroads, he saw it was a person, a woman—a beautiful woman in long silk robes, her hair dressed high with many ornaments." I can picture her perfectly, like a lady in a Tang Dynasty painting, standing gracefully in the moonlight.

Xi-xi continues her story. "'I see you are tired and have come a long way,' the lady said to Fu-ren, waving her beautiful fan. 'Where are you going?'

"'I'm going to the capital to take the examinations,' he told her. Then he said, 'I must be on my way,' because he suspected she might be a fox fairy, even though he didn't know the nearby mountain was Fox Mountain.

"'The capital isn't so far,' she said. 'You should eat and rest to do well for the examinations. Come to my house, where you can have some food and sleep.'

"'You are very kind,' Fu-ren replied, 'but I cannot stay.'

"'Don't be afraid,' the lady said. 'I am not a fox fairy, as you might think. Come to my house and I will prove it to you.' And so he went with her up the road to Fox Mountain"—the chalk moves up the smaller road—"where they came to a magnificent mansion." Xi-xi draws the outline of a house. "There she gave Fu-ren a delicious dinner and they went to bed, and after a while they went to sleep."

This is the conventional part of the story. It happens every time. We prepare ourselves for the denouement in which the student wakes up to find himself lying alone in an abandoned fox's lair next to a desiccated (or smelly, depending on the storyteller) pile of chewed bones.

But Xi-xi has other ideas. "In the morning he woke up," she says, "and found the beautiful woman still beside him."

This is very surprising, we think. Perhaps this is the proof that she isn't a fox fairy? Perhaps the peach is giving him protection?

"They ate breakfast," Xi-xi continues, "and the woman told him, 'You must go and take the examinations. When you return, I will be waiting for you at the crossroads.' So he went and took the examinations and when he returned, she was there waiting for him. She went home with him and they were married."

Xi-xi has abandoned the blackboard, as it is almost dark, and we can hear Mrs. Tou calling for Yuan-mei to come home.

"I'm coming!" Yuan-mei yells, and we turn back to Xi-xi. "Is that it?" we ask.

"Not yet." Xi-xi resumes her storytelling voice. "They had two children. Seven years passed. Then, one morning after the full moon, Fu-ren woke up to find his wife and children gone. They were never found, although the villagers looked everywhere. But there was one old man who said that on the night they disappeared he saw three foxes in the fields, playing in the moonlight. He watched them a long time until finally they ran off toward the mountains and disappeared.

"Afterward, every night of the full moon, Fu-ren went out and looked toward the mountains, waiting for his family to return." Xi-xi's voice fades almost to a whisper. "Some say that even now, a thousand years later, he still wanders around on nights when the moon is full, looking for his family."

We didn't need company going home that evening, because there wasn't any moon.

At some time during our fox fairy phase, I had to memorize long swatches of *The Song of Hiawatha* for my fourth-grade English assignment with the Calvert home study program. I fell in love with the world of Hiawatha. When I lay on my bed on the porch and looked out at the branches of the old toon tree, the murmur of the city faded into the wind sighing through the giant trees of the forest behind the wigwam of Nokomis. I was drawn by the hypnotic rhythm of Longfellow's verses into the deep woods beside the lake where the wigwam stood, a thread of smoke rising from its apex. "Daughter of the Moon." The words themselves evoked a vague longing to be someone other than I was, someone slender in the moonlight, with long black hair, in a soft doeskin dress with fringes and moccasins that moved silently over the moss on the forest floor, someone living with the deer and chipmunks like those in Snow White (only not so excitable), living a charmed life in a teepee under the great trees by the lake—a life far away from the muddy, smelly, noisy, dirty, crowded, busy, ordinary world of Yuanling. When my turn came around again to tell another fox fairy story, I switched to Hiawatha.

Telling about Hiawatha was more complicated than I had anticipated. My audience was willing enough to listen, but they didn't know what I was talking about. My introduction to the story turned into a lecture drawn from my store of inaccurate information about the life of Native Americans before the European settlers arrived. A significant drawback was the fact that I didn't know the Chinese words for much of what I was talking about. To begin with, I didn't know the word for "American Indian" and resorted to a direct translation of "red men," which connotes red-colored people in Chinese. This gave the wrong impression. After the comments died down, I explained that they weren't really red. "Then why do you call them that?" my audience asked. "That's just the way it is," I said, and went on with my exposition.

Drawing on the blackboard was somewhat useful in describing my subject, and acting out various aspects of Native American life helped to elucidate such activities as hunting with a bow and arrow and dancing around a campfire—after I had explained campfires. But I was still telling about the forest primeval, about deer and bear and beaver and Indian braves and maidens and feathered war bonnets and mittens with the fur side inside and the skin side outside, when our mothers called us in for the night.

On my way up the back stairs I had a happy thought and went in to ask my father about it. He was pounding away at the piano, playing his uniquely spirited rendition of Sibelius' *Romance.* Usually when my father played the *Romance,* Mother found something to do in another room. But I went in, right up to the piano. My father was bent over the keyboard, his stubby brown fingers flying over the keys, his foot heavy on the pedal. *Da da da di di da di dum-dum*—the windows vibrated in time with the bass octaves as they rang out the first half of the melody's passionate statement. "Daddy!" I screamed over the din.

"Yes?" he shouted back. His left hand completed the melody's ringing declaration and joined the right hand at the upper end of the keyboard to descend in a noisy waterfall of tumbling notes.

"Do you think we could make a teepee?" I yelled.

He stopped in midwaterfall. "A what?"

"A teepee. I'd like to make a teepee. Do you think we could do it?"

"Of course!" he replied. "What kind of teepee do you want?"

"A real teepee. Like the ones in *Hiawatha*."

He thought a moment. "Why, yes," he said. "I think we can make something like that. Let's see tomorrow what we can do." And he returned to the waterfall.

The next day we found a couple of old rugs in the attic. On the flat ground between the houses, we tied some bamboo poles together at one end and tried to drape the rugs over them. But they slid down. So my father went to the school carpenter and borrowed some long three-by-fours to which we nailed the rugs so that the opening to the teepee looked out to the toon tree and over the city. As a final precaution, we covered the whole thing with stiff *you bu*, canvas made waterproof with tung oil. We laid another piece of *you bu* inside for the floor.

There it was. A teepee—though not exactly like the one pictured in the black-and-white photograph in my geography book. My friends looked at it doubtfully when I announced that it was finished. I took off my shoes, and stepping inside, I sat down cross-legged. *"Jin lai, jin lai!"* I invited, patting the *you bu* with my hand. "Come in, come in." One by one they stepped out of their shoes and sat down on the floor. "Shall we get our stools?" Xi-xi suggested tentatively. I explained that the red people didn't use stools. They didn't use any furniture. This was how they sat. Since most Hunanese do not customarily sit cross-legged on anything, much less the floor, the thought that it was a desirable thing to do had not occurred to the assemblage. But they took my word for it and settled down on the pungent *you bu*. Our Hiawatha phase had begun.

I apprehended that my friends' enthusiasm did not match my own, but I was sure that once started, they, too, would want to participate in the fascinating life of American Indians. I had planned a list of activities for gradual immersion in Native American culture as I understood it, culminating in an evening powwow and a night in the teepee. When I laid out my program, there wasn't much comment. We started with preparations for the powwow, making war bonnets cut and pasted from Chinese newspapers, and we practiced a few times prancing around a rock, alternately leaning over and bending backward while intoning loudly in a monotone, rapidly vibrating the palms of our hands against our open mouths. These practice sessions were not entirely satisfactory, because the participants had an unfortunate tendency to collapse into hysterical laughter from which it was difficult to get back to business.

There was some question about eating a red people feast, which I explained consisted of pieces of raw meat roasted on sticks over an open fire. I overrode the doubts of the prospective celebrants, assuring them it would be delicious. Their most serious questions concerned spending a night in the teepee. They were not used to sleeping away from home, and most of them had always shared a bed with one or more siblings. Only the homeless and the insane spent the night without a solid roof over their heads, exposed to snow, rain, drafts, and fresh air. Moreover, they showed little confidence in my assertion that no bad men, predators, snakes, or fox fairies had been seen in the compound within living memory. I don't know what objections their parents may have had, but only the assurance that Reverend Rugh would spend the night with us persuaded the Tou children and Xi-xi to attempt it.

The evening of the powwow arrived. My father kept an eye on us from the porch, where he worked at the card table. He had lit a small fire on the hard ground in front of the teepee, with a bucket of water nearby, and we sat around it cross-legged in our war bonnets. "By the shores of Gitchee Gumee," I intoned in the original English, "by the shining Big-Sea-Water . . ." The eyes of my fellow tribesmen glazed over as I continued several inches into the poem. When I couldn't remember any more, we got up and danced around the fire. I was pleased that the dance was completed without any giggling. We then sat down and pushed pieces of raw beef onto sticks we had whittled under my father's tutelage, and held them over the fire. It took a long time for the meat to cook. The pieces were tough and messy to eat without benefit of chopsticks, forks, knives, or napkins. To tell the truth, my portion didn't taste as good as I had led myself to believe.

Night had fallen when we finally finished spitting bits of charred beef into the glowing embers, and silence reigned. "When is Reverend Rugh coming?" Xi-xi asked hopefully. "Daddeeee!" I yelled.

My father came and we entered the teepee where our blankets were piled on the *you bu*. By the faint light of the dying fire we each wrapped up in a blanket and lay down. My father poured the bucket of water on the fire and pulled shut the flap of rug over the opening. It was pitch dark. We heard him lie down. *"Nimen hao ba?"* he asked. "Is everyone all right?" The reply was ragged but polite, *"Hao,"* and silence descended. But not for long. The hard ground was knobby under the *you bu*. It took time to find a comfortable position and the *you bu* crackled and rustled whenever someone moved. The pungent smell of tung oil grew heavier in the still air of the teepee. Xi-xi next to me got restless. She moaned, *"Ai ya. Douzi tung!* My stomach hurts!" Then, "I'm going to throw up!" My father got up quickly, opened the flap, and took her outside in the fresh air. I heard her crying. In a few minutes he put his head back through the flap. "I'm taking Xi-xi home," he said. "I'll be back," and his head disappeared. Some moments later Tou Yuan-mei sat up and started to cry. "I want to go home, too," she sniffed. "I'm afraid. I don't like it out here," and she got up.

"Don't be afraid," I said. "It's *nice* out here." There was no response. Yuan-mei was out the door, leaving the flap open and her blanket in a heap on the floor. Her brother stood up. "I'd better go with her," he said, and followed her out.

Alone in the teepee, I sat up and looked out the door at the lighter dark outside. Fresh air poured in the opening. A breeze rustled the branches of the toon tree. I wished Xi-xi would come back. After a while my father appeared in the doorway. "Xi-xi will be all right," he said in Chinese. "But she'd better stay home." He looked in the teepee.

"They went home," I said. "Yuan-mei was scared."

"Oh," my father replied. "Well." He came inside, leaving the flap open, picked up a blanket, and lowered himself onto the *you bu*. "It's all right," he said matter-of-factly. "They're just not used to it." Then he said, "I'm going to get Molly," and went out.

I felt a lot better. It would be fun to sleep with Molly. When my father set her down at the teepee door, she bustled in, licked my face, and sniffed around excitedly. My father wrapped himself in the blanket and lay down across the opening so she couldn't get out without his knowing. Eventually she finished her explorations and settled down with a gusty sigh. I looked up through the open flap where the tree was outlined against the night sky.

"You remember the time you slept outside with Aunt Wini?" I asked.

"I certainly do," my father said.

"How did it happen?" I asked, knowing perfectly well, but wanting to hear it again.

"Well," my father said, "sometimes Uncle Vin and I would take our mattresses onto the terrace outside the living room and sleep out under the stars. Aunt Wini always wanted to come, so finally one night we said she could."

"How old was she?" I asked.

"Oh, maybe five or six," said my father. "Well, it started to rain in the middle of the night, so we woke Wini up and carried the mattresses into the living room, where we went back to sleep on the floor."

"Did you get really wet?" I asked.

"No. Just a little. We were dry by morning. When Aunt Wini woke up, she didn't remember a thing about it, and couldn't figure out why she was on the floor in the living room. She went in and woke up Granddaddy and Grandmummy Rugh, all excited, and told them, 'I just woke up and I was in the living room!' She thought it was magic."

"What did you do?" I said.

"At first we pretended we were amazed, too, as though it really was magic. But then we explained what had happened."

"Did she believe you?"

"Not at first, because she couldn't remember moving. Later, probably, she did."

I could see Aunt Wini as a little girl with tousled hair, dragging her blanket into the living room without really waking up. I snuggled deeper into my blanket. Maybe it would rain in the middle of the night, I thought sleepily. It was good we had put *you-bu* over the teepee.

༐

The next time it was my turn to tell a story at the blackboard, I outlined some mountains and a stream at the bottom of a gorge spanned by a bridge. My chalk traced a path into the scene as I began in my best storytelling voice, "The student, Ming-jun, was on his way to take the examinations when at dusk he came to a footbridge high in the mountains_"

Our Hiawatha phase had ended.

THE CHAPEL

One day I told my father I'd like to have a chapel. I don't know what particular circumstance inspired the idea, but he agreed to it and suggested that the best place would be behind the bookcase in his study. The bookcase covered most of one wall, and pulling it out from the wall made a space in which I put a chair at the open end and a small table against the wall at the other end. On the table I put a candleholder with a candle and a pierced bronze incense burner for powdered incense. Behind the table I hung a scroll depicting, with delicate brush strokes on a blank background, a Chinese Madonna and Child sitting on a weathered rock by a spray of bamboo.

Whenever I visited the chapel, it wasn't for long and I didn't do much. Usually I just sat looking at the Madonna and Child in the shadowed light of the candle's flame and watched the filament of smoke rise past them, filling the quiet space with a hint of sharp fragrance. I was waiting for something to happen. It never did, but I liked being there. In that space behind the bookcase, the Madonna and Child, the candle, the fragrance, the stillness, and I all joined in a circle of interdependence that felt incomplete if one element was missing.

Perhaps my desire for a chapel was precipitated from an environment saturated with religious inclinations. All the foreigners were in Yuanling because of their religion. First there was unambiguous, unadorned, and fundamentalist Protestant Christianity represented by local churches with the support of their founding missionaries. And there were the more liberal versions of Protestantism practiced by the Presbyterians and people like my parents, whose efforts were dedicated to health and education. Then there was the more intricate faith of the Catholics, who had a large church, hospital, and school at the other end of town. I was well aware of these varieties of Christianity and took for granted that they were on the right track—though the Catholics may have wandered off a bit.

I paid less attention to the emanations of Tao and Buddhism throughout the Chinese world around us, evidenced in household and wayside shrines, in temples and in art, in customs and assumptions made about the world—ancestors, evil spirits, auspicious dragons, the kitchen god, the god of war, the emperor of heaven, and many others, including the "goddess" of mercy. Strictly speaking, she wasn't a goddess but a bodhisattva—a Buddhist being who, having reached enlightenment, declined to enter nirvana so she could stay on earth to help others.

The pragmatic Hunanese, hedging their bets, gave recognition to all these deities. We Westerners thought the Hunanese were just superstitious. Yet, through some mysterious process of absorption, I acquired a subliminal sense of the eons of myth and mystery out of which these gods, spirits, and monsters emerged to populate the Chinese cosmos. In the noisy, time-encrusted temples loud with casual conversation and cluttered with charred sticks of incense and offerings of shriveled fruit, a Taoist deity or an obese Buddha loomed like an hallucination in the smoky gloom, and I was arrested by the aura of infinite emptiness and stillness that surrounded each garish image covered with grime.

My father had come to China because of his faith, but Mother often pointed out that she had come to China because of my father. Her faith, she said, was doubtful. As the daughters of the Presbyterian minister in a small town, Mother and Aunt Dorothy had been expected to be models of Christian girlhood as envisioned by influential members of the church. While neither of the sisters was happy with the role, Mother had been the more rebellious, taking refuge in the claim that she lacked both the spiritual resources for religious experience and the intellectual endowment to talk about it. So we didn't talk about religion much in our family. Yet Mother was very much at home among the prayers and hymns with which she'd grown up, and expected them to be part of our daily life.

We always began the day with a reading from the Bible and a prayer. But it was singing hymns with my parents before bedtime rather than morning devotions, or even Sunday school or sermons, that launched my fledgling flights into religion. Evenings settled around us warm and safe when we sang together at the piano the familiar words to melodies so well known that to take part in their harmonies was as natural as saying good night.

One such hymn was my father's favorite, with words by John Greenleaf Whittier—a Quaker, though I didn't know it then:

Dear Lord and Father of mankind
Forgive our feverish ways.
Reclothe us in our rightful mind,
In purer lives thy service find
In deeper reverence, praise

. . .

The hymn ends with a plea:

Breathe through the heats of our desire
Thy coolness and thy balm;
Let sense be dumb, let flesh retire,
Speak through the earthquake, wind, and fire,
O still, small voice of calm.

I especially liked this last verse, possibly because it alluded to something very like the paradoxical stillness I sensed in the clamorous clutter of Buddhist and Taoist temples.

The foreigners in Yuanling were divided about equally between Protestants and Catholics. We Protestants attended Thursday evening prayer meetings as a matter of course. They were always held in the living room of missionaries who lived at the other end of the city, because the living rooms at our end were too small. People took turns leading the gathering. We sat on chairs and sofas, singing hymns, saying prayers, and listening to talks that ranged from definitive statements on sin and salvation by our more conservative brethren to my father's less absolute reflections on acceptance and service.

At the close of the meeting, we had refreshments. Stuffed with cake, cookies, and tedium, I was always half asleep for the long walk home through the night—a walk that was almost magical compared to the plodding reality of the prayer meeting. In a fog of fatigue I held my parents' hands and we paced the dark miles of Yuanling's street as though walking in place while the dim lights in the shops on either side slid behind us and vanished. When our front gate came into view, we paused at the door and knocked, and when it opened, we glided through and floated up the stone staircase to the top of the hill and home.

Usually the prayer meetings were led by seasoned missionaries who followed a predictable format. But one meeting was exceptional. It was conducted by Uncle Art, the youngest of the Yale Bachelors. At that time, five Bachelors lived with a wind-up Victrola and a stack of 78 rpm records in two rooms comprising the other half of the second floor where we lived. After Miss Granner left, they moved downstairs, and my father moved his desk and books into one of their rooms to make his office. But on this particular Thursday afternoon they were still upstairs and we could hear them and their music quite easily through the wall between us.

The opening notes of Beethoven's Fifth Symphony reverberated ominously through the wall. "Hey, Art!" one of the Bachelors called, as if the music reminded him of something. "You ready for prayer meeting tonight?"

"What?" Uncle Art yelled back.

"Prayer meeting!" On our side of the wall, Mother gave my father a mock worried look.

"What about it?" shouted Uncle Art.

"It's tonight. Did you forget?"

Beethoven screeched to a halt. In the ensuing silence, Uncle Art said, "What time is it?"

"It's almost five. What're you going to do?"

Uncle Art didn't reply.

"Oh, dear," said Mother, trying to look serious.

After supper, we started on our walk to the other end of the city. "I wonder what's going to happen," Mother said.

"I don't know," said my father, shaking his head.

Privately, I hoped we would skip prayer meeting and go straight to refreshments.

The Bachelors had walked through the hills behind the city rather than taking the main street, so we didn't see them until we arrived. I ran a critical eye over Uncle Art. He didn't seem to have anything with him that looked like papers or a Bible with which to lead the meeting; on the other hand, he didn't look worried, either. The grown-ups chatted for a few minutes, then everyone sat down and turned expectantly to Uncle Art, who was leaning back empty-handed in an upholstered armchair.

"Tonight," he began, "we will have Quaker Meeting." That sounded interesting. I'd heard of Quakers and the Underground Railroad, but I didn't know anything else about them. He went on to explain that holding a Quaker Meeting meant we would have an hour together of silent meditation and prayer. My hopes for something either interesting or edible plummeted. He added that during this time, anyone who felt moved to speak could do so. When the startled assemblage realized he had nothing more to say, people tentatively started bowing their heads, as though not sure how far down they should go. I noticed not everyone's eyes were closed. I don't recall anyone speaking, but I doubt my memory is accurate. The room was full of ministers, most of whom were rarely silent for more than a few minutes. Any one of them could deliver a ten-minute prayer with no warning whatsoever. My recollection is, however, that silence reigned for most of the meeting, if not all.

Time stretched out indefinitely. Even the mantel clock slowed down. After half an hour, the long hand had progressed only five minutes. I stared at it to see if I could catch it moving, but it doubled into two long hands and I blinked. Someone coughed. Then one of the missionaries—Reverend Colbitt, I shall call him—blew his nose, as though using the cough as an excuse to make noise. The room returned to silence. Holding out one finger in my lap, I shut my eyes alternately and watched the finger jump back and forth without moving. My head itched. Maybe I had lice again and Mother would have to rub my scalp with kerosene to get rid of them. I could almost smell it, like last time. It made me woozy. I crossed my eyes and the lamp across the room doubled. The long hand on the clock had moved five more minutes. . . . Eons later Uncle Art shook hands with the missionary next to him and the prayer meeting ended. It was my first experience of "worship in the manner of Friends," as Quakers like to say. Of all the prayer meetings we attended it was the most unforgettable and the most boring.

My father went to Chinese church services regularly. Each Sunday morning he walked down to the chapel at the bottom of the hill, where Reverend OuYang, of the Evangelical Mission, officiated. Xi-xi and Yuan-mei also went regularly with their families, but Mother and I attended less often. The chapel was a long, low-ceilinged room with dingy whitewashed walls and windows of smudged and wavy glass, pointed at the top.

The room was filled with benches on which hymn books and Chinese-language Bibles were laid at regular intervals for the Sunday service. Next to the lectern at the front of the room was a small pedal organ that whined to a stop whenever a hymn ended. My father, reading Chinese, sang all the words. I pretended I could, too, by singing each word a split second late. Usually I gave up after the first verse and sang "la la," as Mother did, until we reached the "Amen," which is the same in Chinese and English. My father followed the scripture readings in his pocket-sized Chinese-language Bible while Mother and I read the English version. All three of us recited the Lord's Prayer in Chinese. I also knew the Chinese words for the Doxology, but from then on the church service and I parted company. Reverend OuYang had a special voice for addressing God that went up and down soporifically, building up to several climaxes before reaching the peroration. I believe it was during his prayers that I developed the skill of making my mind go blank. As for his sermons, I could understand only a few words besides "Jesus" and "God," and spent the time reading a book or, when I was at an age when I was expected to take an interest, daydreaming.

The Catholic church was much more interesting than our places of worship. It was one of the biggest buildings in town, along with the electric plant and the Catholic hospital. I was in it only twice, but each time I was awed by the height of the ceiling and the opulent decorations. High above the altar Jesus drooped on a cross with trickles of blood running down his forehead, his hands, his feet, and his side, much like the trickles of blood that ran down my legs every summer when my father pulled off the encrustations of impetigo. Off to one side stood a statue of the Virgin Mary with her hands hanging out from her sides, palms open, staring down mournfully at whoever came within her line of sight. She reminded me a little of the Goddess of Mercy, although the goddess didn't have blue eyes or yellow hair showing under her veil, and she didn't look so sad.

The banks of candles burning in front of Mary and various saints reminded me of the candles burning in front of statues in Chinese temples. But I sensed no mysterious emptiness around these images. These looked like what they were—brightly colored statues of painted plaster. I reminded myself that while Catholic churches were very different from ours, basically we believed the same things. Besides, there were definite advantages to being Catholic in Yuanling.

One advantage was food. Once a year the sisters who ran the hospital invited the three of us for tea. There were fifteen of them, but as some were always on duty at the hospital, usually only six or eight were with us for tea, including the mother superior.

The sisters fascinated me. From what I could see of them, they never seemed to sweat, no matter how hot the weather; they led mysteriously regimented lives of dedicated service while wearing very interesting clothes; they were always serenely cheerful; and their food was outstanding. They served cucumber sandwiches (made with cucumbers from their own extensive gardens, so they were safe to eat), delicate rolls of paper-thin ham (something we rarely had), and chocolate—*chocolate*—cupcakes. The sisters weren't allowed to eat with us, so they sat across the parlor while we ate, their hands lying quietly in their laps as they chatted with my parents and beamed at me. I liked the way they moved in one piece when they turned to talk, because their veils blocked their side vision. Mother said they must be homesick for American children, and so it seemed, because they kept saying how good it was to see me and urged me from across the room to take another cupcake, which I did.

Another advantage to being a Catholic was that their church service had a lot of action. We went to Mass once while we were in Yuanling. It was a special occasion because the archbishop of China had come to celebrate Easter Mass and all the foreigners in Yuanling were invited to attend. The archbishop was a large and dignified Chinese man draped in magnificent robes with a double-pointed hat on his head. He walked down the aisle in a procession of fathers and boys in white gowns, up to the altar, where the most intriguing activities took place. We Protestants remained planted on our seats while fragrant smoke billowed and various men and boys up there swung the incense burner, chanted, knelt, stood, walked around, bowed, rang bells, and read books, while the sisters and the Chinese congregation around us knelt and stood and sat and knelt and filed up to kneel again at the railing for Communion. It seemed as though they were playacting, yet obviously they weren't. It was hard to understand how the sisters and fathers, who spoke American English and served chocolate cupcakes for tea, suddenly took part in these strange and alien proceedings held in Latin, a language unknown to anyone else in Yuanling. I couldn't imagine my mother or father or the Bachelors doing anything so outlandish.

Yet I was attracted by all these goings-on. Maybe I would be a Catholic sister someday, in full skirts to my ankles, with a metal crucifix on a string of beads clicking gently at my side. I would dip gracefully in front of the high altar, cross myself, and kneel in a shaft of light to gaze prayerfully up at Mary or Jesus so that my veil dropped in one fluid fall straight to the back of my legs under the long skirt, which flowed in liquid folds over the marble floor. It was an affecting picture—I'd seen one like it somewhere—and I filed it away to admire later with other affecting pictures I was collecting of myself.

One cold morning in November 1943, my father, who'd had a cold, didn't get out of bed. Mother sent Chen Shi-fu across the river to the Yale-in-China hospital for a doctor. When the head of the hospital, Dr. Liu, finally came, he said my father had pneumonia and should be in the hospital. In those days before antibiotics, pneumonia was a very serious business, especially for someone with asthma. The problem was, which hospital? The conditions in the Chinese hospital at our end of town precluded his going there. The journey to the Yale-in-China hospital across the river was out of the question. There remained the Catholic hospital. So Chen Shi-fu was sent again with a message, this time to the Catholic hospital, and came back with two men and a stretcher. By this time my father wasn't answering questions; his eyes were closed and his cheeks sunken, and each hair of the stubble on his chin looked extra black against the grayness of his face under the tan. Mother's face was stony as she got things ready to go with him.

The men wrapped my father in a quilt and held the stretcher while Tou Shi-fu and Chen Shi-fu lifted him off the bed and gently laid him on the stretcher. His eyes stayed closed. "Will he be all right?" I asked Mother. The pupils of her eyes were so big they made her blue eyes look black. "I just don't know," she said. "Mrs. OuYang says you can come over there," she added, gave me a quick hug, and went out the door after Dr. Liu and the stretcher.

I went out to the front porch with its rumpled bed where my father had been, and watched the little procession set out to carry him through the hills and rice paddies to the hospital at the other end of the city. I returned to the living room. The furniture seemed distant and flat, like furniture in a picture. The book I'd been reading lay open, its pages limp on top of my indifferent desk. When I tried to read, the words were disconnected. I shut the book and wandered over to my chapel, where I sat down, but only for a few minutes. The stillness was too quiet without my father's muffled typing on the other side of the bookcase. The space felt cold and vacant, almost strange, and the Madonna and Child distant and alien. I left without lighting the candle or the incense, and went to Xi-xi's house.

The following week was strangely empty, though we kept to our usual schedule in the morning. In the afternoons Mother visited my father in the hospital while I stayed home and did homework and practiced the piano. There were daily *jin bao,* and if Mother was at the hospital, I went to the dugout with the OuYang family, or sometimes with the Bachelors. The Japanese were stepping up their activity in Hunan, spreading south and west from Dong Ting Lake and bombing the cities down river from us.

One afternoon Mother took me to visit my father on the second floor of the Catholic hospital. We walked into a very long room lined on either side with white metal beds backed against the wall. Each bed had a man in it. A few beds had screens around them. Charcoal braziers glowed at intervals along the center aisle to take the chill off the frigid air. I saw my father propped up in a bed halfway down the aisle.

"Well!" he exclaimed softly as I walked toward him. "Look who's here." He didn't move his head from the pillows. I stopped at the foot of the bed because Mother had said I shouldn't get closer. He smiled. "How are you?" His voice was oddly soft, as though all of it wasn't working. I felt strange; I didn't know how I was. I looked at his Chinese-language Bible next to a thermos bottle on the bedside table.

"When are you coming home?" I asked, and looked at him again. His cheeks were hollow under his cheek bones, his eyes looked like dark holes in his face, but his chin was smooth and his hair was combed "Soon," he said. The head nurse, Sister Ursula, came up, her white habit rustling gently as she stopped next to me. She was a small woman with a sweet face. "In a while," she said to me, smiling.

A Chinese nurse in a white apron and cap showed up at my father's side and handed him a small glass of liquid. He thanked her and looked at it in mock consternation. "Again?" he asked in Chinese. Then he drank it down in one gulp and pretended to shudder at the taste. The nurse giggled and took the glass. Suddenly I felt better. Sister Ursula smiled indulgently. "It's very nice to have Mr. Rugh on our ward," she said to Mother. "The sisters have been praying for him every day. We're all grateful the good Lord has spared him."

As the Japanese advanced that week, Mr. Ying, the dean of Yali, and Mr. Lao, the principal, hired boats to evacuate the school in case the enemy got too close to Yuanling. By the end of the week, the Japanese had taken two large cities a hundred miles downriver. Now there were three *jin bao* a day, and everyone expected we would be bombed at any time. Mother, with Mr. Lao and Mr. Ying and the doctors, decided my father would be safer at home than at the big Catholic hospital looming over the rest of the city. Ross Dixon, one of the Bachelors, was in the hospital also, so early one bone-chilling morning, before the usual time for *jin bao*, eighteen Yali students with stretchers went to the hospital and carried my father and Uncle Ross home.

The *jin bao* were now lasting several hours at a time. Uncle Ross was carried out to the dugout on a stretcher, but my father was too sick to be out so long. Mother wouldn't leave him alone in the house. That morning when the siren went off, Mother wanted me to go with the Bachelors, but I refused. I knew with absolute certainty that if I went to the dugout, I would never see my mother and father again.

So they let me stay. And when the city emptied and everyone had left the compound and all was quiet except for the distant cries of hawks circling above the river, Mother and I sat by my father's cot in the living room and she read to us from old copies of *Reader's Digest* and the *Atlantic Monthly*.

There were two long *jin bao* that day, both with urgent alarms soon after the initial siren. The second one sounded so soon after the all clear from the first that people hadn't reached home and just turned around and went back to where they'd been. With two *jin bao* in close succession, Japanese airplanes must have been swarming all over Hunan, and I knew they'd bomb Yuanling this time. Mother started reading again, but after a couple of minutes the bugle sounded. "Listen," she said, and in the silence we heard faint droning in the distance. Mother put down the magazine. The droning got louder. Then very loud. Without warning the ceiling disappeared. There was nothing between us and the planes about to drop their bombs. Open to the sky, the three of us held hands and waited. My heart was pounding in my throat. The droning continued, louder, then softer, then louder again. Finally it faded away. Without warning the ceiling returned. Mother picked up the magazine and resumed reading until there wasn't enough light to see. Then we sat in the dark until the all clear sounded, when we turned on the light and got ready for bed.

The *jin bao* continued at least twice a day while the Japanese advanced within eighty miles of Yuanling. For three or four days there were no Chinese troops between us and the Japanese. Missionaries and thousands of refugees fled to Yuanling from the towns downriver. When they had stopped at night along the way, Japanese planes came early the next morning and strafed and bombed them. Although many boats were sunk and hundreds of people were killed, all the missionaries made it to Yuanling. Soon thereafter the Japanese pulled back, and the missionaries and refugees returned to their homes. We didn't know why the Japanese stopped their advance or why they didn't bomb Yuanling. Perhaps Yuanling wasn't worth it. We hoped so. Over the next days the *jin bao* slacked off, and I became very busy making up the schoolwork I'd missed and preparing for another Christmas play with Xi-xi and Yuan-mei. By Christmas my father was well again and life was back to normal.

Shortly before Christmas, Mother took a batch of Tou Shi-fu's springerle cookies to the sisters to thank them for taking care of my father. At supper that evening Mother said with a twinkle, "Well, Dwight, I sure am glad you're not Catholic!"

I looked at her, surprised. Daddy a Catholic?

"Me too," said my father. "Why?"

Mother explained. When she had finished her visit with the sisters, Sister Ursula had accompanied her to the door. "Mrs. Rugh," Sister Ursula said earnestly, "if only Mr. Rugh was Catholic . . . he'd be a saint!"

There was one hymn Mother disliked intensely, so we never sang it at home—"Nearer My God to Thee." At the piano, Mother would flip over its page on her way to another selection in the hymn book. "Just imagine," she'd exclaim, looking as though she smelled something bad. "They played it when the Titanic was sinking!"

I wasn't sure why that made her dislike it, but her disapproval gave me permission to look at the hymn critically when we sang it in church or at missionary gatherings. I decided I didn't like it, either; the tune was boring and people always dragged it out—especially Reverend Colbitt.

In fact, another reason I didn't like the hymn was that it was one of Reverend Colbitt's favorites. I avoided Reverend Colbitt. There had been a time when he would touch me whenever I was near him. Once, in someone's living room when no one else was there, he lifted me onto his lap and started to slide his hand up my leg under my clothes. I didn't want to be rude, so I pretended I had to go somewhere, slid off his lap, and went out. He didn't scare me. Nor did I dislike him. I just didn't *like* him. Grown-ups were often unaccountable, and I took for granted that this was how he was unaccountable. What he did was embarrassing, so I didn't tell my parents. I just stayed out of his reach.

It was Reverend Colbitt's love of the hymn, as well as Mother's aversion to it, that started to open a crack in Christianity for me, though I wasn't aware of it at the time. One day I would discover the crack grown wide and, looking through it, see that there is more than one way to seek what some call the Truth, and more than one way to share—as we sang in the Quaker hymn —"the silence of eternity."

On a day well into the new year, I realized I hadn't visited the chapel since my father was in the hospital. I stepped into the shadowed space and smelled the stale scent of old incense. The candle was a dusty stub. Through the gloom I looked at the Madonna and Child sitting in tranquil solitude on their rock. I felt sorry for them, waiting so patiently there in the dark, and yet I didn't feel like keeping them company.

I came out from the behind the bookcase and told my father I didn't want the chapel anymore. "All right," he said thoughtfully. He didn't ask me why, which was just as well, because I couldn't have told him. The next day I put everything away—the candleholder and the incense burner, so reminiscent of Catholic Mass and Chinese temples, and finally the scroll where the Madonna sat with her Child, surrounded by stillness and empty space, like the Goddess of Mercy.

SUMMER PALACE

Not far from Peking, just before the end of the nineteenth century, the last empress of China rebuilt her summer palace beside a lake. It was a magical place of towers with scarlet-lacquered balconies and buildings with curved roofs of yellow-glazed tile—a color no one but the imperial family could use. Inside the buildings were rooms with furniture of rosewood and ebony, cupboards inlaid with shell and semiprecious stones, screens of carved wood and silk, vessels of gold, and mythical bronze beasts crouching on their pedestals. Outside the buildings, pavilions stood mirrored in ponds, their reflections hanging upside down below lotus blossoms with leaves like jade platters floating on the surface. Moon gates revealed vistas of gnarled pines and peonies and weathered rocks. On the side of a freestanding wall, nine ceramic dragons pranced on a blue ceramic sea. An outdoor colonnade, almost half a mile long, stretched along the lakeside where the empress strolled under ceilings covered with thousands of paintings. Marble bridges linked the shore to islands and curved over creeks, their reflected arches completing circles in the water. In a corner of the lake, a marble boat stood stationary, two stories high, with balconies from which to view the scenery. To this retreat the empress brought her court to escape the heat, noise, and diseases of summer in Peking.

We, too, had a retreat—a place away from the noise, the festering heat, and the almost daily air raid warnings of summer in Yuanling. We, too, had walks and vistas, a pond, a boat, a bridge, and treasures unmatched by anything the empress owned. We even encountered beasts more impressive than her famous dragons. In place of her scarlet-balconied towers and roofs of Imperial yellow, our summer dwelling was a small house of coffee-colored mud and plaster over bamboo lathing, with a packed-dirt floor and a roof of rough gray tiles. It was tucked in at the top of a secluded valley several miles downstream from Yuanling on the other side of the river. The back windows looked up to a saddle between two hills where a stand of tall pines sighed and whispered with the slightest movement of air. The front windows looked out to the sky edged by green hillsides. Instead of balconies overlooking a lake, we had a packed-dirt terrace in front of the house, shaded by an awning of woven bamboo matting. The valley was too steep and the vegetation too thick for us to see the rice paddies descending in steps below us, but from the terrace we could see a sentinel pine on an outcropping over the valley and beyond that the Yuan River glistening silver in the distance. We called the place Shi Qiao (pronounced "shr chiao") after the village at the bottom of the valley; the name means "stone bridge."

When my parents agreed to extend our stay in Yuanling to four years, the prospect of spending every summer in the city persuaded them to acquire two rice paddies at the top of the valley above the village. There, for the sum of ninety U.S. dollars, they paid for the land and built the house on the upper rice paddy cut into the yellow-red clay of the hillside. On the lower paddy, backed by a retaining wall of gray stone, they planted a vegetable garden. To tend the garden and mind the house when we were away, they hired a caretaker, Zhang Shi-fu.

Our boat was a sampan hired for the summer from a middle-aged couple who took my father up the river in the morning to work at Yali, and back in the evening in time for supper. He always whistled the oriole's call when he reached the last stretch of the path, to let us know he was almost home. Tou Shi-fu used the boat every day to go to market across the river. Once or twice Yuan-mei came on the boat to spend a few days with me, but her mother usually wanted her home to help out. Xi-xi came once but got homesick after one night, and my father took her home the next day.

Both Yuan-mei and Xi-xi seemed relieved to go home, perhaps because they hadn't slept so far from home before, or perhaps because our life at Shi Qiao was too different—the quiet may have been too eerie and the sounds too strange, what with the rustling of unknown things in the underbrush, the lonely cry of the Indian cuckoo calling its insistent question up the scale in the evening, and the whispering of the pine trees outside my window after we went to bed. I was sad and a little hurt when I watched my friends walk down the path for home. But I also knew they would be waiting for me when I returned to Yuanling.

So Shi Qiao became a separate place for me alone, but I wasn't lonely or bored. It was a magical place no less enchanting to me than the Summer Palace must have been to its courtly visitors. Each summer when we climbed past the sentinel pine and turned into the valley, we stepped into a quiet so profound that it was like an ancient presence. The valley was not silent; rather, each single sound stood out like a jewel set in stillness. It was a tranquil world of pine-drenched air where gnats danced out their tiny exuberance in the sunlight and other denizens of the valley marked the hours with song—a tentative antiphony of waking birds at dawn, the shrilling of cicadas in high unison at noon, the Indian cuckoo's solo query ascending the valley at dusk, and after dark the chanting of a hundred thousand frogs.

At the corners of the house were large wooden tubs, as high as my chest, to catch rainwater from the eaves. My father borrowed a microscope from the biology department at Yali, and in a drop of water from the tubs I saw wonders the empress never dreamed of—paramecia shaped like tiny shoeprints with fibrillating fringes shimmering in the light, or the blob of an amoeba stretching its border to form a miniature ping pong paddle and then pouring itself into the new outline until it became a blob again. Unidentifiable strings of things waved themselves in solo performance or pas de deux across the microscope's bright stage. A piece of algae or a tiny fractal frond of fern revealed a structure more elegant than any artifact the empress might delight in. Once my father and I caught a gnat no bigger than a speck of dust and carefully covered her with a cover slip on a slide. We gazed at her as through a spyglass, and while we looked, she started to lay a string of eggs. We called Mother, and the three of us took turns watching the gnat create a minute necklace of pearls more exquisite than any brought as tribute to the imperial court.

In the tubs, mosquito larvae—"wigglers," we called them—jerked like animated commas, hanging on to the underside of the water's surface to breathe until I poured in a little of the tea oil Tou Shi-fu used for cooking. As the opalescent film spread over the water, I watched them sink to the bottom of the *kang*, there to die from lack of air. When it came to mosquitoes, I was as unforgiving as the empress, known for her vindictive nature. I showed them no mercy, for they showed none to me. To them, I was the most savory of snacks—especially in the outhouse.

The outhouse was tucked up against the hill to one side. A visit to its shadowed interior was not an occasion for relief. Rather, it was a race to see who could accomplish their purpose first—the mosquitoes or I. One factor in my favor was the smoldering stick of incense stuck in the dirt floor. It repelled most of the mosquitoes except for one or two whose smoke-detecting apparatus was defective. The healthy, normal mosquitoes took refuge in the pit below the hole in the seat, and I could hear them humming hungrily as soon as I opened the door. Hastily, I would ready my clothing, pick up the stick of smoking incense, insert it into the hole, and wave it around inside, holding my nose and hoping that the defective mosquitoes would not attack from the rear. When I estimated that the mosquitoes in the pit were sufficiently stunned, I pulled out the incense and sat down as fast as I could to keep the smoke inside, hoping to finish before they recovered. By the end of my first week in Shi Qiao, I had developed a strong antipathy for the outhouse. But my technique rapidly reached such facility that I usually escaped its precincts unscathed.

A partner in my battle against mosquitoes was a gray gecko, no more than two inches long, who lived up near the ceiling on the whitewashed wall of my room. Thanks to him and the netting over my window, I didn't need the mosquito net hanging over my cot. Another ally against the mosquitoes was a tree frog who came every year to settle at the top of a corner post holding up the bamboo awning over the terrace where mosquitoes lurked during the day. If I climbed on a chair, sometimes I could spy him in the shadows—a patch of apple green with toes like little spoons. He chirped every now and then, a friendly little sound that assured me he was on duty even when I couldn't see him. When we sat on the terrace in the evenings, Zhang Shi-fu helped him keep the mosquitoes at bay by placing two or three smoldering sheaves of aromatic plants around the terrace where they burned until long after dark.

On the hillside opposite the outhouse, the house carpenters built a tall wooden swing to my father's specifications. There I spent many hours alternately standing on the board to pump up as high as it would go and plopping onto the seat to watch the river swing up and down beyond my feet and to "let the cat die" until the swing almost stopped and the heat became unbearable. Then I climbed to my feet and started over again, cooling off in the rushing breeze as I swept out over the hillside and back—almost as Daddy had done, I thought, when he was my age and had swung on his one-rope swing way out over the Los Gatos hillside in the foothills of California's Santa Cruz Mountains. Whenever he told the story of that swing, he stretched the words, "w-a-y out," and spiraled out his hand so that I could see a boy twirling gloriously over the golden slope of the hill and feel the breeze in his hair, just as I did here in the foothills of Hunan's western mountains.

It was a hot climb to our house. The path started at the river and meandered through thickets of bamboo until it suddenly became steeper in groves of old pine trees. Steps were cut into the hillside, some lined with slabs of rock, but most were just yellow clay, which turned slick when it rained. We rarely saw other people on the path, but now and then we heard a distant shot, which my father said came from a rifle, and we knew that Nationalist soldiers were in the hills looking for fuel and game, and perhaps deserters.

One day when we started up the steep part, we saw gobbets of congealing blood on the path ahead. They continued as we toiled up the hill. "Oh, dear," Mother said. "Are they going to our house?" My father speeded up to go on ahead. "Dwight," she exclaimed, "do you think you should go?"

He stopped. "Of course," he said. "I'll just go a little way and see what's happening."

"Please be careful!" Mother called after him as he disappeared up the path. We continued to climb, and after a while he came back and said it was all right. Whatever it was had gone over the hill.

"Is Zhang Shi-fu at the house?" asked Mother.

"No," he said, and added nothing more. We continued the rest of the way in thoughtful silence.

Zhang Shi-fu returned later that night. A wild boar had been wounded by some villagers and finally killed further on toward the mountains. They brought home enough meat to feed the entire village. Zhang Shi-fu had joined the hunt as it passed and brought back some meat as well, but he didn't offer to share it and we didn't ask.

Zhang Shi-fu was a member of the Miao tribe, known in Southeast Asia as the Hmong. He was a taciturn man with the profile of a Sioux Indian chief—bronze leathery skin, hooked nose, and deep crow's feet. His accent was so thick that what few words he spoke were barely comprehensible to me. He was very much at home in the hills around Shi Qiao. Dressed in a black tunic and trousers, a black turban wound around his head, and straw sandals, he moved silently along the trails, appearing and disappearing without greeting, farewell, or explanation. Yet he kept the house in good repair and was a gifted gardener. When he finished his work, he spent the remainder of the day squatting on the edge of the terrace or the vegetable garden, looking out over the valley and smoking a long pipe with a tiny bowl that he kept stuffed with tobacco he had grown and cured himself.

In my opinion, the most interesting thing about Zhang Shi-fu was the fact that he ate squash blossoms. He dug a small pond at the back of the vegetable garden, put some fish in it, and planted squash vines against the wall at the back of the pond. All summer long they bloomed—floppy orange and yellow trumpets that together with their jade-green leaves made a colorful display against the gray stone of the retaining wall. They bloomed profusely. Almost every day Zhang Shi-fu picked some and cooked them in his *cai*. After a couple of years I persuaded Tou Shi-fu to cook one or two in our *cai* as well. Once was enough. The blossoms had no taste and turned slimy in my mouth.

In Zhang Shi-fu's pond there were water beetles, whose comical antics didn't seem to interest the fish. Sometimes I caught a clutch of the beetles and put them with some pond water in a mason jar to watch at nap time (which Mother seemed to remember more frequently in Shi Qiao than in Yuanling). My bedroom was at the back of the house, and there I lay on my army cot by the window with the jar on the sill in a shaft of sunlight coming through the trees above the house. Until nap time was over, I watched the beetles busily trundle around in the water, using their feet like little oars. Then I returned them to the pond, where they hurriedly rowed their way down to the comfortable dark of its murky depths. There were usually one or two scooters skating on the shaded surface of the pond— delicate spiderlike insects with long jointed legs thin as silk threads. Dragonflies, too, stopped by and hung for seconds over the water before darting away. Now and then a bee flew in and burrowed in the heart of a squash blossom and then buzzed off heavily, her legs fat with yellow pollen.

The garden featured vegetables Mother nurtured from seeds mailed in letters by Aunt Dorothy, who got them from the Burpee seed company in America. Most of the garden was devoted to rows of tomato plants. They grew to be as tall as I. All our foreign friends who came to visit oohed and ahhed over them, as if they were the only tomatoes in the whole of Hunan, which was possible. They certainly were the only vegetable we ate raw— twice a day at least. My father liked to pick a ripe one, sun–warmed, off the vine, wipe it on his shirt, and bite into it right then and there. "Wonderful!" he'd say, wiping his chin with the back of his hand. His enthusiasm didn't convince me. Eating raw vegetables was un-Chinese. I would have preferred them cooked into *cai* if we were to eat them at all. But Mother quoted Aunt Dorothy, who had said that vegetables had more vitamins when they were raw than when they were cooked. Stoically I ate my daily quota raw, sprinkling the slices with generous helpings of *bien-tan,* the local unprocessed sugar.

Mother kept insect pests off the tomatoes by spraying them with soapy water. The birds were another matter. They relished tomatoes. That was when Molly came into her own. From early morning on, she stationed herself at the edge of the terrace overlooking the vegetable garden. If a bird was so foolish as to fly directly to the tomatoes, Molly exploded into action and dashed down to the garden, where she ran up and down the rows, barking hysterically, ears flapping wildly, and the bird—or, better yet, birds—took off in a frantic clatter of wings. Mission accomplished, Molly bustled back to the terrace, several inches of tongue out the side of her mouth, and resumed her vigil with an air of pleased competence.

As the summer progressed the birds became wiser, and rather than flying directly to the garden, they walked in from the far side and quietly attacked the tomatoes from underneath. To counteract this tactic, Molly took to making regular sorties into the vegetable garden, streaking down silently and bursting into barks only when she reached the rows of tomatoes. If she saw the birds before they knew she was coming, she was very happy indeed, and erupted into barks of such explosive volume that Mother said the birds were lucky they didn't get heart attacks. After Molly had succeeded in surprising a bird, she came to us for congratulations before resuming her station. It truly was a fine accomplishment. We made much of Molly's success, to which attention she responded with ever more enthusiasm for her job. In the evening, as soon as she heard my father whistle the oriole's song, she abandoned her post with a happy bark and scampered off to meet him. After giving him an extravagant welcome, she would dash to the vegetable garden and go through the motions of flushing the birds, perhaps to demonstrate how faithful she'd been at her job while he was gone, or perhaps from an excess of joy.

Molly loved to go on walks. So did my parents. I was less enthusiastic and went only because Molly and my parents expected it. We usually walked in the evening after supper, along the only horizontal path leading away from our house and around the edge of our valley into the next. With

Molly exploring ahead, we strolled along the trail on the steep hillside, looking at wildflowers and admiring the view—the *same* flowers and the *same* view we'd looked at the evening before and most evenings before that. Mother pointed out every little change—a flower or bud, a touch of blight, a butterfly. "Oh, see that butterfly," she'd say softly, pointing to one resting briefly on a rock. "Isn't it *exquisite!*" Or "Oh, dear. Something is killing that beautiful anemone. How sad!" Or "Look at this," pointing to a cluster of tiny toadstools. "They weren't here yesterday. Isn't it wonderful!" My father always responded with appreciation, but my interest had long since worn thin, looking at so many exquisite, sad, and wonderful things every evening. It was years before I realized that on those evening walks I had absorbed, however reluctantly, some portion of my mother's wonder and sensitivity to the beauty of nature's small creations, whose tiny perfection and diminutive disintegration often go unnoticed.

The walk I liked best took the better part of a day. It entailed hiking down to the village of Shi Qiao, across a stone bridge, and following a path up the side of the stream into a series of narrow valleys, like small gorges, where the walls became almost vertical and were decorated with trees and plants growing out of the rock. Walking along the base of those walls, I felt like a figure in a Chinese painting of mountains and water. The stream was deeper where the walls came close together and flowed swiftly into the more shallow areas where the walls were farther apart. There the water rushed over the pebbles so noisily that I could almost hear voices in the multiplicity of sound, as though water sprites were conversing under the foam.

We always stopped for a picnic where the stream was wide and shallow just below a sharp bend between two cliffs. We waded out to a flat rock in the center of the stream, where we ate our lunch, the dappled water chuckling around us. Molly was convinced she was a water spaniel, and it was all we could do to keep her out of the stream to forestall a soaking from her energetic shaking after an invigorating dip.

One day we brought along Mother's last bar of Fels Naphtha soap, used for bathing Molly because it was lethal to fleas. After our lunch, Mother went back to the shore to sit with the picnic basket while my father and I stayed on the rock to wash Molly. We had just gotten her lathered up when Mother called urgently over the sound of the stream, "Dwight!"

"What?" he called back, busily rubbing soap around Molly's ears.

She pointed upstream.

We looked. Swimming around the bend toward us was a herd of water buffalo. Their broad backs almost filled the stream from side to side, confined by the walls of the narrow gorge. A boy was sitting on one of them. When Molly caught sight of them she exploded into frantic barks. Slippery with lather, she shot out of our grasp into the stream and paddled valiantly toward the herd, leaving a wake of soapy water behind her. Obviously her weeks of chasing birds had been mere rehearsals for this, her greatest challenge. The buffalo snorted and swung their heads, the buffalo boy yelled, and my father jumped in the water after Molly. He grabbed her hind legs and pulled her to him, clasped her to his chest, and plowed through the water to the bank.

I stood mesmerized in the moment. I had never seen water buffalo so close before. I had never seen so many together, nor from such a low angle, now that they had come to their feet in shallow water. I knew they were the mildest of creatures, but from my position, their size outweighed their purported placidity. They looked as big as trucks, the spread of their horns wider than my arms could stretch. "Betty Jean!" cried Mother as they approached the other end of the rock. I jumped into the water, landing on my hands and knees, and splashed to the bank as fast as I could, where Mother pulled me up. All the while, Molly, in my father's arms, was barking convulsively, egged on by the echoes from the valley walls, which amplified her volume to unhoped-for proportions.

When we looked back at the stream, the herd was flowing over the rock where we had been. Molly continued to hurl insults at the offending interlopers from the security of my father's firm grasp, but they ignored her, moving slowly and smoothly through the water until they disappeared around a bend further downstream—all except for one. It was a picturesque sight. There in a shaft of sunlight was a lone water buffalo on the rock, repeatedly licking the spot where we'd left Mother's last bar of Fels Naphtha. He ran his tongue in slow strokes over the stone with the lingering satisfaction of a gourmet cleaning his plate after a particularly delectable repast. Finally he stepped off the rock and leisurely followed the herd down the stream and around the bend.

When the last buffalo had disappeared, Molly stopped barking, and my father put her down. She wiggled her rear and pawed his foot, modestly asking for congratulations. Obviously her bravery had successfully rid our stream and our rock of dangerous intruders. Because of her, the place was restored to us. Indeed, when we returned to that spot in later times and bathed Molly on that very rock, never again were we disturbed by unwelcome visitors. On those peaceful occasions, Molly got washed with Chinese soap, which, we discovered, was also lethal to fleas.

Shi Qiao gradually changed over the three summers we were there. The influx of refugees and Nationalist soldiers caused an acute shortage of firewood, and soldiers started cutting down the trees in the valley for fuel, while farmers cut them down to make charcoal for sale. Whenever we heard the sound of chopping behind the house, my father or mother went up and asked them to stop, which they did so long as we were there. Each time we returned to Shi Qiao, we were relieved to see that the sentinel pine was still standing. After a couple of years, about the only trees left in the valley were the sentinel pine and the grove of pines immediately behind our house, but even there, many of the trees were gone. Up on the saddle behind the house, streaks of red soil started showing among the remaining trees. Erosion had set in.

I loved the rain at Shi Qiao. The air became fresh, and it was both cool and cozy in our house with the water drumming on the tiles and pouring off the eaves in front of the windows like a silver curtain closing us in. One night there was a downpour. It was so cool I had to pull up my sheet, and went to sleep lulled by the sound of water rushing over the clay bank outside my window. I had always wanted to sleep next to a waterfall.

The next morning I woke up with a feeling that something wasn't right. The water had stopped pouring over the bank and the rain had ceased. In the quiet half-light of dawn I swung my feet over the edge of the cot and stepped into cold water almost up to my knees. The floor was covered with bloody water. After a wrenching moment of dislocation, I realized the water was red with the soil from the hillside. My straw slippers floated forlornly in the slow current which flowed toward the door of my parents' room at the front of the house. I waded through the door to their bed. They were just waking up. "There's water all over!" I announced, halfway between fear and satisfaction. They sat up and took in the situation immediately. "Oh, Dwight!" Mother said. She looked around. "Where's Molly?" and without a further word, they got out of bed into the water, and the three of us splashed to the living room, where we found Molly miserably curled up on a chair, her love of water forgotten. By that time, Tou Shi-fu and Zhang Shi-fu were awake, and all of us got busy pushing the water out of the rooms with whatever we could find and through the front door. The awning had come down, so we couldn't see the front of the terrace, but we could hear the water pouring down into the vegetable garden below. After a while we were down to the slick dirt floor. The storm had washed the sky, and the morning dawned bright and clear. In the steaming sunlight of full day, we saw that the house and the bank behind it still stood firm. We returned to Yuanling for a couple of weeks to give time for repairs and for the house to dry out. I thought it had been very exciting—actually a lot of fun—having water in the house. But Mother started to worry that we might lose the house in another storm.

Our last summer in Shi Qiao was much like the others. I had brought some favorite books to read, did some arithmetic with my father (it was my hardest subject), played cards, went on walks and picnics, and made a landscape in the bank at the side of the house by cutting a tiny path into the clay. I erected toothpick bridges over miniature chasms and fashioned little pavilions overlooking gigantic cliffs. As I worked, I became very tiny and entered a Song Dynasty landscape in which I was a footsore traveler on the path along the cliff. I imagined a waterfall right *here* on the path, where I sat to rest and cool my feet. Further on, I became a beautiful lady in a long silk robe, with jeweled combs in my jet black hair, sitting in a pavilion high above the mist and listening to the plaintive notes of a *xiao*—a Chinese flute—calling across the chasm.

That summer we borrowed the Bachelors' Victrola with some records, and one moonlit night my father moved my cot and mosquito net to the terrace. He set the Victrola in the open window of the living room, and while he and Mother played their favorite card game, Russian Bank, by the light of an oil lamp in the living room, I lay on my cot and listened to Beethoven's Moonlight Sonata. Propped on my elbow, I looked past the silhouette of the sentinel pine to the moon, and below the moon, to the silver road it laid across the river. Everything stopped to listen. Even the chorus of frogs muted their chant as the tranquil notes floated slowly into the night and sailed in serene succession over the dark valley to the moonlit path on the distant river. For one long lyrical moment the river and the moon, the pine tree, the valley, the house, my mother and father, and I all came together in the music.

૪

Although the war was still raging in 1944, the tide was turning toward Allied victory. When we left Yuanling that year for furlough in the States, my parents gave the house and land to Zhang Shi-fu, for it seemed likely that when we returned to China, we would not come back to Yuanling. After our return to the States, when we were living in a three-room apartment over a variety store in New Haven, word came from Yali that the house had burned down and Zhang Shi-fu had disappeared. When I heard the news, I couldn't believe it. Although I was busily occupied with my new friends, my new school, my sixth-grade classroom, my piano lessons, although I didn't tell my classmates I'd lived in China, although I had barely thought of Shi Qiao since we left, I needed it to be there. When this American world seemed alien and puzzling, I needed to know that the house was there to surround us with its inanimate love. I needed to know that the valley and the pines, the gecko and the tree frog, the Indian cuckoo, and even the mosquitoes in the outhouse were waiting to welcome us back with an acceptance that expected nothing from us except to be there. I never fully believed the claim that Shi Qiao was gone.

Half a century later, the Summer Palace of China's last empress still lies by the lake outside Beijing, preserved almost as she left it. It is there for the whole world to visit and admire. But Shi Qiao exists for me alone.

THE BROKEN CIRCLE

The radio we had in Yuanling was a state-of-the-art Hallicrafter short-wave receiver my father had bought in Shanghai when he came to get us. It sat at the back of his desk—a squat gray metal box not at all like the Art Deco construction of sleekly curved wood sitting in Uncle Ed and Aunt Dorothy's California living room. Their radio had housed orchestras and tenors and emitted oracular voices announcing the news and the merits of Ivory Soap. Our radio emitted static. If one listened carefully, a distant voice sometimes could be heard behind the noise, fading in and out, stuttering faintly. Once a day my father inserted a sheaf of papers and carbons into his typewriter, switched on the radio, adjusted the volume, and typed out the news as he heard it. Then he gave the copies to Chen Shi-fu to deliver to the Bachelors, the Yali administration, and sometimes to the missions at the other end of town.

I didn't pay much attention to the news. The fact that it was mostly bad didn't bother me, for I lived inside a circle where I knew nothing could hurt us. It was unlikely that Japanese bombs could harm us—if they ever came. For one thing, we Americans weren't in the war and therefore weren't their targets. More important was my faith in my father. I was in the process of disconnecting the magical proposition I'd made between my mother's anxiety and my father's reassurance. Now her anxiety seemed pointless. We had always come through safely in the past, hadn't we, just as Daddy said we would? "Dearest," he would say to Mother, "of course it'll be all right" (whatever it was). "We'll be fine." But Mother was disgusted with what she saw as my father's unfounded optimism. "You always say that!" she invariably replied, her blue eyes bright with frustration. Shaking her head, she'd add, "You just don't know!" Whenever I heard one of these exchanges, I reminded myself that Mother's worry was needless; Daddy was always right in the end.

In spite of Mother's aptitude for anxiety, I didn't hear much talk about the war during our early days in Yuanling. My father kept track of the fighting on a map pinned to the wall, but the map meant no more to me than those in my geography book, which was rather boring. But by our second year in Yuanling, as the war news got worse and rumors more rampant, even I could see that the Japanese forces were spreading like a bloody stain over the map of China.

One morning in December 1941 I had just come into the dining room from playing outside with Molly when, through the door to the living room, I saw my parents sitting at their desks. They were unnaturally still. Under the radio's crackling static, a muffled voice rose and fell with portentous British detachment, but my father wasn't typing. Mother wasn't correcting papers. When I started into the room, they didn't move. Then Mother saw me. "Betty Jean." she said. I stopped in the doorway.

Mother said, "The Japanese just bombed Pearl Harbor." The Japanese were always bombing some place or other, but her words didn't sound right.

"The Japanese bombed what?"

"Pearl Harbor," she said. "At Honolulu."

"The Japanese bombed Honolulu?" Our house in Manoa Valley flashed through my mind—and our avocado tree, and my kindergarten, where I'd learned to tie my shoelaces.

My father finally spoke. "Not Honolulu, as far as we know," he said heavily. "They bombed Pearl Harbor near Honolulu, where we had a lot of battleships."

"But we're not fighting Japan," I said.

"We are now," my father said, looking very sad.

That day people moved slowly and spoke in low voices. Mother worked with me as usual on reading and composition, geography, and history, my father taught me arithmetic as usual, and the day unfolded as usual, except that the safe circle around me had suddenly become fragile and undependable. Even I, uninterested in the geography of the war, knew that we were now isolated in a small and vulnerable enclave of deceptive tranquility, ringed by mountains beyond which lay a circle of implacable hostility. There was no way out. I vaguely sensed what the grown-ups experienced with sharpened awareness: We Americans in Yuanling had precipitously joined the Chinese in a round of dormant terror where familiar objects were seen with greater clarity, happenings were more memorable, gatherings more close, friends and family more precious, and goodbyes more thoughtful. At the same time, everything seemed not quite real, but rather transparent and temporary, giving literal meaning to the words "for the time being."

I began to suspect that bad things actually could happen to us, although it didn't really sink in—especially as time went on and nothing very bad happened. In fact, the war brought some very exciting events to Yuanling. One was the showing of a British propaganda film of the London blitz brought to Yuanling by a visiting English teacher from Britain. Movies were a novelty in Yuanling, and each showing of this film was an event of great interest. When it was shown at Yali, the students made room for Xi-xi and Yuan-mei and me in the front row of a very crowded room. There we sat with our eyes glued to the flickering screen.

The ancient projector had no sound system but produced enough noise on its own to make up for it. The electricity wasn't all it should have been, either, but there was enough to show buildings burning, searchlights moving against the night sky above St. Paul's, ambulances careening around Trafalgar Square, and brave men with washbasins on their heads putting out fires and digging people out of rubble. The film featured a fearless nurse in a spotless white uniform and a short stiff veil decorated with a red cross over her forehead (I knew it was red, even though the film was black and white). She looked like Aunt Dorothy, who had been a nurse before she married Uncle Ed. Well, she almost looked like Aunt Dorothy, except that she was taller and thinner, her face was longer, her eyes and nose were different, and from what I could see of her hair, Aunt Dorothy's was darker. But like Aunt Dorothy, she knew exactly what to do and always showed up with an ambulance to succor whatever victim had been dug out—man, woman, or child—while in the background buildings tumbled, smoke billowed, flames leaped, and antiaircraft tracers floated up toward German bombers pinned in beams of light. I determined then and there to be a nurse when I grew up.

The areas of occupied China fluctuated with the ebb and flow of fighting. What was occupied one week might be free the next and then reoccupied. But no foreign combatant, Japanese or American, ever reached Yuanling, with the exception of Captain Costello. We learned of him one morning when we heard that an American pilot had made an emergency landing in the mountains and had been brought to Yuanling at night by Chinese guerrillas. For once, the rumors were not exaggerated. Captain Costello had indeed been taken to the Catholic hospital at the other end of the city. During his recovery, he was inundated by grateful visits and homemade delicacies from the foreign community. In fact, the whole town rejoiced in his survival, for he was living proof of America's stand against the horror of Japan's depredations.

Long after that exciting time, Captain Costello's name evoked for me the image of a dashing pilot nonchalantly swooping his fighter plane through the skies and shooting down enemy aircraft with casual but deadly accuracy. Actually, Captain Costello didn't look very dashing. He was a short, mild-mannered young man with a smooth, square face and honey-colored hair, who responded to all the adulation with quiet courtesy and few words. One day an assembly was held for him with speeches and presentations and Chinese patriotic songs, ending with Mother directing the Yali Glee Club in a ringing rendition of the first verse of "God Bless America" in English followed by a repetition of the first verse, this time starting with "God bless Jung Hua Ming Guo"—the Republic of China. Shortly after that celebration, Captain Costello left Yuanling as inconspicuously as he came.

One afternoon several weeks after he had gone, I was on the swing next to our house when the air raid siren started to sound, then stopped abruptly. When it stopped, I heard airplanes. Their angry hum rapidly expanded to a deafening roar, and two fighter planes streaked low over the town, circled out above the river down to the other end of town, returned, zoomed down again, waggled their wings, screamed up into the sky and disappeared into the haze toward the western mountains. Everyone ran out to see what had happened. We soon learned that the planes had dropped several large bundles onto the Catholic compound at the other end of the city—Captain Costello's tender of gratitude. Their contents were distributed to all the missions in town—K rations and delicacies we had long forgotten, such as cheese, powdered coffee and cocoa, tinned butter and meat.

My share of the bonanza was a one-by-three-inch block of U.S. Army chocolate—the most delicious chocolate ever created. It was crammed with enough nutrition to provide a whole meal's fuel for a GI with a sixty-pound pack slogging through the hottest jungle or perched on the coldest mountain—so hard that it could be broken only by banging it with a cleaver and so dense that it stayed firm even in direct sunlight. Its color was charcoal brown, and it was packed with such fulfilling flavor that one thin fragment scraped off by my upper incisors flooded my entire body with dark delight—barely sweet and not really bitter, just Chocolateness. I kept the dwindling cube under my pillow for weeks (it was of such inherent integrity that it left no smudge on the bedlinen) and shaved off one flake every night before sliding off blissfully into the very sweetest of dreams. Later we heard a rumor that Captain Costello and his partner in generosity had been demoted for leaving a flight mission to deliver his thank-you bundles. I hoped it wasn't true.

The years passed, and still the Japanese planes ignored Yuanling. One day in our fourth year at Yuanling, we were at lunch when the siren sounded at noon. Its warning howled up the river like a great lament, and into the foothills. It seemed to last longer than usual, and it was still wailing when I went onto the porch to see what was happening. When the siren finally stopped, there was an ominous silence. The town lay still, trapped between the river and the hills, like a rabbit motionless with fear. Then the murmur started again, tentatively at first, and quickly expanded to an agitated roar.

I went back to the dining room, where Chen Shi-fu was reporting that the ball was red. Tou Shi-fu broke up the fire in the kitchen stove and went home. We left our lunch on the table and quickly got ready to go. My father got out our air raid bag, I picked up Little Bear, Mother gathered our hats and her bag, and we were on our way, joining the rest of the school population up the back path out of the compound, down into the ravine. I saw Xi-xi and Yuan-mei, but they stayed with their families in the ravine while we took one of the trails into the hills.

We had walked farther than usual when we stopped near the top of a hill to catch our breath. The heat was accentuated by an uncertain noontime breeze. In the bright sunshine we looked down over the steps of rice paddies and grassy hillsides and saw meandering lines of people moving up from the town, with leaves and branches in their hats. There was no noise up where we stood except for the fitful whisper of the breeze blowing past our ears. When it lulled, we heard the distant cry of hawks endlessly tracing their circles above the river.

While we were looking, the people suddenly vanished. Uncomprehending, we stared at the empty hillsides baking in the sun and the gleaming rice paddies quietly reflecting the blue sky. Then we heard the faint notes of the bugle warning that the airplanes were coming, and realized that the people had squatted down, their leafy hats blending into the hillsides. We, too, crouched down by the path, but I felt conspicuous without their camouflage. I listened for the airplanes, but all I heard was the restless wind and rustling grass. After a while, the lines of people on the hillsides appeared again and we got up and went on.

We came to a single grave on a hillside, facing downriver toward the other end of town. The wall of the grave circled around a worn tombstone carved with characters barely discernible under scabs of lichen. Dried goat droppings lay in the stubble on the ground. We walked in and sat down with our backs against the wall. The stubble pricked my legs. It was still and hot in there, and a little smelly, but it provided protection if fighters strafed the hillsides. My father took out the book we were currently reading, *The Robe*, by Lloyd Douglas, about a Roman centurion who crucified Jesus and later wandered the hills of Galilee, trying to learn about him. Those hills, I thought, must have been like these, and I settled down to listen.

My father started to read to us. Suddenly we heard footsteps and a soldier rushed into the center of the grave. He stopped short when he saw us, obviously not expecting to see two foreigners with a child sitting against the wall. He brandished his rifle and scowled horribly. Then he noticed the white pages of the open book and jabbed at it with his bayonet. "Get rid of that!" he shouted, his country accent so thick we could hardly understand him. "The airplanes will see it!" My father closed the book, remarking mildly that there were no airplanes. "Shut up!" the soldier shouted again. "They'll hear you!" and he flung himself down by the wall, laying the rifle across his lap so that it pointed at us. We sat there, very still, for what seemed like a long time.

Then I heard humming, faintly at first, like the summer sound of bees around a hive. Gradually it became more sure, a droning song sustained on one note. The soldier began to chant softly, "O-mi-to-fu, O-mi-to-fu," invoking the name of Buddha. My father put his arm around my shoulders, and Mother took my hand. The droning song grew louder rapidly until it filled the whole sky and the air between the hills with malignant ecstasy. A monstrous vibration invaded the wall around us and throbbed in my ears like a gigantic earache. Shadows flickered across the grave. The song faded rapidly. Through the opening in the wall, I saw tiny airplanes turning in the sky over the far end of the city. Raindrops glinted under them. There were distant whistles and thuds that steadily grew louder as the song returned. "O-mi-to-fu! O-mi-to-fu!" shouted the soldier, and the noise grew even louder. Only when I was pushed down on my stomach did I realize that those raindrops were bombs. My mother and father put their arms over my back. I felt their weight pushing me down. The droning and pounding got louder and louder, then softer, then louder again as the planes made their bombing runs up and down the river. The air shivered in time with the thuds. I wanted to curl into a ball, but I clutched Little Bear and stayed still, breathing as lightly as I could while the bombers sang and the bombs whistled and thudded. I don't remember when it stopped.

I next found myself walking outside the grave. The all clear must have sounded, for the soldier was gone. As we started down, I saw plumes of smoke standing over the town. When we arrived at the compound, my father left us to join the teachers and students going into the city to help put out the fires and dig people out of the rubble. Mother and I went home.

During the days that followed, the bombing didn't seem to have much effect on me or my friends. At first we told each other about what we had seen and how we had felt. We took turns describing our fear at the most awful moment or what gruesome scene we'd heard that someone else saw down in the city. Our favorite phrase was "*Ngo pa si da*—I was scared to death!" declared with wide-eyed drama and received with appreciative murmurs from the others. But we soon stopped talking about it and resumed our usual activities and enthusiasms. In fact, I put it all away as something that was finished, until one night sometime later.

In bed on the sleeping porch, I looked out at the faint outline of the town against the lighter darkness of the river and decided to think about the bombing. It was like opening a forbidden package. Tentatively at first, I pictured the bombers turning over the city like hawks circling over the river. Then I imagined the pilots inside the planes. They had sharp bird faces and sat immobile, staring straight ahead and humming to themselves as silver raindrops whistled down beneath them. I remembered how their song reached into our space and throbbed in my ears. I remembered how shadows had flickered over the grave and the air shivered with heavy thuds. I felt the weight of my parents' arms on my back. What if we are bombed again and Mother and Daddy are killed? My breath stopped. What if I am left alive?

It was then that I reached the terror wrapped in the package of my remembering. Now I knew. I knew Mother and Daddy would be killed the next time. They would die and I would be left behind. No one knew who I was. I was left behind with nothing known, nothing loved, nothing familiar. When the bombers came again Mother and Daddy would die. *Please, make me be killed, too.*

My father must have heard something because he came onto the porch and sat down on the edge of my bed. He laid his hand on my head. "What's the matter?" he asked. "What is it?" I found it hard to talk, but I turned over and clutched his hand. At last I managed to sob out my fears. "Oh, dearest," he said gently. "Nothing will happen to us." He paused. "We'll be fine," he said. "You and Mother and I will always be together."

I didn't think to question how he knew. It was enough that he was there to say it. Under the slow, soothing strokes of his hand on my hair, I fell asleep. But below the level of sleep I knew that his hand would not always be there to comfort me. The circle around my childhood was broken. What I had only suspected at the time of Pearl Harbor I now knew for sure—that there was a world outside the fractured periphery of my security, one not defined by my parents. It was a world where safety was ephemeral, where someday my mother and father would die, and where finally I would be left by myself, with no one who knew where I came from, wrapped in an envelope of solitude.

DEPARTURE

During the four years we were in Yuanling, Aunt Dorothy sent me two new dresses, brought by a Bachelor on his way through California to Yuanling. Otherwise, I wore what we'd brought when we came. Fabric was scarce, so over the years my mother artfully enlarged what I had by putting in strips of white sheeting around the waist and hem. I also had some clothes left in the house by previous generations of missionary children. Early in 1944, a missionary who was returning to the States gave Mother several yards of figured American cotton she hadn't used. With a borrowed sewing machine—the kind that had to be cranked with one hand while the other hand guided the cloth under the needle—Mother made three dresses. They were alike, except one had a blouse made of white sheeting, because there wasn't enough figured fabric to go around. The dresses were for Xi-xi, Yuan-mei, and me. They were beautiful.

My father had run out of film for his camera, so at Easter that year he took us to a portrait studio that had recently opened on Yuanling's main street and had a picture taken of us in our dresses. I called them our "sister dresses," as if they would help keep us together, for by then we weren't seeing so much of each other. We were spending most of our time on schoolwork, and now that Xi-xi and Yuan-mei were older, they had to help out more at home. But we still could get together on Saturday afternoons after their school let out for the weekend.

One Saturday afternoon I came in from playing with Xi-xi to find my mother and father sitting at the dining room table, not doing anything. Their faces were strange, their eyes wide and glistening as though they had tears in them. Mother told me to sit down. Then she said, "Betty Jean, dearest." She paused. "Something very sad has happened."

My mouth went dry.

She said, "Molly suddenly got very sick. When Daddy found her, she was already gone."

"What do you mean—gone? Where did she go?"

"Dearest. Molly got sick and she died."

She was wrong. Molly was fine. I had just played with her that morning, right before lunch.

159

"No," I said "It can't be. It isn't true." I looked at them for confirmation. "Is it?" Of all the bad things I believed I could prevent by thinking of them ahead of time, this I hadn't thought of. "How can it be? She was fine this morning."

My father explained that it had happened very fast. She must have gotten out and eaten something bad. He had found her lying outside her box on the back porch; she'd thrown up and had stopped breathing. He'd just gotten back from the hills where he'd buried her before I got home.

"She ate something bad?"

"Well . . ." My father stopped. His eyes were very dark. Then he said it looked like she had eaten poisoned meat. He didn't tell me until much later that her tongue was swollen and stained black.

I said, "Poison? No! Who would poison *Molly*?"

Mother said, "She didn't suffer long."

I felt like crying but no sound came out.

I saw Miss Ting shoving the little boy into the tiger's closet. Then the sound came.

I cried until I didn't remember why I was crying. Then I remembered, and it was like learning the truth all over again. Mother held me close, rocking back and forth. She was crying, too.

When we stopped, I said, "Molly's gone?"

"Yes."

Molly was gone. Her happy welcome, her eager presence no matter how I felt, her warm body wiggling with joy wasn't there anymore. We could no longer say "Where's Molly?" because there was no "where'" with her in it. From an unknown hand she had trustingly taken poison.

After that day, Yuanling no longer seemed such a friendly place. Something was missing at the center, and something malevolent lurked under the edges. When Molly died, I started to leave Yuanling.

It was also during that final year that one afternoon I heard children's voices chanting on the path in front of our house. I went out to the porch to see what was happening. They were looking up at the porch, and when I came out their volume increased. I didn't understand what they were saying, but suddenly I realized they were chanting at me. After one quick glance I shrank back from the screen just as Tou Shi-fu came out from around the house and shouted angrily at them. I couldn't believe that children were calling me names here, where my friends lived, where I'd been standing next to my own bed on the porch. They could not have been street children. Had any of my friends been among them? They couldn't have been, but I wasn't sure. Maybe they *wanted* to be there but couldn't because their parents would be angry. I was confused and ashamed— ashamed of being me, of being different, of being someone my friends wanted to chant at if they could. What had I done to make them do that? I must have done something wrong, but I didn't know what it was. Too ashamed to talk about it, I never mentioned it to my parents or tried to find out why it happened. Tou Shi-fu didn't say anything, either.

I went back to being with my friends whenever I could, pretending nothing had happened. I pushed the incident down into that dark place with other memories that lived on without my attention. But when we were packing for our trip back to the States, a thought occurred to me. "When we go home," I said to Mother, "I won't be a foreigner anymore."

"That's right," she said. "You won't."

We had lived in Yuanling for four continuous years, except for a time around my tenth birthday when we had returned to Changsha for several weeks while my father took care of some business and Mother saw the dentist. Then we went back to Yuanling for our first bombing, for our last Christmas, our last lunar new year, our last Easter, and our last days at Shi Qiao. In June 1944 the Japanese began their long-expected drive through central China. They took Changsha again, and again Nationalist soldiers burned the city before they left it to the Japanese, as they had burned it six years before, killing thousands of their own citizens. In areas of Hunan unoccupied by the Japanese, Nationalist soldiers were turning to banditry and raiding the countryside, including villages around Yuanling. The American and British consulates urged women and children of their nationalities to leave China as soon as possible, because escape routes out of the country would soon be cut off. My father did not want to leave until Brank Fulton arrived—the man from Yale-in-China who was to replace him. Mother would not leave without my father, so we waited for Brank to arrive from the States. But once he got to China, his travel was delayed because of the shifting conflict and the difficulty of getting transportation inland. After some weeks it still was unclear when he would reach Yuanling. Finally my parents decided to depart while there was still time. So, on a day early in July of 1944, we left Yuanling for good.

It was about five in the morning when we crossed the river to the "bus station"—an open area with a bus standing in the middle. We were going to Zhijiang, a city about a hundred miles away over the mountains, where the nearest U.S. air base was located. There we were to catch a plane for the first leg of our journey out of China. Before we got on the bus, my mother and father shook hands with people who had come to see us off, saying, *"Zai-hui"*—perhaps best translated as "May we meet again," but meaning goodbye.

Xi-xi, Yuan-mei, and I were wearing our sister dresses together for the last time. We stood, not looking at each other, not touching, not saying anything, for the few feet between us seemed almost too far to talk across. Besides, there were no words for what was happening. We watched the grown-ups say *zai hui* so many times, so easily, so firmly, so finally. When it came time for us to say it, we said *zai hui* softly to each other, as though that somehow made it less real. Then I turned and followed Mother across to the bus and up the steps.

Chen Shi-fu had saved seats for us by physically occupying a bench on the left side alongside some of our bags. I sat down at the window and looked out, but I couldn't find Yuan-mei and Xi-xi in the crowd. More and more people piled into the bus with some good-natured yelling and some less good-natured pushing. Chen Shi-fu saw us settled on our bench, then pushed his way off. The bus rumbled and roared and we started to move. As we pulled away I spotted Xi-xi among the people outside, but I couldn't find Yuan-mei. Xi-xi was waving her left hand limply at shoulder height. I waved back until the bus turned a corner.

Our vehicle was a converted truck crowded with people sitting on the benches and more sitting in the aisle on stools and bags and boxes. By ingenious adaptation, the gasoline engine used charcoal as fuel. Up by the front window on the right was a large metal cylinder with charcoal burning inside. A pipe from the cylinder fed the fumes to the engine. It wasn't very powerful, so we climbed through the mountains no faster than one could walk, but we racketed downhill fast to make up for it, swinging around corners with the horn insistently declaring our right of way no matter what was coming from the other direction. Every now and then we stopped and the driver stuffed more charcoal into the cylinder from a supply he had on the roof. It was a hot day, and with the windows open, charcoal fumes blew into the bus from the right. Many of our fellow passengers were carsick. Now we understood why Chen Shi-fu had gotten us seats on the left. Even so, I got a headache and felt queasy until I knelt on the bench with my head out the window, and thereafter I spent most of the trip in that position.

We got to Zhijiang in the late afternoon and arrived by rickshaw at a mission compound in time for dinner. We were to stay at the mission until we found a plane to take us to Guilin, then another plane to Kunming and thence over the southern part of the Himalayas to India.

I was tired after the bus trip and not at all hungry, but I started to revive when a pair of American GIs who had been invited to dinner asked us if we would like to see the weekly movie at the air base that evening. Not counting the British propaganda film about the blitz, we hadn't been to a real movie since we'd seen *Snow White* in Hong Kong four years before. I felt better immediately. Although there was a full moon that night, the men said it would be completely safe, for the Japanese never bombed after dark. So we hastily swallowed our dessert and climbed into their jeep, which took off for the air base like a jackrabbit—at least that's what my father said as we bounced over the road out of the city.

It was exhilarating. The night was sweltering hot, but the top of the jeep was down, and as we bounded along the high road between rice paddies, the wind of our motion cooled us off. When we slowed down, there was a delicious smell of gasoline that reminded me of Hong Kong and Shanghai and, most of all, California. This was America, or at least a part of it, and something inside loosened that I hadn't known was tight. Everything now was under control and predictable. The Army Air Forces would take care of us.

It was dusk when we entered the air base and the jeep skidded to a stop at a large Quonset hut. There was a low roar inside the metal building, where several hundred men were gathered for the movie. Our hosts guided us to the door at the back and started us down the middle toward the front. As we walked down the aisle the noise became deafening, punctuated with whistles and calls. They were all looking at us. One of the GIs explained to Mother later: "They haven't seen an American kid in three years," he said. "And she has braids."

By the time we got near the front, the noise lessened and the lights went out for the movie. But I didn't see it. Men came to our row to say hi, how was I doing, and take this, handing me a candy bar or gum. Others passed candy bars and gum up the rows, adding to the growing pile in my lap. I couldn't see very well in the flickering dark, but the candy bars felt thin and long and flat in their wrappers, which I dimly saw said "Hershey" on one side. I tried one. It was limp from the heat and drooped weakly over my hand as I opened it. My teeth went through it without resistance; soft, and cloyingly sweet, it oozed over my tongue and melted submissively—a very distant cousin to that unforgettable hunk of dusky rock-hard brown-bitter *hint* of sweetness from Captain Costello. I nibbled politely on this pitiful excuse for chocolate and said thank you very much while the movie blared away and the GIs' contributions to homesickness built up in my lap to the point where Mother had to transfer some to her bag. I switched to chewing gum.

Some GI's asked us to come over to their row, so Mother and I moved over and they asked me where I'd come from and where was I going, and said that their little sister in Iowa had braids just like me, and maybe we could come have a Coke with them after the movie, and what would I like from the PX? I didn't know what a PX was, but I tried to answer their questions and said thank you. After the first surprise, I wasn't at all embarrassed. It seemed quite natural to be talking with them. It was nice to look like someone's sister.

I hardly noticed when the movie stopped abruptly in midscene. The lights went on and suddenly the building emptied as everyone walked quickly out the doors at the sides and back. Our hosts said that Japanese planes had been reported heading toward us, and not to worry, they never bombed at night, but we should go back to the city to get away from the air base, "just in case." One of our hosts said goodbye and the other quickly ushered us out a side door to the jeep, where he and my father helped Mother and me into the back.

With my father next to the driver, we dashed back the way we had come, this time without headlights. The full moon was so bright that we could see the road and the rice paddies on either side. The noise of the engine and the wind was so loud we had to shout to be heard. Suddenly, ahead on our left, the huge shape of an airplane appeared, flying low toward the road. I caught a glimpse of its propellers on the front of its wings, round circles in the moonlight. Its landing lights were on, making parallel lines of brightness running ahead on the water of the rice paddies. As we sped down the road, the giant shadow flickered overhead, followed by the mammoth roar of its engines. Then the world exploded in sound and light.

I found myself slogging through the water in the rice paddy in water up to my waist with Mother pulling my hand. "Dwight!" she called frantically, and I glanced behind us, expecting to see him there. But he was still in the front seat of the jeep. Our host was holding Mother's other hand. He dropped it and started back to the jeep, but my father jumped into the rice paddy in one sliding bound and ran toward us. Another shadow flickered overhead, and the world exploded again on the other side of the road. A huge earache punched the sides of my head and we ran on, splashing through water up to my knees. Another shadow—the sky lit up with flashes of deafening pressure—and our guide shoved Mother and me into a deep ditch running along the edge of a rice paddy. He and my father followed. More sky shadows flickered past and I heard our guide yell in a lull between explosions, "We'll be okay here." Suddenly the air was filled with loud chattering, and a myriad white and red lights floated up toward the shadows that swept overhead again and again, as though churned out by a giant machine just over the horizon. I started to shake and clung to Mother. "Those are antiaircraft guns, dear. They're not shooting at us," Mother said reassuringly, and pulled me closer. I remembered the antiaircraft fire in the movie of the blitz in London and briefly saw the brave nurse in her white uniform and veil jump out of the ambulance. I felt better. Then the world exploded again, and we crouched in the water on the bottom of the ditch, our arms over our heads with my father's arms over our backs. And so it went on with lulls between spasms of explosions for two hours.

Gradually, our ditch filled up with GI's who came running across the paddies, so that by the time the air raid was over, the ditch seemed crowded. I was still shaky at the end, and numb, with a dull ache in my ears. All was quiet. We waited for a time, but the planes didn't return. Slowly we stood up and climbed into the rice paddy. "Is everyone okay?" someone asked, and then the men disappeared into the night. When we got to the road we found the jeep where we had left it. Our host looked it over, turned on the engine, and after a few minutes we got in and drove to the mission, where we thanked him for the evening and for taking care of us.

When we got to our room, Mother said to my father, "Dwight. What were you *doing*, sitting in the jeep like that? You didn't pay any attention to *us*!"

"I was watching the planes," he replied. Because their landing lights were on, he had thought they were ours. "And then there were all those fireworks," he said. "Beautiful!"

"*Honestly*, Dwight!" Mother said, shaking her head in hopeless exasperation. "You could have been killed!"

My father went back to the airfield the next morning to see when there would be a plane going to Guilin. He came back to tell us that the ditch where we had sought shelter was actually parallel and quite close to the runway. While bombs had landed all around in the neighboring paddies, little damage had been done to the runway itself. Only a few planes had been hit, and by afternoon the bomb craters on the strip itself would be filled in. There was a plane leaving for Guilin the next day, and we were to take it, for the sooner we got out the better. Once they started, the Japanese were likely to try again.

Our night at the movies in Zhijiang became a family legend. Whenever Mother finished the story, Daddy joined in the laughter at the picture of him sitting in the jeep, "like a dodo," he'd say, "admiring the show." He'd shake his head wonderingly between chuckles and add, "We sure were lucky! That airfield was put out of commission for days after we left."

Perhaps it was the laughter, perhaps it was because we had not been on our home ground, perhaps it was the fact that the Japanese hadn't done much damage, but for whatever reason, the bombing at Zhijiang, terrifying as it was, never took on the mythic significance for me that the bombing had in Yuanling. It never reached into that secret place where I harbored long-lived fears like a low-grade fever. Unlike the bombing in Yuanling, the bombing at Zhijiang turned out to be just an adventure.

THE LAST LINK

We flew from Zhijiang to Guilin in a C-46, the workhorse of the Army Air Forces. Bundled in sweaters and coats, we sat on metal bucket seats strung along the metal sides of the airplane, too hot to touch, and chewed gum vigorously in the sweltering heat as the plane rumbled down the airstrip, past the coolies who had just filled the last bomb craters with dirt. At the end of the runway we lumbered up a few feet above the rice paddies and then we were soaring over the countryside, the engines taking on the familiar drone I'd last heard from the Japanese bombers over Yuanling. This time the throbbing song was friendly, steady, and reassuring, filling the immense tube of the plane with sound so full and all-enveloping I could almost touch it. It was too loud to talk. I turned around and knelt on the seat to look out the window, which was a piece of scratched Plexiglas. In the center of the Plexiglas was a hole filled with a black rubber stopper on a chain. The hole was just large enough for my fist, so I pulled the stopper from the window, letting in a roaring torrent of cold air. No one noticed. Quickly I thrust my hand through the hole and spread my fingers. They waved loosely like noodles in the wind. When my fingers got numb, I pulled in my hand and replaced the stopper. Heedless of the noise and cold, I pressed my nose to the Plexiglas, watching the sunlit countryside turn slowly beneath us and pillows of clouds pass leisurely by just above the window.

All too soon the plane started to bank, and my father gestured for me to sit down. I held on to the edge of the metal seat as the air grew bumpy, my bottom alternately light then heavy with my stomach going the opposite way. Mother handed me another stick of gum. The plane leveled off, and I twisted around to look out the window again, down onto the fantastic mountains of Guilin—gnarled fingers of stone reaching up from a flat quilt of rice paddies so green that the color vibrated. A wisp of cloud floated between two unbelievably vertical mountains, just like the improbable landscape of a Song Dynasty painting, and the plane tipped sideways again, leaving the mountains for an airstrip. We landed heavily and taxied up to a Quonset hut, shimmering in the sunshine. With my ears stopped up, everything was eerily quiet when we walked down the steps into a sweltering heat bath.

We spent the night at a hostel among pine trees, and the next day we took off again in another C-46 for Kunming in Yunnan Province, the southernmost province of China. From there we would fly over the southern Himalayas to India—a flight course of legendary fame called "the Hump." Ten thousand tons of supplies for the Chinese and American forces were flown into Kunming each month over these soaring mountains near the roof of the world. Hundreds of American fliers, navigating mostly by sight and the seat of their pants, were shot down or flew off course, ending their lives abruptly or slowly among the mountains and hostile hill tribes of the Hump. But hundreds of fliers took their place and the lifeline stayed open. By now there was no other route in or out of free China. The Burma Road, a wonder of engineering threading its unlikely way through the mountains, had been taken by the Japanese two years before. Now the Ledo Road was being cut slowly through the mountains of Burma, from India toward China, by Americans with bulldozers and hill men with shovels and baskets working under the constant threat of Japanese fighters and bombers. But the Ledo Road was a long way from completion, and the aerial bridge over the Hump remained the sole connection to the free world. To save China from disintegration it had to be kept open at all costs. In Kunming we saw rows of General Chennault's famous Flying Tigers lined up along the edge of the runway with sharks' teeth painted savagely white on the sides of each fuselage. Their job was to escort the incoming C-46's from the farthest point their fuel would allow and fight off the Japanese Zeros that attacked out of the sun like swarms of monstrous mosquitoes.

The tide of the war had turned in the Pacific as American forces island-hopped their way toward Japan. The Japanese reacted by moving to attack American airfields throughout southern China. But even as they approached—they took Guilin a few weeks after we left—there seemed to be a kind of exuberance, almost ebullience, energizing the Americans, so different from their dispirited counterparts in Chiang Kai-shek's army, sick and underfed. Mine became a Norman Rockwell war peopled with American "boys" in khaki, their smooth faces friendly and innocent of profound thought, army caps pushed back on their heads, chewing gum while they casually went about their business with effortless expertise. Their manner said they could afford to be casual because they knew we would win in the end.

We stayed several days in Kunming, waiting for a plane to carry us over the Hump to Calcutta. Some Yali graduates came to see us and took us out for delicious meals in the city. One of them who came to see us off at the air base had remembered how Mother loved flowers, and at the bottom of the steps to the plane he presented her with a great sheaf of long-stemmed blossoms. They already looked slightly limp in the early morning heat. I felt limp, too, with an undershirt under my dress, two sweaters, wool stockings, and my winter coat. We were wearing as many clothes as we could, partly in anticipation of the drop in temperature at high altitudes and partly to keep our baggage within the weight limit of forty pounds each. Our aircraft was fitted with regular seats on each side of the central aisle, and the window at each row of seats was disappointingly devoid of hole and stopper. My father put our bags in the rope rack above our heads and placed the flowers on top of them. I sat down by the window with Mother next to me; my father sat across the aisle. After takeoff, the engines settled into the familiar drone as we spiraled up over the airfield and headed toward the mountains. I rested my forehead on the cool window and watched China spread out and recede beneath us.

Soon it got cold and my clothes grew clammy with congealed sweat. I started to reread *Little Women*—one exception to my usual rule of forgetting a book so that I could read it again as though new. *Little Women* was my favorite book, and I knew most of it by heart. But still I read it slowly, as though savoring a favorite food, reliving each well-worn scene as comfortable and comforting as cocoa and buttered toast. Now and then I looked out the window at the terrain below, not realizing that it should be terrifying, that at any moment we could be attacked by Japanese Zeros, that in an unavoidable cloud bank we could run into the side of an unknown mountain. We flew past gigantic perpendicular ridges running thousands of feet down the mountain sides and sailed besides steep valleys cut deep into the mountain, their walls furred with forests where the tribesmen of the Himalayas lived in an era thousands of years before the one in our aircraft. We flew over the Ledo Road, thrown in tiny loops up the flanks of the mountains, and soared over the plains of the Brahmaputra in Assam, the northeast province of India near Tibet, Burma, and Nepal. There we landed to refuel.

We stepped from the frigid air of the plane into a furnace silently booming with gigantic waves of moisture-laden heat. Our skin was instantly slick with sweat, the air too humid for evaporation. The shadowless plain was glaring white under the sun, so bright that I had to squint my eyes almost shut. The whole scene was indistinct, blurred by heat waves that shimmered off a vast and treeless expanse of ground. Through the wavering air, we could vaguely see the outlines of a structure in the distance where, we were told, we could get something to drink. My tongue felt thick and sticky in my mouth. The thought of something cold and wet sliding down my throat was irresistibly alluring; otherwise nothing could have induced me to leave the shade of the airplane's wing. Under the weight of that immense heat we made our way like wounded insects across an endless plain until we arrived at the structure, which turned out to be a roof of corrugated iron resting on poles. There in a hot black square of shade was a table with tin cups and thermos bottles of scalding coffee. That was all. No sugar or cream, and nothing to sit on. It was there that I had my very first cup of coffee. It would be many years before I had another.

Back in the airplane it was hotter than outside. Mother's flowers drooped over the rack as though they'd been boiled. Fortunately, the plane took off as soon as everyone was seated, and within a very short time I was shivering and pulled on all the layers of clothing I thought I'd never want to touch again.

The plane landed at Calcutta in the late afternoon, and we stepped out into another giant sauna. Moisture instantly sprang out on our faces, and our clothes soon turned soggy under our winter coats. Night had fallen by the time we got through customs. We were getting into a taxi when a man in a turban came running toward us with something draped over his arm. At closer proximity, we saw it was Mother's moribund bouquet. "Madam!" he called. "Madam!" He spoke in the lilting Indian English that is perfectly clear, but which makes one think that words are piling up just behind the lips. "You left these beautiful flowers!" he said, and presented them to Mother with a wave of his hand reminiscent of a salaam. She thanked him faintly, my father gave him a tip, and we squeezed into the taxi for the long ride to the Calcutta Girls' School, where we were to stay. Time slowed to a standstill while the car progressed erratically through the night streets of Calcutta and the scents and sounds of India fluttered in through the open windows like tatters of a dream.

At last we arrived at the school guest house, where we were to stay. An Indian man in white shirt and trousers ran out to help carry our suitcases up the steps to the front hall, where we were greeted by the hostess, an Englishwoman of ample proportions and firm manner. She was telling us about our accommodations when the taxi driver appeared at the door. "Memsahib, these were left on the seat!" he said reproachfully to Mother, and handed her a bundle of limp vegetation. It hung lifelessly from her hands, looking faintly translucent at the ends as though about to enter the more advanced stages of decay. Our hostess looked at it with some surprise. Mother said, "These were beautiful this morning. Now look at them! They've followed me all the way from China!" She laughed apologetically. "Do you think we could get rid of them here?"

"Certainly," our hostess replied, and gestured to the Indian man to take the rotting flowers away. Our last link to China was gone.

Becoming American

"One nation, indivisible, with liberty and justice for all." My voice merged rhythmically with the rest of the class, ending on a note of satisfying solidarity. Miss Stone said, "You may sit down." Amid the rustles and bangs of some thirty other sixth-graders, I removed my right hand from my left chest and slid into the seat behind my desk. I'd been in this class several weeks now—five months after that sweltering night we arrived in Calcutta. We had spent two months in India and six weeks on an American troop ship from Bombay to California. Now, on this gray December day in New Haven, I was too occupied with being an American sixth-grader to think of that trip. I was waiting with the rest of the class for the next item on the morning's agenda.

It was Jimmie Quinn's turn to give us the quiz question of the week from the latest issue in the 1944 series of the *Weekly Reader,* an educational newspaper designed to attract the attention of preadolescents. We looked forward to these questions because no one could possibly be expected to know the answers—a condition that appealed to our sixth-grade intellects.

Jimmie walked to the head of the class and, grasping the *Weekly Reader* with both hands, read the question.

"Where does it rain blood?"

Silence. There was the customary pause while the class waited for Jimmie to turn to the back of the *Weekly Reader* for the answer. I gazed at the blackboard and thought of red raindrops. For an instant the blackboard split open and I glimpsed a place so different from this New Haven classroom that it was like a streak of color in a black-and-white movie.

"Yes, Betty Jean?" said Miss Stone.

Startled, I found my hand was up. "Peking," I said.

Jimmie, who had already referred once to the back of the *Weekly Reader,* looked again. "Right," he said.

The class stared at me.

"It rains *blood?*" someone asked.

I explained that in Peking, the rain looked like blood if it was raining when red dust blew in from the Gobi Desert.

"So it doesn't really rain blood," remarked Aaron Teitelman from the back of the room.

"That's what she *said*," countered Vince Falade. They always took opposite sides.

"All right," said Miss Stone. "Please raise your hand if you have something to say. Now, who can tell us where Peking is?"

All hands remained down.

"Betty Jean?"

"It's in China," I answered reluctantly. I was beginning to feel uneasy. I had broken a precedent and revealed knowledge that a regular sixth-grader wouldn't have. To explain this aberration, I hastened to add, "My father told me about it." That was true. I had never been to Peking.

I hoped Miss Stone wouldn't ask me more questions, and she didn't. She told us to get out our geography books and look up China and Peking and the Gobi Desert on the map. She talked about how we were helping the Chinese fight the Japanese, and we looked at Japan on the map. Eventually we went on to something else, and I relaxed. The word *China* had stayed just that—the name of a distant place in our geography books.

Miss Stone knew I'd lived in China, but she also must have known I didn't want to talk about it. If someone asked me where I was from, I said, "California," because it made me less of an outsider than coming from China. To my classmates, having lived in California was sufficient to account for occasional lapses of speech and behavior.

Now that I was here in New Haven, it was California, not Hunan, that felt like home. When we'd arrived in San Mateo, south of San Francisco, a few weeks back, the dim images of our relatives I last saw five years ago sprang to life again. The adults looked just the same. But my closest cousin, Phyllis, had magically changed into that most mysterious and desirable thing to be—a freshman in high school. My other cousins, too, looked different, but they were all my very own cousins and that would never change. And so, like sinking down on a soft sofa, I settled into the web of familyness that held us together and in which each of us had a place.

When I had walked into Aunt Dorothy and Uncle Ed's house in San Mateo, the furniture in the rooms was just as I remembered from when we'd lived there on our last furlough. But the glassed-in front porch seemed empty. That was where Phyllis' brother, Bob, kept his miniature squadron of airplanes hanging from the ceiling. Now they were gone, and Bob was in the Army Air Forces, learning to be a rear gunner in one of those new Superfortress bombers—the B-29's. I remembered his model aircraft better than I remembered him. Nevertheless, he, too, was an anchor point in our network of relatedness.

My first days "back home in the States" had been punctuated with small thrills of sudden familiarity: the steaming thunder of running bathwater, the satisfying scent of car upholstery, the ringing crash of an opening cash register, the urgent clanging of a bell as a yellow-and-black bar descended at a railroad crossing—the list went on and on. But more lasting than these happy starts of recognition was the sure knowledge that when we went out no one would stare at me, or laugh, or call out "Hey, big nose!" or "Foreign devil kid!" Here I could get lost in the crowd. At last I was like everyone else.

After a week or so on the West Coast, we took a train across the country to New Haven and moved into a furnished apartment over a variety store that sold everything from candy and hair nets to notebooks and pins. Our third-floor walk-up was dark, small and noisy. My parents slept in the living room on a fold-out sofa, and trolleys stopped outside every twenty minutes until after dark. In the evenings, the people who lived below us played jazz on the radio so loudly that the floor vibrated and we had to bang on the radiator to get them to turn it down.

> In Yuanling at the end of the day, after the murmur from the
> town died down and the lights winked out, I could occasionally
> hear from my bed on the porch the diminishing thuds of an oar
> in its oarlock as a boatman sculled his craft across the dark
> current until the only sounds left were the sleepy comments of a
> cricket slowly stitching up the night.

In New Haven, I didn't think of how we'd lived in Yuanling. The difference was too great to make any connection.

As the newness of things in New Haven wore off, I began to suspect that I wasn't like everyone else after all. I first noticed it with food. Take those two most American of delicacies that people were always offering as treats—ice cream and Coca-Cola. I never did learn to like ice cream. It was too cold and not worth the discomfort—unless the flavor was chocolate.

As for Coca-Cola, it felt like a mouthful of prickles and tasted like the fumes at a gas pump.

We were invited to Thanksgiving dinner at a Cape Cod cottage belonging to the Smith sisters, two maiden ladies, old friends of Mother's. The house was all that such a dwelling should be—white woodwork, dimity curtains, braided rag rugs of indeterminate colors, a crackling fire in the fireplace, and the irresistible aroma of roast turkey. At a dining room table laden with food and crystal water glasses, I discovered that this quintessential American meal was actually a trial of bland poultry flesh sawed off a large and naked bird, soggy bread spooned from its eviscerated carcass, and, a long time later, orange-colored paste cut with geometric precision from the inevitable pumpkin pie.

> *In Yuanling at lunchtime, Xi-xi, Yuan-mei, and I took our rice bowls and chopsticks and strolled down the paths of the school compound, shoveling down mouthfuls of hot fragrant rice and, with the tips of our chopsticks, picking up morsels of cai nicely spiced to a potential state of numbness with Hunan's fiery red peppers.*

In New Haven, I avoided remembering how we ate in Yuanling.

The American language also took some getting used to. When we first arrived, I read the traffic signs and advertisements carefully in order to absorb their meaning. And once I understood their significance, I wondered at their tone: "STOP" at intersections seemed abrupt and rude; "Smoke Lucky Strikes!" seemed bossy rather than inviting; "Send your blood to the front" was surreal. I learned the hard way when not to take people literally. If they asked you to wait "a couple of minutes," they usually meant much longer—yet they themselves didn't like to be kept waiting more than the promised amount of time. And, no matter how you felt, when they asked "How are you?" the correct answer was "Fine."

> *In Yuanling we never asked "How are you?" When we came across friends or acquaintances, we commented courteously on what the other ones were doing so that they could answer truthfully with an agreeable "Yes." "Oh, you're shopping!" we'd say to someone met in the market, or "You've finished school!" to a friend carrying her schoolbooks down the path toward home, or "You're walking down the street!" to an*

acquaintance passed on the street. But the most civilized
greeting of all was "Have you eaten?" to which one could
answer either in a positive mode, with "Yes," or in an
anticipatory mode, "Not yet." Thus, even a brief encounter in
Yuanling was a moment of mutual validation.

The greetings we exchanged in Yuanling would be unthought of in New Haven, so I didn't think of them.

But what was most surprising about Americans was not their food or their conventions of speech, but the things that bothered them. It was hard to predict what they might not like. They did not mind tasteless food, but if there was a delay serving it, they were unhappy. They usually had more than one of something, like a watch or a radio, but they got impatient if one couldn't be fixed right away. They made a fuss about things that I'd always taken for granted, like bad smells, cold rooms, tepid hot water, no ice cubes. I began to think that some of the things Americans thought critical really weren't so important. But I wasn't sure of this. My own standards had suddenly became unreliable.

So I entered sixth grade in New Haven on the edge of bewilderment, antennae out to catch every hint of what was happening, every nuance of speech, every change of expression, while trying to act as though I was comfortable and knew what was going on. It was most important not to be "different." There was no way my classmates could relate to memories of the years past, which I could recall more easily than last night's dreams—if I wanted.

Timeless days on the back of a river
in a junk with a sail like a moth's wing . . .

Dead men in open coffins
spied through a mist of plum blossoms . . .

Fox fairy stories heard in the dusk
punctuated by fireflies . . .

A madwoman running after me
up an endless staircase . . .

Shadows flickering over a ditch and
the world exploding in light and sound . . .

or, from our recent trip across India—

> *The Taj Mahal*
> *floating in the sky*
> *like music . . .*

But I didn't want to bring back those memories. The events they recalled were so irrelevant to sixth grade in New Haven that it was as though they were not mine to remember. If I thought of them, they might make it harder to fit in.

I already had several strikes against me. In addition to coming from out of town, I had entered the class two months after school started. I was one of two Protestants in the class besides Miss Stone; most of the class was Catholic. And I was the only sixth-grader who stayed at school for lunch. My father was at the Yale-in-China office all day and Mother had a job as substitute teacher in the public school system, so I drank my milk and ate my sandwich and apple and hard-boiled egg at a table with Miss Stone at the back of the classroom. Then I practiced the piano in the auditorium until the others came back from lunch at home.

With these differences to overcome, I tried not to show that the schoolwork was easy for me, thanks to the Calvert home study system. I rarely raised my hand, and when we took tests, I was careful not to put my pencil down until someone else had finished.

My best friend was Lucy Felicello, whose desk was next to mine. We always walked to school and went home together, usually stopping at the variety store downstairs to replenish our supply of spicy Red Hots before coming up to my apartment to do homework. In the coldest weeks of winter, I walked with Lucy to her house, where we could ice-skate in her tiny backyard covered with a sheet of ice after her brothers had flooded it with the hose.

I went to Mass once or twice with Lucy at the big Catholic church a few trolley stops up the street, she with a lace doily bobby-pinned to the top of her head and I with a kerchief knotted under my chin. While she genuflected and crossed herself with easy grace, I sat ramrod straight in the seat, wanting to copy her yet knowing that it would be make-believe for me, and besides, I wouldn't do it right. I admired Lucy; she was all I wanted to be—large dark eyes, ivory skin, wavy black hair, pristine notebooks filled with beautiful handwriting that she had learned from the nuns at parochial school before transferring into the public school system. By the end of the school year, my handwriting was almost the same as hers—the closest I could get to be like her, with my blue eyes, blond braids, and plain Protestant ways.

After we'd been in New Haven a couple of months, Mother met with Miss Stone to find out how I was adjusting to my new school experience. At the supper table Mother told us that Miss Stone said I was "a real addition" to the class; I got along well with my classmates and my schoolwork was excellent.

"I'm so proud of you, dear," Mother said.

My father said, "Good work, BJ!"

I didn't think of what I'd done as work—sixth grade in New Haven was easier than fourth grade had been with the Calvert system the previous year in Yuanling. Under the glow of my parents' praise, I suspected I hadn't earned it. It made me feel blurred, indistinct. I often felt that way here in New Haven, as though when people talked to me they were really seeing someone else.

"There's just one thing," Mother continued. "Miss Stone says you have a tendency to jump to conclusions."

I snapped into focus. Maybe I'd been doing something wrong. "What does that mean?" I asked. It couldn't be too bad, or Mother wouldn't bring it up so casually.

Mother looked at my father. "You explain it, Dwight. I'm not good with words."

If Mother couldn't explain it, it must be bad.

"Well . . ." My father paused to think. "Jumping to conclusions means doing something before you know enough about it."

"Like what?"

He thought again and I sat very still. "Like diving into water before you know where the bottom is."

This took a moment to absorb. Was that all it was? Suddenly the picture his explanation evoked struck me as excruciatingly funny, with all the slapstick humor of a Tom and Jerry cartoon. He started laughing, too, and soon we had pushed back our chairs and were doubled over, hooting, howling, and sobbing with mirth. When we slowed down, Mother said, straight-faced, "Honestly, you two!" which set us off again.

I never did learn what I did to make Miss Stone say I jumped to conclusions. Perhaps that was the easiest way I could decide how to behave when I didn't have enough information to read a new situation accurately. But as I became familiar with the meaning behind people's words and behavior, I found them less surprising. After a while I was saying things without wondering beforehand if a regular sixth-grader would say them. I could even disagree with someone if I did it so they wouldn't lose face. And I was putting down my pencil as soon as I finished a quiz. I didn't notice when I started to do all this. It just happened.

The longer we stayed in New Haven, the further my life in China sank toward the bottom of my awareness—except for piano lessons. Piano lessons were such an ordinary part of American life that I could safely recall the lessons I took in Yuanling, when I trudged with my music books down the city street to the Presbyterian mission at the other end of town. My teacher had been Miss Bayless, who taught music at the Presbyterian Girls' School and played the piano in violin and cello trios with my mother and father. Auntie Bay was tall and lean and elegant, gracefully erect in drab missionary dresses, wire-rimmed glasses perched firmly on her nose, her hair in a loose bun at the back of her head. She didn't say much, but her eyes crinkled at the corners when she smiled and she had a contagious chuckle. When she played the piano, she sat very straight but looked relaxed, moving only slightly as runs and arpeggios, chords and melodies and grace notes dropped effortlessly off her fingers into the keyboard.

In New Haven I carried my music books on two trolleys to lessons with Mrs. Loefski. Mrs. Loefski looked very pregnant when I started with her, and had expanded to unbelievable proportions when I finished seven months later. The hems of her dresses swooped up several inches in front and a stray strand of hair hung down from the bun on the top of her head. In those days before deodorants, she exuded a strong body odor.

For her students' recital in June, Mrs. Loefski decided I should play Debussy's *Clair de lune*. Since I'd been raised on the four-square solidity of hymns and the classical precision of Bach, Mozart, and Beethoven, I didn't immediately catch on to the dreamy suggestions of musical Impressionism.

One Saturday morning as I was marching through Debussy's hazy harmonies, Mrs. Loefski abruptly took over the keyboard. "It's like *this*," she said. I leaned out of the way as far as I could. "Here's the moonlight," she intoned over the keyboard, sinking her fingers into the keys and waving her elbows. "And here"—her voice grew louder as her left hand stretched down in front of me to begin the arpeggios and her right hand reached up to counter with the melody—"are a man and a woman making love in the moonlight. . . . She murmurs softly, 'I love you' . . . and he answers her." Mrs. Loefski began to sway as the music encompassed the whole keyboard with accelerating passion. "'I love you!'" she fluted breathlessly. "'I *love* you!'" As if caught by a gust of wind, she swept her hands off the keyboard, bent sideways like a bulbous ballerina, and flung her arm out in a curve, wafting waves of body odor.

I was a little stunned by this onslaught of musical emotion and Mrs. Loefski's emanations. When I recovered, I thought of Auntie Bay and how *Clair de lune* would emerge coolly from under her fingers. The next time I practiced in the school auditorium, I tried to play it as I thought she would. In the end, I played the soft parts of the piece sitting still and cool like Auntie Bay, with the notes dropping off my fingers (I hoped), and the loud parts like Mrs. Loefski, alternately leaning over the keyboard and rocking on my hip bones like an impassioned metronome. It says much for Debussy's genius that in spite of this eclectic approach, *Clair de lune* possessed enough inherent coherence for me to get a satisfactory round of applause at the end of the recital. In that applause, Yuanling and New Haven momentarily came together, and briefly I felt distinct, as though the clapping really was for me, not someone else.

In New Haven I learned more about the war than I had ever known in Yuanling, where the news was mostly rumors and our focus had been very local. In New Haven we sat in the living room after supper and listened to the news on the radio, my father following the fighting on a National Geographic map of the world. By 1944 the war in the Pacific had definitely turned in favor of the Allies, but there still was a long way to go. American forces continued their grueling leapfrog progression up the islands of the Pacific toward Japan, encountering suicidal opposition from the Japanese at every stop. Over the years, the names of those encounters had dropped one by one through the evening news like a string of bloody pearls—New Guinea, Guadalcanal, Tarawa, Kwajalein, Eniwetok, Saipan.

I remembered a newsreel we saw in Bombay showing a Japanese soldier on fire, charred black like charcoal, running out of the cave from which he'd been flushed by flamethrowers. After a couple of seconds he stumbled and fell, still burning, to the ground. Perhaps that had happened on Saipan. The island fell to American hands in July at the cost of sixteen thousand Americans wounded and thirty-eight hundred dead; twenty-three thousand Japanese died, including hundreds of civilians who had thrown their children over the cliffs to the sea and jumped after them rather than surrender.

It turned out that Saipan was important because it was near enough to Japan for the new superbombers, the B-29's, to reach Tokyo and return nonstop. By the end of November 1944 the airfield for the B-29's was completed and the giant bombers were taking off for Tokyo. Bob was there with a B-29 that he and his crewmates christened the *Wugged Wascal*.

My father and I looked up Saipan on the map—a barely discernible speck among others scattered in a thumbnail curve on a vast expanse of robin's-egg blue. I gazed down at the speck labeled "Saipan" and thought, *Bob's right there.* Tokyo was four inches away.

One day in January of 1945, the *Wugged Wascal* was on a bombing raid over Tokyo when an engine was hit and caught on fire. On the way back to Saipan the plane flew for five hours with the engine burning until finally it dropped off and the aircraft gradually lost altitude. The radio man kept in contact with headquarters as long as he could. Just before they hit the water, he told the base they were going down and tied the radio key in position to continue transmitting their location. The navy started a massive search of the area, but a storm blew up, so they had to stop until the weather improved. The next day the searchers came across an oil slick, an inflated life raft, and some life preservers. But Bob and his crewmates were never found.

The night we got the news, I tried to think about Bob and what it must have been like. But I couldn't remember him. I only saw, over my bed, a dim squadron of miniature aircraft all heading in the same direction as though for a common destination. But Bob would never reach that destination, and now our family's web was ripped, his place in it tattered, loose, and empty.

Before the war there had been several Japanese-American families in the Congregational church where Aunt Dorothy and Uncle Ed were members. In 1942 President Roosevelt had approved an order to send all the Japanese-Americans in California to internment camps. The church members were sent to Tanforan Racetrack, not far from San Mateo. Aunt Dorothy and Uncle Ed were able to visit them every Saturday to bring them supplies. Several of the families had sons who, as GIs, fought up the spine of Italy in the most decorated battalion of the war, and when they came home on leave some stayed with Aunt Dorothy and Uncle Ed at their house in San Mateo.

A few weeks after the news about Bob's death was published in the local paper with his picture, Aunt Dorothy and Uncle Ed's neighbors of seventeen years presented them with a signed petition demanding that they leave San Mateo because, it said, they had "harbored Japs." A day or so later, people carrying torches gathered outside their house at night, shouting and threatening to burn down their house. Uncle Ed called the police, who dispersed the mob before they could do any damage.

Over the following weeks, Aunt Dorothy and Uncle Ed visited each of the households that had signed the petition. I don't know what they said on those visits, but eventually all except one family apologized.

In China I had learned a proverb that says, "Within the four seas, all men are brothers." Now I learned something new—new, at least, to me: within the four seas, men are also bigots. Bigotry was not confined to one side of the world, as I had thought. Now I knew that those familiar words yelled in the busy streets of Changsha and the narrow streets of towns along the East River could be heard here in the quiet suburban streets of America as well: "Foreign devils!"

In the summer of 1945, as the Allies moved ever more surely toward victory, we left New Haven for California, where Mother and I would live for another year at Aunt Dorothy and Uncle Ed's new home in Burlingame. My father would return to Hunan, where we expected to rejoin him after the war.

Rather than take the train to the West Coast, my parents decided to drive across the country so that, as Mother said, "Betty Jean can get to see this wonderful country of ours." And I did. From New Haven we set out in a 1941 blue Ford sedan for Niagara Falls, and from there we drove two hundred miles through Canada, where we bought our tourist quota of twenty gallons of ration-free gas. We drove through the varicolored spires of South Dakota's Badlands and marveled at the colossal faces on Mount Rushmore. With a hot wind thundering through the open windows of the car, we sang our way across the prairies, all the way from the Revolution to the Second World War—"Yankee Doodle" to "God Bless America," and every other song we knew in between. At the end of the Great Plains, we drove up the untamed mountains of the West, and when it wasn't too steep, we coasted downhill in neutral to save gas. At Yellowstone, we glimpsed fleeting rainbows in Old Faithful, and we fished from a rowboat on the river, where Mother accidentally reeled in one more trout than our quota and had to throw it back. In the Tetons we stopped for a thunderstorm at the top of the pass, and that night at the bottom of the mountain we inched our way for two hours through a drive of at least two thousand sheep. In the Sierras we gazed down in silent wonder at the gigantic vista of Yosemite, and finally we cheered when we came over the coastal hills of California and saw at last the gracious expanse of San Francisco Bay.

In the time it took us to journey two hundred miles up China's East River, we had traveled four thousand miles, by my father's reckoning, through North America. Over those miles we drove under the spacious skies of the song, through its waves of grain and over its mountains, into an

American universe where one always moved ahead, freed from the past into space and time and endless potential. It must have been then that I sensed the promise of this land and first felt a deep affinity for not just California but America: for its beauty, its abundance, its thrumming assurance of endless possibility, and most of all for its dream of hospitality, its dream despite Aunt Dorothy and Uncle Ed's neighbors—or its dream, perhaps, because of them.

Yet when my father left for Changsha, I wanted to go with him. I wanted to wake up again to the acrid whiff of toast smoke drifting into my room from the kitchen. I wanted to walk barefoot over cool black lacquered floors and feel the woolly contrast of Peking rugs under my feet. I wanted to go out on the porch and take in the scents of Changsha in the morning and at lunchtime feel the tingle of hot chilies on my tongue. I wanted to hear the hearty accents of Hunan and walk down Changsha's busy streets, both vibrant and mundane. I wanted to smile back into the familiar faces of friends. I wanted to hear again my father whistle the oriole's song at the end of the day, telling us he was on his way home and we three would be together again and everything would be all right.

One evening before my father left for China we were invited out to dinner at the home of an eminent China scholar. Toward the end of the meal, the conversation turned to the Chinese language and its variations. Knowing I'd grown up speaking the local language of Hunan, our host asked me to say something in that dialect. Only twelve months before, I had said goodbye to Xi-xi and Yuan-mei, speaking in Hunanese so natural that it was indistinguishable from theirs. Now I sat silent while the others waited.

What should I say? *"Have you eaten?"* I could remember saying it, but how did the words go?

"This food is very good"? Actually, it wasn't.

"Goodbye"? I remembered the last time I said that, across the immense distance of the few feet separating me from Xi-xi and Yuan-mei, just before I followed my parents onto the bus that took us away. I remembered the meaning conveyed by the Chinese words for "goodbye": *may we meet again.* But I had left those words in Yuanling. I couldn't say them here.

Finally, a sound drifted up to where I could reach it—one word doubled to convey its heartfelt import. I said it tentatively at first: *"Xie-xie."* Then once more:

"Thank you."

FALLING INTO PLACE

In two years I was back in Changsha. After a year of seventh grade in California, I had completed eighth grade with the Calvert home study system at home on the Yali campus. Now I was about to leave Changsha again to enter high school in Shanghai.

The night before I was to leave for Shanghai, I was homesick. I hadn't expected it. After all, I was fourteen, and until I'd gone to bed that night, I could hardly wait to leave. I had been looking forward eagerly to ninth grade at the Shanghai American School ever since Mother had enrolled me the previous year on our way from the States to Changsha. Here in Changsha, I had been very busy. Besides studying, I'd made some attempts at learning Chinese calligraphy, practiced the piano, played trios with my parents, and sang in the Fu Xiang Girls' School Chorus at the Presbyterian mission. I had ridden my bicycle around the city and, when the Keplers came to live at the Presbyterian mission, I'd gone biking with Tommy and Mercer, also in their teens, and accompanied them on hikes and picnics. I'd spent a memorable summer with the Keplers, and Mary Newman from a nearby city, and Teddy Heinrichsohn, whose father had given me Molly seven years ago. With an assortment of younger siblings and long-suffering parents, we had shared a large summer house on Nan You San, a sacred mountain about ninety miles from Changsha. Now, at the end of the summer, the five of us would travel together to the Shanghai American School, or SAS, with my mother as chaperone.

Home from Nan You San, I had packed my trunk, which now stood at the foot of my bed. Among its contents were Little Bear, my toy koala, who had accompanied me wherever I'd gone since I was seven, and an ankle-length dress with a full skirt for dances, copied by a Changsha tailor from a picture in a magazine. Armed with these talismans, one from my past and one for my future, I felt ready for anything that SAS had to offer. The prospect was totally enthralling.

But now, on this hot August night, it dawned on me that I was leaving home for good. Never again would I live with my parents—I would only visit them from somewhere else. I lay on the bamboo mat atop my bed, pajamas soaked with sweat, face wet with tears. This was the end of my life as I knew it. This was goodbye. Forever.

I turned over and looked out the window at the silent bulk of the camphor tree against the lighter darkness of the night. I shut my eyes and found myself in a strange and empty world where nothing was familiar, nothing known. It was a place not empty of people but, somehow, empty of *me*. No one recognized me, not even my friends. My mother and father were only distant memories. In a panic, I realized I couldn't recall their faces. I knew what they looked like theoretically—Daddy had dark hair and brown eyes, and Mother had light brown hair and blue eyes—but I couldn't *see* them. I got out of bed and headed for the door.

There was the sound of typing from the living room. On bare feet, I padded through the dining room and saw my father working at a card table in a cone of light from a floor lamp at his shoulder. With his familiar shape and face, the known world returned and the tears started up again. When I reached his table, I couldn't speak. He looked up, his hands stopped in midair above the typewriter keys. "What's the matter?" he asked, his face a mask of concern. I started to sob. He dug in his pocket for a handkerchief and handed it to me. "What is it?" he asked again. The warmth of his tone made me cry all the harder. Finally I managed to tell him I didn't want to leave.

"Oh," he said, somehow conveying in that one quiet word a sense of sudden and sympathetic understanding. "Then don't go. You don't have to. You can stay home."

I hadn't thought of that.

My tears dried up as I considered this new idea. I couldn't go to Chinese school; although my spoken Chinese had returned, I could not read or write enough for first grade, much less high school. And I couldn't study at home—we didn't have the Calvert system for high school.

"What about school?" I said.

"We'll work something out," my father replied, as though it was the easiest thing in the world.

I thought of the next day, waving goodbye to the others as they went off to SAS without me. I'd be staying in Changsha—by myself, as usual. Suddenly there was nothing I wanted more than to be on that train with the others.

"That's all right," I said. "I'll go."

"All right." Again my father spoke as though it was the most natural thing in the world. "You'd better try to get some sleep. It'll be a long day tomorrow."

A great load dropped away. I felt like jumping up and down with relief. I was going to SAS! I danced around the table to his chair and gave him a big kiss on the cheek. "Good night!"

"Good night," he said. "Remember, you can always come home if you want."

From then on, I didn't look back.

The Shanghai American School was an enclave of idealized American education, housed on a campus reminiscent of an eastern prep school. The colonial-type buildings of red brick and white trim were connected by colonnades around a large quadrangle of well-tended lawns, trees, and bushes—all behind a fence on Avenue Pétain in the French Concession of Shanghai. The students were mostly the offspring of American missionaries, businessmen, and diplomats, but there was a sprinkling of pupils of other nationalities as well, including Chinese whose parents could afford to send them to SAS. Here, for the first time, I was with others my age who, like me, had lived in more than one language and inhabited more than one world and knew, without speaking of it, what it was like to be home at not-home. Although I was in another new place again, I could describe it with unconscious authority, as though I had been there for a very long time. In one of my first letters home I wrote,

> We elected officers of the class last Friday. Jimmy Thoroughman is president. He really is very nice. He is so shy he hardly ever dances. . . . The secretary-treasurer is Shirley Asseier. She is one-fourth Chinese and the prettiest girl in the class. . . . We all like her. . . . Our class is really very nice; next to the junior class I think ours has the most unity. . . . The kids are really swell. . . . There is no prejudice of any kind . . .

Academics at SAS were rigorous. Four hours of homework a day were not unusual and exams were three hours long. In a roster of outstanding teachers, Mrs. Merritt, my ninth-grade English teacher, was the most memorable. There was a false rumor that she had once been a

Shakespearean actor at the Old Vic in London, but it was hard to imagine what parts she would have played. Aside from her voice, which carried her British accent effortlessly as far as she wished, there was nothing Shakespearean about her. She was short, with a barrel-shaped body and bowlegs. Her hair was orange and her mouth a slit of scarlet lipstick crowded between her nose and her chin. When she wasn't in class, a cigarette drooped from her lower lip, its wisp of smoke drifting up past her left eye, narrowed to a sinister squint. As a teacher, she was superb and merciless. Every Friday we had to hand in an essay of between three hundred and five hundred words, and every Monday she read one or two of our efforts to the class, sprinkling them liberally with acerbic asides or helpful commentary—one was never sure which was coming next. She introduced us to Dickens and hooked us on Shakespeare, and I got into college on the English I learned in her ninth-grade class. She was an inspiration and a terror.

Another terror in my life was George Wittsack, the hockey coach, who made us run a mile around the track every day and swore at us when we did something wrong. When I started tenth grade, he put me on the A team as center forward, but I wasn't happy. I was convinced I couldn't play as well as the rest. I wrote home that George was mad at me most of the time and that I didn't blame him. I couldn't seem to do anything right. I would scamper down the field dribbling the ball, and he'd shout, "What the hell are you doing?" and I would pass it to Woogie Pickens on the right, who would pass it to Harry Refo coming up on the left, who would hit it to Anne Lockwood on the wing. Anne's expert stickwork, speed, and strength would get the ball back in front of the goal at just the right time to hit it in.

We played league games at the racecourse in downtown Shanghai, and a good number of our schoolmates, both boys and girls, came out to cheer us on, all of which made the contests feel much more important than they would have seemed if we'd played on the school grounds. George whipped us into being the top women's team in the city, so we had few, if any, losses that year. But I endured the ride to each game in a jellylike state of anxiety, which I managed to conceal, and returned from each game a little weak with relief that we'd won and that the next contest was a whole week away.

In one game against a team of large and muscular British women, I stopped a hard-driven ball with my jaw and was knocked momentarily senseless. Since we were playing thirty-minute halves with no time out and no substitutions, I resumed play as soon as I could see straight, but I wasn't much use. Back in the dormitory, I lay on the bed with an ice bag to my chin, barely able to open my mouth, and insisted between clenched teeth that I would not play in the piano recital that evening. Mary Clark, my roommate, kept pestering me to play, and finally in exasperation I donned my recital dress and walked on stage with a grossly swollen jaw reminiscent of Popeye, decorated with shades of color from a black patch on my chin to a faint blue wash in front of my right ear. As I made my opening bow, someone tittered. Consumed with fury, I ripped through *Liebestraum* in record time, bowed briefly, and was stalking off the stage when a fresh wave of applause stopped me. I turned to see someone in front of the stage reaching up to present me with a large sheaf of flowers. My parents had arranged for them through the school, and Mary, in on the secret, hadn't known what should be done with them if I refused to play. Hence her insistence.

Insulated from what was going on in the outside world, our life at SAS was marked by the intense camaraderie of dorm life and dining hall, studying, sports, the school newspaper, dances, and trying to break the rules without getting demerits. The boys were especially gifted at inventing offenses for which rules had yet to be written, many inspired by Teddy Heinrichsohn's creative genius. Their feats were the stuff of legends, such as electrifying a toilet seat and moving a slumbering dorm mate, bed and all, onto the roof of the colonnade, where he reportedly woke up sometime later. The guardian of the boys' dorm was Captain Wilkes, who had been in the U.S. Army during the war—a man of enduring character, firmness, and resilience, highly respected by his charges. Although they must have tested his mettle, Captain Wilkes remained at his post for the whole time I was at SAS.

By the boys' standards, our infractions in the girls' dorm were mild indeed. We short-sheeted beds, held midnight feasts by flashlight, balanced cans of water atop doors carefully left ajar, and lowered messages to boys from the upper floors after lights-out. Nevertheless, by the time I left SAS, we had gone through four dorm mothers in two years.

The most demerits I earned were garnered in my freshman year, when Mary Clark, I think it was, and I were dateless for the first formal dance. To assuage our sorrow and avenge our single state, we armed ourselves with flashlights and, while most of the school was at the dance, climbed the forbidden water tower—a red brick edifice that rose above a grove of trees where couples tended to wander off the lighted colonnade on their way back to the girls' dorm. The faint strains of Bing Crosby singing the evening's signature song wafted up to our station at the top of the tower. "Now is the hour," he crooned, "when we must say goodbye. . ." We readied our flashlights. Soon we spotted the outline of a single couple strolling in the dark below us, and, synchronizing our attack nicely, we simultaneously illuminated Mr. and Mrs. Gibb, the principal and his wife. They, too, had anticipated an influx of couples seeking the sheltering shadows of the trees and were patrolling the area to correct any untoward wandering. I was of the opinion that Mary and I were helping them with their job, but I accepted in silence my allotment of demerits—almost but not quite enough to get me grounded.

The dormitories at SAS became unnaturally quiet and orderly during exam week. Three hours long, each exam required not just cramming, which was easy, but hours of study and review. I believe it was the final exam week of my freshman year that the novel *Gone with the Wind* appeared in the girls' dormitory. In the presence of this siren saga, such pedestrian matters as exams, meals, and lights-out became irrelevant. If the book was within reach, no healthy young woman could possibly do anything but read until she fainted from hunger or finished the book. We passed it around like a hot potato. When I had it in my reluctant possession, I had devoured the first couple of hundred pages before I managed, at the end of a chapter and with great effort of will, to leave it in the communal bathroom. On returning from lunch another day, I saw it on my bed. Without breaking my stride, I picked it up while making a U-turn back into the hall and tossed it through the transom of the nearest room, to the howls of protest from its hapless occupant. Thereafter, we all shut our transoms and locked ourselves in our rooms as time ground inexorably on toward our final days of reckoning. I didn't finish the book until the following year.

By the time I started tenth grade, in the fall of 1948, the Communist Eighth Route Army had taken over most of the west and northern parts of China and was moving east and south. The situation became so tense in Changsha that American women and children were evacuated from the city, and Mother, very reluctant to leave my father behind, came to Shanghai, which at that time was still some distance from the fighting. She and I spent Christmas at SAS that year. But things calmed down, and early in January of

1949 she returned to Changsha. In fact, it looked as though the Communists would be a boon to China's recovery from the depredations of the Japanese and the corruption of the Nationalists. Whenever the Communist Eighth Route Army took over a city, order was quickly restored and the populace, including foreigners, was generally treated well. My parents decided that when China finally did become totally Communist, they would stay in Changsha and I would continue at SAS

As conditions became more chaotic ahead of the Communist advance, students began to leave SAS for the States at the direction of their mission boards or at the behest of their parents. Mary Clark, my roommate, much to my sorrow, was among them, and I moved in with Anne Lockwood, whose parents were with the YMCA in Canton.

That Easter of 1949 Anne and I, along with some others, took the train to Nanking, where we spent the vacation with classmates whose families lived in that city. On our way back to Shanghai, we took a train that was almost empty of passengers, as most people were trying to get out of Shanghai, not go into it. Increasing numbers of Nationalist troops were deserting and changing sides while their leaders scooped up their wealth and fled to Taiwan. Incipient panic, not yet overt, was spreading over southern China like the silent diffusion of an epidemic before the disease breaks out—a loosening of the expected interactions between people and a slacking off of the usual restrictions on behavior that make a civilization work. Chaos was in the air we breathed, but it had not yet settled in. Perhaps that explains why, when we tired of playing cards, we decided to visit the engine—something I would not even have imagined doing in more normal times. But that evening, once we thought of it, it seemed a reasonable thing to do to break the tedium of the trip.

We were in the first car behind the coal car, so I didn't have time to change my mind before I was standing at the rushing gap between cars. The noise was so loud we could barely hear each other shout. The tracks and cross ties whipped past below my feet to the frantic rhythm of the wheels and the wind blew my hair straight up from my head. The coal car swung rapidly back and forth, unsynchronized with the tiny platform on which I was planted. I didn't dare shut my eyes to step over the shifting space between the cars, but somehow I put my foot across without willing it, and threw myself onto the short ladder at the back of the swaying coal car. Following the boy ahead of me, I managed to climb up to the top without my feet coming off the slippery rungs, crawled over the coal on all fours, and jumped down into the cab. The engineer and his helper looked surprised. It was too noisy to talk, but they accepted our presence without visible objection and even allowed us to blow the whistle. At the train station in Shanghai that night, we hopped down from the cab, well pleased with ourselves and covered with coal dust and soot.

With the Communist army moving toward Shanghai, the Nationalists made moves toward its defense. Unrest grew in the city over the following days; inflation burgeoned, order broke down, and rioting broke out as the social fabric of the city started to disintegrate. People were robbed openly on the streets. The very wealthy and those who were just wealthy scrambled to leave. U.S. dollars were the currency of choice, and on the streets in downtown Shanghai, a stolen U.S. passport sold for hundreds of U.S. dollars. But on the broad, tree-shaded boulevards of the French concession, where SAS was located, all was quiet. We felt what was happening elsewhere in the city only as the faintly moving air of shock waves from a series of explosions too distant to hear.

What occupied our attention was the approaching end of term. Final exams were a scant month away, dominating the landscape like the Himalayas in the middle distance. One morning a few days before the end of April, Anne and I were summoned to Mr. Owens' office—he was the principal that year. Although we had recently received recognition for having the messiest room in the dormitory, we could not think of anything we had done to warrant such attention, and seated ourselves with puzzled trepidation.

Mr. Owens told us that the U.S. hospital ship *Repose* was leaving Shanghai the next day, taking some wounded British sailors either to Hong Kong, Japan, or the Philippines, depending on circumstances. A number of SAS students would be leaving on the ship, under direction of their mission boards. Since Anne and I were not under any mission or guardian, he said we could leave or stay. The school would continue to operate with the few remaining students and faculty until the end of the school year.

With Mr. Owens' words, a vista opened before us of sunlit meadows, larks singing in a clear blue sky, and no mountains anywhere in sight. Given the choice between staying and leaving, we thought we should leave. Since Anne's parents were with the YMCA in Canton, Mr. Owens advised us to consult with the executive secretary of the YMCA in Shanghai before making a final decision. With our passports in our hands, we took a rickshaw through the streets of downtown Shanghai to see the secretary, who, to our heartfelt gratitude, also thought we should leave. Not being used to that section of town, we didn't think the activity on the very crowded streets was unusual, though we heard later that there was rioting. Blissfully carefree, we made our way to the U.S. consulate, where we were given typhoid and cholera shots and our papers for departure.

Sometime during that day, I sent a telegram to my parents in Changsha:

LEAVING TOMORROW ON USS REPOSE DESTINATION UNKNOWN WILL LET YOU KNOW WHEN I ARRIVE.

I didn't know at the time that my mother had been in the hospital with pneumonia when she and my father heard the news of the impending battle for Shanghai. They had sent me a telegram telling me to go to Hong Kong, but I didn't receive it. By the time they got my message, Mother was out of the hospital.

Back at SAS, all was hurried as we disposed of the things we couldn't take, said our goodbyes, washed our hair, and packed late into the night. I was in a daze from excitement and fever from the shots, and I have no clear memory of our last hours at SAS. The next morning we departed for the ship on a bus with the others.

I said goodbye to SAS almost without thinking. Perhaps I could afford to do so because I took with me, at last, a sense of permanent belonging. In Changsha and Yuanling I had felt I belonged, but I had also known it wasn't permanent—I would always be a foreigner. In the States, although I had learned how to fit in, I was always something of a visitor—an outsider.

But at SAS I was neither foreigner nor outsider. I was with others like me, whose traditions and worldview were a combination of the country we lived in and the very different country from which our parents came, and yet not totally of either. From the common experience of partial belonging and our intensely shared lives at SAS, we created, in those years between world war and revolution, a heritage unique to us—a third culture from the precincts of which we would gaze out at the rest of the world. Wherever we were, our point of view would always be slightly outside of the norm for that place. But within this third culture *we* were the norm. Within this third culture we had forged bonds that held across time and space and change and race so that when we came together again, we did not have to grope for understanding. At reunions in later years we picked up where we'd left off forty, then fifty years before, and although we were delighted to find out what had become of each other, we were not surprised. What we had become seemed inevitable, because we *knew* where each of us was coming from. SAS was our home country, the place of our full belonging. At last I had found a group that shared my origins. No longer suspended between two worlds, at SAS I fell into place.

Five days after the *Repose* steamed down the Whangpoo River from Shanghai, it docked in Hong Kong. Anne and I took the train to Canton, where I stayed with her family at the YMCA until my parents came to join us. Then we talked about what to do. Finally we decided that Mother and I should go to Los Gatos while my father would return to Changsha for a few months to see the school and hospital through the change of government. Then he would join us in the States.

A few days later Mother and I flew to California by Pan American Airways, taking three days from Hong Kong to cross the Pacific. My father returned to Changsha. We thought it would be only a few short months before we were together again. We were wrong.

LOS GATOS AND CHANGSHA

My father's letters from Changsha took about three weeks to get to us in Los Gatos. For a year and a half, he had written to Mother almost every day and to me about once a week. This letter was for me. I slit open the flimsy envelope carefully and pulled out some tightly folded sheets the consistency of old tissue paper.

The letters were always several pages long, with faint typing, single spaced on both sides of paper so thin that the lettering showed through into the words on the other side. As usual, I opened the envelope with mixed feelings—pleased to hear from him and guilty because I didn't write him more often. I wrote him maybe every month or so. I knew he looked forward to hearing from me. I knew I should write regularly, like Mother. But there was always something else to do. Besides, it took a long time to write him because, once started, there was always so much to say.

With a mental sigh I unfolded the brittle pages, then stopped. Instead of densely packed typing, the paper was covered with rows of random marks, some curved, some straight, some curved and straight, some twisted, and others wavering off between the lines. I stared at them, momentarily disoriented. *What's happened to Daddy?* I thought. Then I realized I was looking at shorthand.

I didn't know he could write shorthand.

Over the past couple of months we had been discussing my final semester of high school. Since I had completed all the courses I needed to graduate, I thought I should concentrate on taking secretarial classes. The fact that they required very little homework was purely accidental. What was important was that I could use the skills if I needed a job, and what's more, shorthand would be useful for taking notes in college.

My father was unpersuaded by these excellent arguments. Yes, he'd written in reply, it might be good to get those skills sometime, perhaps in summer school. But, referring to his own college years, he thought I should continue to take academic courses so that I wouldn't get out of the habit, as he claimed he had, to his sorrow. In my next letter I pointed out that taking easy courses didn't seem to have hurt him, since he had a Ph.D. from Yale. With that, I signed up for Shorthand, Office Skills, Basic Accounting, and

Typing (even though I'd learned to type when I'd taken eighth grade at home in Changsha).

My father said no more on the subject, but somehow he'd learned how to write shorthand. I pulled out my copy of *Gregg's Shorthand* and settled down to decode his squiggles, laboriously learning that he had found an old copy of *Gregg's* in the attic, and this was the result. Maybe he'd give up by the next time he wrote, I thought hopefully. But under my counterfeit exasperation I enjoyed the joke, then felt the sudden sting of unshed tears.

The attic of our house in Changsha was an endless source of subject matter for my father's letters. In its dim reaches were piled books, old magazines, records, chests and trunks, and furniture, our own as well as some brought in from other faculty houses when their occupants had returned to the States. Stored in the corner farthest from the dusty dormer windows were crates of ancient Chinese artifacts, some over two thousand years old, that had been dug up outside the walls of Yali when a road was built back in the thirties. My father hadn't wanted the boxes stored in our house, but the Yali administration (all Chinese) was of the strong opinion that our attic was the safest place for them in the uncertain days before the Communists arrived.

At first my father's letters had not been inspired by the contents of the attic. Rather, they were full of news about friends and what he was doing—going to meetings or to church, teaching English classes, going out to dinner or having people in, or seeing off the few remaining Americans on the train when they left for home. Soon we learned that he had moved most of his things into the bedroom he and Mother had shared so that another family and some single teachers could move into other rooms in the house. Now he spent most of the time in his room and ate his meals there, prepared by Da Shi-fu, the cook, who, along with the gardener, Ho Shi-fu, had stayed on with my father after Mother left.

After the Korean War started, my father rarely mentioned our friends, and when he did he referred to them through their children—"Rosemary's father," he'd write, or "Teddy's dad." Instead of reports of his own activities his letters were full of jokes culled from the attic's supply of *Reader's Digest*s and pages of long quotations from books on religion and history, science and nature, that he wanted me to think about. Friends in Changsha say that my father was often heard typing late into the night, and later some people were to claim he was actually typing out secret information as a spy.

In addition to writing us long and chatty letters, my father wrote poems, sometimes setting them to music. He played records on the Victrola and practiced his *xiao,* a Chinese flute. He played hymns on our old piano. He described what he saw outside the window—children playing on the lawn, a thrush bathing in the pedestaled birdbath, or a blackbird singing his heart out on a misty morning. He tried to transcribe the blackbird's song onto music manuscript and sent it to me so I could play it on our new piano in Los Gatos.

It didn't occur to me to wonder why my father's activities, like the blackbird's song, were now all solo occupations. Engrossed in my own preoccupations, I undertook to educate him on what life was like for teenagers in these modern, postwar times. I sent him sheet music of current popular songs, my favorites being "Zena, Zena, Zena", which he liked, and "La Vie en Rose", which he said didn't have a *real* melody like the songs from the good old days when he and Mother had the leads in their senior class operetta. In reply I sent him a copy of the senior play in which *I* had a lead, the title of which was the most memorable thing about it: *Out of the Frying Pan.*

Recently we had exchanged views on using makeup, which I insisted did not go against nature but "complemented the work of the Almighty, if applied judiciously and artistically." In his next letter my father said he put his trust in my "innate good sense and good taste." To sustain that trust, I did not mention the magenta lipstick, the scuffed saddle shoes, the bobby sox, and the pin curls into which I tortured my naturally curly hair, covering it with a dish towel knotted under the chin. These were all *de rigueur* when the usual group of us seniors piled in someone's convertible on Saturday afternoons to visit the soda fountain, where we played the jukebox and consumed hot fudge sundaes and banana splits and Cokes (from which I took token sips only).

If it took me a long time to read one of my father's letters, it must have taken even longer for the Chinese censor in Changsha—a comforting thought. I'd had that censor in mind when I sent my father a valentine with a rubber band you twisted in such a way that a cardboard heart on it whirred out when you opened the card. It must have whirred out at the censor, I thought with satisfaction. Now I wondered what this long-suffering individual must think of my father's shorthand. Could the censor read it? If he couldn't, why had he let it come through? Out of exhaustion?

The year 1950 came and went, but there was still no sign of my father's return. At the request of the Yali administration in Changsha, he had been able to obtain funds from New Haven for a new gymnasium to replace the one destroyed by the Japanese. After the funds arrived, it became obvious that there was nothing more for him to do at Yali, so he applied to the foreign office for permission to return to the States. But while the other Americans, and indeed most of the foreigners in Changsha, left after the first few months under the new government, my father's permission to leave did not come through. Nevertheless, I knew he'd come home eventually. He didn't seem to be worried. In fact, for the first time in his life, he was doing things he'd always wanted to do but hadn't had time for. "Being alone so much," he wrote, "and fooling with things by myself, I find myself enjoying the simplest and queerest things, and then, with a start, I wonder if it's a sign of mental deterioration or if I really am having a good time!" In another letter he wrote about the birds at the birdbath:

> "They hop around the edge, trying to make up their minds to plunge in, and then they finally do, give one or two shivers, and hop out on the edge and fluffle all over. . . . After half a dozen times they really go to it and do a real job of it. It is so much fun to watch them."

When I read those words, I could see my father's single silhouette at the bedroom bay window, looking out at the birdbath. I did not know that he truly stood alone, for by this time it was unwise for his friends to be seen with him.

Many years later, a Chinese friend connected to the hospital told me of another of my father's activities during that time. By private arrangement with one of the hospital administrators, he gave blood whenever someone needed his type, for the Chinese were reluctant to donate even for relatives.

He usually walked over to the hospital at night so no one would know that the blood had come from a foreigner.

卐

Meanwhile, Mother and I were living in a bungalow in Los Gatos, rented from friends. While I completed my junior and senior years at Los Gatos Union High School, Mother taught third grade in the same building where she had been a third-grader herself. With most of our friends we attended the same Presbyterian church where her father had been pastor for twenty-five years, until his death. Mother was very busy. She spent hours in the evening preparing her lessons, wrote my father almost every other day, cleaned house, did the cooking and shopping, and worked long hours in the garden under the windows of our bungalow. In the evening we always listened to Lowell Thomas, a nationally known commentator who delivered the nightly news on the radio. Otherwise, except for breakfast and supper, we didn't see much of each other.

If Mother was busy, so was I, with schoolwork and piano lessons, running for secretary of student council (I lost), attending meetings of the local chapter of the World Federalists, singing in the church choir, cutting apricots in the orchards around Los Gatos alongside migrant workers, going to the movies or to dances with Ralph or George or Dennis or John, or driving with the youth group from church to ice skate in San Francisco, to ride the roller coaster at Santa Cruz, or to picnic on a favorite beach accessible only through a tunnel at low tide. There we girls swam, sunbathed, and talked while the boys practiced rock climbing on the cliff behind us. One memorable night we stayed around the bonfire too long. In the dusk, the tide rose until we noticed the tunnel was underwater, and we were trapped on a shrinking beach. The only way out was up the cliff, but it quickly became too dark to climb with safety. The water was nudging the foot of the cliff when the moon finally appeared over the top and we could see the pitons the boys had placed during their afternoon climb. With ropes tied about our waists we scaled the vertical rock and then drove home with only the vaguest of explanations to our parents why we were so late.

Absorbed with such felicitous adventures, I didn't have much time to help Mother around the house or to worry about my father. After all, he was fine. He said so in a letter to Mother:

"I am perfectly all right, and getting along a thousand times better than I deserve. . . . There isn't a day goes by that someone doesn't make me feel sorely ashamed . . . for my failure to have lived up to what they say in being kind to me and expressing their friendship. I can see thousands of ways I have failed them and how wonderful they have been to me. So don't go worrying about me."

But Mother did worry. Sometimes even when we weren't talking about my father, her face became anxious, her breath would catch, and she would sigh and look out the window, her eyes bright with tears. Just being alone with her sometimes made me anxious and angry for no reason that I could explain. Once I woke up at night to hear her muffled sobs from across the bedroom we shared, and I was filled with helpless fury at her for making such a fuss. My chest and throat swelled with silent screams, but I stayed quiet so she wouldn't know I was awake. I didn't want her to talk about missing Daddy and wondering why he didn't come home. I didn't want her even to hint that she was afraid he might *never* come home. I didn't want to be the one to say that everything would be all right.

🕊

In the summer of 1950, before my senior year, I was sent by the local chapter of the Daughters of the American Revolution (who I believe were unaware of my membership in the World Federalists) to "Girls' State" in Sacramento—a popular program for civics education in the '50s. There I spent a week with girls representing high schools throughout California, learning something of the intricacies of state government and having a noisy good time attending caucuses, organizing campaigns, cheering at parades and booing at the convention. Several hundred of us slept in double bunks set up in a large gymnasium. Each morning we woke to announcements broadcast over loudspeakers followed by the morning news amplified from the radio.

One morning I was lying on my top bunk, dreamily gazing up at huge sunbeams slanting down from the windows, when I heard the words "North Korea" boom through the buzz of a hundred conversations. The happy noise faded to silence while the newscaster told how the United States had just entered the Korean conflict. Then the voices in the gym started again, rapidly rising to an uproar. I lay very still on my bunk. In the midst of that cacophony, I felt the first cold trickle of fear. What would happen to Daddy? The question seeped like tainted groundwater under my remaining days in Sacramento, and at the end of the week I left, worried about my father and about how much more anxious Mother would be when I got home.

But when I returned to Los Gatos and started my senior year, Mother was much the same as before. Nothing seemed to have happened to my father. His letters remained as long and chatty and cheerful as ever. He never even mentioned the Korean War. My anxiety subsided.

In the middle of January 1951 a letter came to both of us written on the previous Christmas day. I read it to Mother while she got supper. My father was writing to share the day with us, he said, and to explain why he'd spent Christmas in his room rather than joining the usual activities in church and on campus. He'd been wanting to explain for some time, but there was very little to report beyond the fact was that he had received permission to leave Changsha on the previous November 11.

November 11. That was two months ago. Why hadn't he left?

I didn't look at Mother for fear she would confirm my sudden clutch of alarm. Careful to keep an ordinary tone of voice, I continued to read.

Three days before he was to leave, he was packed and ready to go. He took a list of all he was taking—books, clothes, slides and a projector—to the police to facilitate their search of his baggage. At that time they told him he should delay his departure a few days. On the next day, a Thursday, they came and went though all his baggage and made no objection to it. But they did take his radio, saying it could used for receiving messages other than regular broadcasts. They also took the extra tubes and tools he had for the radio. "That was all there was to it after a day or two of questioning about it," my father wrote. "During the examination time, they found some 18 cases of old clay grave things upstairs and were of course surprised at that." But, he went on to say, the school administration had documents and pictures of all that was in the crates, so it looked as though there would be no problem.

What did he mean by "examination time"? And who were "they" that found the old clay things in the attic?

I thought about the radio. It was probably that Hallicrafter shortwave set we'd had in Yuanling. What could possibly be wrong with that? We'd had it for ages; everybody knew about it. And why did they question him for two days? My father's casual explanation gave no clue to the answers.

It was many years later that Chinese friends told me what really happened that Thursday afternoon. Everyone in the Yali community knew my father had been given permission to leave Changsha in November. In a brave gesture of friendship, his colleagues reached across the isolation of recent months to get together one last time. Mr. Ying, the dean of Yali; Mr. Lao, the principal; Mr. Sheng, the treasurer; and other colleagues and faculty got approval to arrange a farewell dinner to be held at my father's house rather than the more usual venue of a restaurant. The circle of friendship was briefly restored as the dinner got under way. Suddenly armed troops burst through the front door and ordered everyone not to move. For the next four hours the guests sat motionless at the tables while the soldiers searched the house from basement to attic, wrote down what they "found, "and took the names of those who were there. Finally they ordered the guests to leave, and everyone departed without saying goodbye. My father would be with them only one more time.

In December the results of the raid were made public. Newspapers in Changsha, Beijing, Shanghai, and other cities across China published articles accusing my father of having been caught trying to rob the Chinese people of their heritage by smuggling artifacts out of the country. My father wrote that since this news aroused

> ...a great deal of natural indignation, friends have suggested that it is better for me not to go out much for a while. This, then, is the explanation for why I have been staying at home. . . .It is very unfortunate and I am extremely sorry there has been this misunderstanding, but when the thing has been entirely worked out to the satisfaction of the authorities, the matter will be settled.

Friends in Changsha have since claimed that actually he was put under house arrest. But the restriction could not have lasted long, because in later letters he mentions shopping in the city and going to church again.

When spring came, our correspondence turned to long discussions about which college I should attend out of the four to which I'd been accepted—two in California, one in the Midwest, and one on the eastern seaboard. It was hard to decide. For fear of hurting Mother's feelings, I didn't tell my parents I wanted to get away from home—far enough away so that I'd be completely on my own. At the same time, I couldn't bear the thought of leaving Mother by herself in the house. She hated to be alone—not like Daddy, who made the best of it. And if I left California, our family would truly be separated by thousands of miles with no idea of when we'd be together again. That thought brought me to the edge of panic.

What should I do? Mother did not indicate in any way where she wanted me to go. My father used at least thirty pages in three letters to weigh the pros and cons of each choice, finally suggesting I take a bus across the country and visit the colleges before making a final decision. "All my love to you these important weeks ahead of you," he wrote at the end. "As high school winds up, keep close to God and be your own true self." That was the last letter I received from Changsha. It was written on May 10.

What happened with my father after that day will never be fully known, as he made no written account and the stories of that time are told by different people from sometimes conflicting memories of fifty years ago. We do know that on May 17 police or troops or officials came to the house and took my father to a mass "meeting," the first event to be held in the newly built gymnasium. When he entered, the hall was reportedly packed with about two thousand people—from Yali, from the hospital, the medical and nursing schools, and from the Presbyterian Girls' School. He was escorted to a straight chair on one side of the stage and there he sat while the master of ceremonies led the audience in choral shouting of anti-American slogans. Then he pointed at my father and announced through his loudspeaker that my father was a spy—a spy who had tried to hide a radio receiver in his luggage. And he was a thief—a thief who had been caught planning to rob China of her heritage by smuggling ancient relics out of the country.

These accusations were evidently lost on my father. He leaned back in his chair, crossed his knees, and took a long, slow look around the interior of the newly completed building, funded at his personal request by a donation from Yale-in-China. Friends later told me that my father's preoccupation infuriated the master of ceremonies, who then yelled even more angrily at my father to sit up straight and pay attention.

And so my father uncrossed his knees, sat up straight, and paid attention as his friends and colleagues with whom he had sat in countless other meetings over the years, with whom he had lived and worked, had endured danger, loss, and hardship, with whom he had shared vision and hope and hard-won accomplishment, with whom he had sat at that last farewell dinner, came one by one up on the stage and denounced him.

The proceedings finally came to a climax with the announcement that my father was to be expelled from the People's Republic. The sign that had hung over the front gate to the school was brought onstage. It was a black lacquered board on which were written in gold the large and solid characters for "Yali," two words taken from a well-known quotation of Confucius. There is no exact equivalent in English for the quotation, but to any educated Chinese of the time, the two words resonated with fundamental Confucian precepts—*ya* for elegance of expression and civility and *li* for propriety and right conduct. Mr. Lao, who had been the principal of Yali for over twenty years, then came on stage with an ax and to thundering applause chopped the board in two.

It is said that my father was taken back to our house, where he stayed for about half an hour. Some thought they heard him playing the piano. Then he came out with his suitcase in one hand and his furled umbrella of oiled paper and bamboo in the other. He walked down the steps from our screen porch, down the front walk past the birdbath onto the path leading to the main walk between the faculty houses, around the soccer field into a gauntlet of shouting people lining the way, past the chapel on the hill, past the new gymnasium, past the dining hall, the dormitories, and the classroom buildings to the front gate.

Outside the gate, the Ma Lou was lined with people. My father's route to the train station had been published in the paper and the people along the way were well prepared. Almost as soon as he stepped onto the road, someone threw something at him, and the crowd's roar swelled. A few steps later, the leader of his escort abruptly turned off onto a side street. Leaving the crowds behind. they walked through sparsely populated back streets to the train station, where my father arrived unharmed.

When the train pulled in and the platform filled up with people, his escort hung a sign around my father's neck, and made him kneel on the platform while they harangued him and announced his crimes to the crowd.

At every stop on that trip to Canton, he was brought out on the platform and the scene was repeated to assembled crowds, regardless of the time of night.

When they reached Canton the next morning, he was put in prison. Three days later, on the morning of May 21, he was taken to the courtyard of the prison and made to kneel on the ground. A guard put a gun to his head.

On the evening of May 21, Mother and I were listening as usual to Lowell Thomas when I suddenly became alert at the words "Dwight Rugh." Mother and I looked at each other. What was he saying? Something about being "released from Red China to Hong Kong"? We listened for more, but Lowell Thomas had gone on to something else.

What happened? We had no idea that my father would be leaving Changsha. His letters had given no hint of an impending departure. In fact, it seemed that he would be staying there indefinitely. Lowell Thomas must be wrong. Maybe he was somehow saying my father had been *expected* to be released to Hong Kong but wasn't? Had something else happened to him?

Mother tried to call long distance to New Haven to find out if the news was true, but the office was closed. Then our phone began to ring as friends and family called who had also heard the broadcast. They were saying my father had been released. Sometime during the evening the doorbell rang. It was Western Union with a telegram from the Yale-in-China office in New Haven. They had received a cable from my father. He had arrived in Hong Kong safely. He was well and he would be coming home soon. He sent us his love.

Mother and I started to cry and then we laughed and held on to each other in the middle of the living room and cried some more, engulfed by happiness. I kept saying, "I can't believe it!" but at the same time I did believe it. Under that tremendously thrilling relief and excitement I felt as though this had happened before. It was inevitable. Of course my father was coming back. He always did. I'd known all along that he would, that the three of us would be together again. I'd known all along that everything would be all right.

ENDINGS

Home in Los Gatos, my father told his story in bits and pieces over several days. He had arrived less than two weeks before I finished high school. In spite of the excitement of his return, I must have been distracted by my high school graduation and all the preparations it involved, for although I remember listening to him with rapt attention, I retained only a few vignettes from his extended account.

I remember his telling about the soldiers of the Communist Eighth Route Army, many of whom seemed to be no older than twelve or fourteen, carrying rifles almost taller than they. Soon after the Communists took control of Changsha, these little warriors would come, three or four at a time, pounding on the front door and swaggering a bit as they walked into the living room. Most of them had come from the countryside and had never seen a foreigner before, much less upholstered furniture. *"Qing-zuo, qing-zuo!"* my father would say, inviting them to sit down. Holding their rifles, they sat down gingerly at first, but when the cook appeared with refreshments, they propped their guns beside their chairs and settled back in their seats to consume generous quantities of tea and peanuts and Da Shi-fu's cookies. My father would play the piano and ask them to sing some of their songs, and soon they were asking him for American songs. "We'd have a very good time," my father chuckled reminiscently. "They were just kids, you know."

One morning after he had moved into the bedroom, my father heard a noise on the front lawn. Looking out the window, he saw that some boys in uniform were about to push over the birdbath. Quickly he opened the casement and leaned out, calling sharply, "Stop that!" They only pushed harder. He tried again: "You break that and you destroy the people's property. That's not mine. It belongs to the people!" They stopped. After talking it over, they apparently decided not to take any chances; picking up their rifles, they departed, leaving the People's birdbath intact.

My father spoke at length about a man I will call Comrade Wu, since my father didn't tell us his name. He was the official in charge of the foreigners in Changsha and came regularly to the house to question my father. At his first visit, he had brought an interpreter with him, in case my father needed him to translate during the formal interrogations in

Mandarin. My father agreed to the interpreter, for although he could understand Comrade Wu's Mandarin perfectly well, he wanted the time during translation to think how he would answer the questions. This arrangement worked satisfactorily for my father but not so well for Comrade Wu. After the Korean War started, he showed up at the front door one day without the interpreter. "Today," he said in English, "I come just as a friend. Let us sit awhile and visit."

"Of course," said my father with some surprise. He had not known Comrade Wu could speak English. After they were settled with tea and Da Shi-fu's cookies, Comrade Wu started the friendly conversation with a question: "Now tell me. What is your opinion of the United Nations' action in Korea?"

"I am not sure what my own opinion is," my father replied carefully. "All I know is the opinions I read in your newspapers."

After that, they always spoke in English without an interpreter, and soon the interrogation sessions changed to long conversations ranging over many topics. One day early in 1951, Comrade Wu arrived with a scroll he had painted for my father—a spray of bamboo with a line of fine calligraphy from the classics alluding to friendship. He had come to say goodbye; he'd been transferred to Korea and was leaving the next day.

Given China's tactics in the Korean War, where Chinese troops attacked in human waves—mostly against American positions—and were killed by the thousands, it is unlikely that Comrade Wu survived very long. In Changsha he was replaced by another official whom my father didn't get to know so well. But it was this second official who would change the route of my father's final walk through the city so that he arrived unhurt at the train station.

My father's visitors dwindled to a very few as China's losses in the Korean conflict mounted. But there was one person, my father said, who came to see him faithfully each month. "You know who it was? It was Tou Shi-fu!" Tou Shi-fu, who had been our cook in Yuanling. He had moved to Changsha, where he ran a successful bakery downtown. By now he had eight children, ranging from Tou Yuan-fu and Tou Yuan-mei, my cohorts from our Yuanling days, through Tou Yuan-an, Tou Yuan-li, Tou Yuan-lo, Tou En-lai, and Tou Zu-sen to little Tou Yuan-ling, less than two years old—six sons and two daughters. On my father's birthday and at

Christmas, Tou Shi-fu would arrive bearing a beautifully frosted cake and accompanied by all his children dressed in their best. They trailed up the front walk behind their father and sat down politely, very well behaved, nibbling cake and sipping tea until Tou Shi-fu, assured that my father was well, said it was time to go. Then they would say goodbye and file out.

A Chinese friend told me decades later that when the foreign office required my father to have a sponsor or guarantor to be responsible for him and ensure his good behavior, Tou Shi-fu was the only one who came forward. When asked why he was doing this for my father, Tou Shi-fu had replied, "Because he is a good man."

I don't know what happened to Tou Shi-fu. Of all the people we lived with and knew, he and his family are the ones I don't know about. No one seems to know. Perhaps some of the family succumbed to starvation during the great famine of 1959. As guarantor for my father—almost too painful to think of—Tou Shi-fu would have received especially harsh treatment during the Cultural Revolution. Perhaps he disappeared in the maelstrom of that insanity and the family was scattered over China in the dislocations mandated by the maniacal policies of the time. I don't know what happened to annihilate this family and cause Tou Shi-fu to vanish as though he had never lived. But I do know this: He was courageous, he was honest, he was loyal, and above all he was faithful to what he believed was right. He was a good man.

The day after my father arrived in Hong Kong the Chinese press reported that on May 17, at a mass meeting of the People, the Changsha Bureau of Public Security ordered

> *...the deportation of Dwight Rugh, American teacher in Yali Middle School and representative in China of the Yale Association of the United States, who allegedly concealed radio reception sets and attempted to smuggle out of China Chinese cultural relics. Chinese coins and radio reception set and tubes were found in his luggage.*

The paper claimed that the "Changsha military control committee had explicitly ordered that no alien resident was allowed to install or use radios or equipment. He was instructed to put up an advertisement in the newspaper to announce his repentance." After four or five tries, which seemed to be the norm for such statements, his profession of regret had been finally accepted.

The *Da Kung Pao,* a mainland newspaper available in Hong Kong, reported that my father's radio was a "military radio receiving set" and that the two hundred cultural relics were contained in eighteen boxes that he intended to smuggle out of the country. It did not say how he planned to accomplish such a feat.

I listened to the rest of my father's improbable story in a state of suspended belief. It was hardly credible that his "trial" was the first event to be held in the new building that he had made possible at the request of those who accused him of being a thief. Like watching a movie, I saw him up on the stage with hundreds of people yelling at him and friends looking at him with strangers' eyes. But from what my father said, he didn't seem to mind. He was more interested in seeing what this new building was like. "You know, they used up all that money just for a big shell, about two times bigger than what we planned for. They didn't want a gymnasium—they just wanted a place to hold a lot of people!" He paused and smiled. "The man in charge didn't like the way I was sitting. I'd sat back with my knees crossed, having a good look around. He got very angry and told me to sit up and pay attention."

"So what did you do?" I said, feeling a little better because my father had upset this person.

"Well, I uncrossed my knees and sat up." He went on to say that the master of ceremonies then invited people to come up and testify against him, and some of our closest friends came up and spoke. "They said things like, 'I used to think this stinking imperialist spy was a friend of mine but now my eyes are opened.' And they made up stories about things I'd done to them."

"How terrible," Mother said, her face paralyzed in sadness.

"But that was all right," my father said. "They had to protect all of us by saying these things. They didn't mean it. They had it all written out in advance and stood up there and read it because it helped things go more smoothly to get me out. We'd seen it coming—it had been done many times before all over the country. So we had agreed long beforehand to say anything that would help make things safer for all of us."

My father must have described how Mr. Lao had chopped the Yali signboard to pieces, but I promptly forgot that part of the story. It was only when Chinese friends reminded me of it years later and I felt a familiar wave of sick emptiness that I realized I had known about it before.

But I remembered well my father's account of what happened a short while later. As he walked through the gauntlet of jeering people to the front gate, a man stepped onto the path in front of him. Here my father stopped speaking for so long that I thought he was going to skip this part of the story. But then he continued. "It was Mr. Lao. He stopped right there in the middle of the path, in front of everyone, and he *smiled* at me." My father's voice broke. "Just think of it," he said, and shook his head in wonder at such bravery.

I said, "And?"

"He just walked across the path to the other side and I didn't see him again." My father's eyes were dark with pain.

At the Yali gate my father looked down the Ma Lou, lined with angry people, and realized he would not survive its length. "But then," he said, "the man in charge turned us off onto a side street. Can you believe it? You know, he took some risk doing that." And my father shook his head again at such risk taking on his behalf.

They reached the train station too early for the train to Canton. While they awaited its arrival, his escort took him to the guard room where the station guards were playing cards. They invited him to join the game. So, he sat at the table with them until the train arrived. The men then laid down their cards, hung the sign around his neck, and took him out on the platform where they forced him to kneel. In spite of this, however, it was their unexpected hospitality in the midst of mindless and malicious animosity that seemed to impress my father more than anything else.

The next few days were grim. When he and his escort arrived at Canton at two in the morning, my father had expected to be put on the first morning train to Hong Kong. Instead, he was arrested and taken to prison, where his suitcase was confiscated. He was put in a room so crowded with men that there wasn't enough room for all of them to lie down. He had nothing with him but his clothes. Everyone spoke

Cantonese, which he could not understand, but sometimes he thought he heard his name, Yu Dao Cun (pronounced "wru dao tswun"), blared out over the loudspeaker. Now and then guards would come in and take a man out. The men who were taken did not return. On the third day the guards came for him. They tied his hands behind his back and took him to the prison courtyard, where they pushed him to his knees and put a gun to his head.

A gun to his head? This was like reading Kafka. Things like that didn't really happen, didn't happen in the real world—the world of this serene living room with its graciously comfortable furniture, our Peking rugs, the piano, the glowing lamps, the Chinese painting on the wall. My eyes went to the delicate black-and-white brush-and-ink scene suggesting mountains and mist, with a tiny man forever crossing a bridge arched over a raging torrent.

My father, too, may have felt that what happened was unreal, for he said, as though surprised at himself, "You know, I wasn't afraid." There was a long pause. "In that courtyard I felt Jesus right next to me. . . . When they put the gun to my head I felt very peaceful. . . . Whatever happened, it would be all right."

What happened was that the gun was abruptly withdrawn and my father was jerked to his feet. They untied his hands, gave him his suitcase, and put him on a train bound for Hong Kong under the guard of two young soldiers carrying long rifles.

It was a blazing hot day, and when they reached the border there was a long line of people waiting in the sun to be processed through a gate to the British colony. On China's side of the gate, an official was inspecting the papers and baggage of people going into Hong Kong. On the Hong Kong side of the gate there was another long line of people waiting to be processed by a burly British officer in a pith helmet.

My father, on the Chinese side, was very tired and thirsty. He wondered how long he would be able to stand there in the noonday sun. After a while his guards evidently gave up and left. As my father inched forward, he thought the Chinese official at the gate looked familiar, but it was hard to see clearly in the glaring sunlight.

"Then, when I got closer," my father said, "I *knew* him! He was one of our old students!"

Mother and I both said, "No!"

"Yes! I knew him well."

"Did he recognize you?" I asked—a stupid question.

"He didn't give any sign of it, and I didn't either. He just looked at my passport and gave it back without changing his expression. Then he had me put my suitcase on the table and told me to open it. And there"—my father slapped his thigh—"sitting on top was a radio!"

"What?" we asked, totally bewildered.

"A radio. Right on top. In the suitcase. I just stood there. Flabbergasted." He paused, remembering. "They must have put it there while I was in prison." We waited for him to go on.

I said, "*Then* what happened?"

"Well, he just looked at it calmly, closed the lid, and handed me the suitcase."

"Didn't he say anything?" Mother asked.

"No."

"Did you say anything?" I asked.

"No. I just walked on through the gate and there I was. In Hong Kong."

I have since wondered about that former student and the choices he faced when he saw the radio in my father's suitcase. I have wondered what happened to him as a result of the choice he made—not to "discover" the radio. I have wondered whom it is we should thank for my father's return to us. But my father never told us his name.

The British officer was obviously in a bad mood, shouting at the Chinese who came up to him, grabbing their papers, and pushing them on. When he saw my father come through the gate, the officer motioned for him to come to the front of the line. When my father hesitated, the officer looked disgusted and waved again, so my father went up to him. Evidently he thought my father was in bad shape, for he had someone carry my father's suitcase and show him to a room in a nearby building. There he sat in the breeze of an electric fan and drank orange squash—an insipidly sweet bottled drink faintly reminiscent of orange juice—while they asked him questions and looked at his papers. Then they put him on the train for

Kowloon.

Later, feeling much better, my father walked up Nathan Road from the train station toward the Presbyterian Guest House, where he planned to stay. Along the way, he stopped to look in a shop window. "There I saw this bum looking straight out the window at me. He was a mess. Then I realized he was me! It was my reflection!" My father—who had always been careful to keep his hair neatly trimmed, who shaved twice a day, and wore a tie even to picnics—thought this was very funny. He went to a nearby shop that took passport photos and had his picture taken. Now, laughing, he pulled a picture out of his wallet and handed it to Mother. She looked at it and cried.

About a month after he came home, my father's trunks arrived in Los Gatos. The authorities in Changsha had instructed his servants to ship the trunks to Canton, but they never arrived. The prison officials in Canton had angrily questioned my father about their nonappearance, but he couldn't tell them where they were because he didn't know. In an extraordinary act of courage, the servants had sent his trunks directly to the Hong Kong border, where, probably by surreptitious arrangement, they were passed without inspection. When he opened them in Los Gatos, my father found, lying at the top of one of the trunks, a diagram for changing a radio receiving set to a sending set. He had never seen it before.

In trying to make sense of what happened, we could only conjecture that the purpose of the stopover in Canton was to wait for that trunk with its damning evidence to arrive by train. When it didn't come, the radio was planted in his suitcase to be "discovered" at the border. Only it wasn't.

Among my father's papers in the archives at Yale there is no written account of his final days in China. In a letter from Hong Kong to the head office, written shortly after his release, he said, "My heart is crushed at the possibilities that may occur to Yale-in-China staff members and their families." In another letter he wrote, "I prefer not to say anything in public. In fact, the less said the better." The Yale-in-China records revealed one mention of the final talk my father made at a trustees' meeting in New Haven following his return from China. In those brief remarks, he only expressed his admiration and gratitude for the work and character of his co-workers and the Yali students; he spoke also of his hopes for China's future under the new regime. In one of his final letters to the office, he said he thought it was very likely that someday Yale-in-China would be able to return to Changsha.

$\mathcal{Y}$

In Los Gatos, my father was as calm and cheerful as ever, interested in everything we were doing, his sense of humor intact. It did not occur to me that he should be any different. *All's well that ends well,* I thought, and immersed myself in preparations for college.

One evening, the three of us went to see the film *The Great Caruso,* the first movie my father had been to in a long time. The years since we had last seen a movie together were erased as we took our usual places, with me in the middle. Toward the end of the film, as the glorious music from the opera *Martha* flooded the theater, suddenly my father covered his face with his hands and bent over to his knees. He stayed there while Mario Lanza's tenor soared and sobbed through the last duet with Dorothy Kirsten. Shocked, I sat immobile, not knowing what to do. I don't think Mother moved, either. When my father sat up, I didn't dare look at him until we walked out of the theater. By then, he looked as though it had never happened.

I don't know if Mother talked with him about it. I didn't—it seemed too intrusive and embarrassing, like asking him something very personal. Whatever kept me from asking him about it also kept me from asking any more questions about his last days in China. For now I knew that under his calm acceptance and good cheer, my father had been profoundly shaken. So I heard his story only once, when he told it to us for the first—and last—time. That was enough for me to know that I, too, was now expelled from the world that had been my first and only real home.

With my father's return to the States, my parents' connections to China ended. They went on to work in Idaho, Israel, and Taiwan, and after their retirement they taught as volunteers in community organization and preschool education in West Virginia, literacy in the Job Corps in Kentucky, and special education in public schools in Ohio. They never really retired until my father died at the age of eighty-one from some liver disease probably contracted many years ago in China. My mother lived, mind and body active and completely focused on reality until she died of a stroke at the age of ninety-four.

As for me, I went to college, to graduate school, got married, and with my husband raised a family. We lived and worked in Cleveland, Tokyo, Hong Kong, and Philadelphia. In those places China was irrelevant, except as a foreign country in the evening news or as a mysterious monolith looming on the other side of Hong Kong's impassable border. Like the Yali signboard chopped in two, my childhood years were severed from adulthood. My past and my present remained separate and unreconciled, But wherever I lived, however long I stayed, however rich my life in experience and friends and family, I harbored a persistent suspicion that I really dwelt elsewhere. Yet I did not hope, did not expect, did not want to return to that native place. For although at heart I had never left China, China had left me.

With Rosemary Ying and Shung-ma, my amah (1937)

The soccer field with the toy ricksha, Freddy Brandauer is on right (1937)

Clockwise (from l), Grandfather Rugh, Mother, Uncle Ed, Aunt Dorothy, Phyllis, BJ (1938)

In a new dress for my seventh birthday, Shanghai

Hawaii, 1938. Shortly before my father returned to China and Mother and I left for California.

Mr. Ying (ca. 1939)
photo by Edward Gulik, Yale Bachelor, 1937 (1939)

View of the chapel (lower l) and front gate from the top of the Yali campus
photo by Grace Brandauer

The last flight of steps in the stone staircase to our house
photo by Grace Brandauer

Our "Summer Palace" in the valley above Shi Qiao

The Catholic hospital in Yuanling
photo by Grace Brandauer

Outside our house with Molly

The "sentinel pine" of Shi Qiao

Cousin Phyllis Lupton (1948)

Cousin Bob Lupton in uniform as gunner,
U.S. Army Air Corps (1944)

In our 'sister' dresses (l to r) Xi-xi, Yuan-mei, BJ

My year in Changsha before going to the Shanghai American School (1944)

Tou Shi-fu's children in Yuanling
(back row) my friends Yuan-mei (l) and Yuan-fu (r) (1950)

My father in Hong Kong (May 21, 1951)

CHANGSHA

I thought I would never return to Changsha. But here I am, almost against my will. I wouldn't have come if it hadn't been for Mr. Ying. My taxi pulls up to his apartment building, and I see him waiting outside the entrance. I would have known him anywhere—in any century, any millennium. Like the faces of my parents, his is a fact of existence. I knew it before I recognized him.

My arms are around him, breaking all Chinese protocol and custom in a very American 1980s-type hug. Through his clothes I feel his bones, and I remember a skeletal soldier in a hillside dump, looking through rotting garbage for food. Mr. Ying pats my back a little awkwardly, as if he hasn't touched anyone for a long time.

"Mr. Ying," I say. "Are you well?"

"Of course!" he replies. "I am very glad to see you."

It is eight years after our family's visit to Changsha during the Cultural Revolution, and now six years after its end.. Earlier this year, Dave and I, along with another couple, received an invitation from the Chinese Academy of Medical Sciences in Beijing to visit some of the hospitals which were given large supplies of up-to-date pacemakers as a result of Dave's work in humanitarian aid. This opportunity to visit China was too good to miss. I decided to go. After all, as a nurse practitioner, I had some professional interest in the pacemakers and a rather academic interest in seeing how China had changed since we were last there. Changsha was not on our itinerary, and that was fine by me. I wasn't interested in Changsha.

But once we were in China, I realized I had to see Mr. Ying. My father had died the previous year, at the age of eighty-one. Mr. Ying was also in his eighties. I would never forgive myself if I left without seeing him. To the consternation of our hosts, when the rest of the party flew to Xian to visit hospitals and to view its famous army of terra-cotta soldiers, I left Beijing for Changsha, to stay twenty-four hours—just long enough to see Mr. Ying.

Now, in his modest apartment, we talk long past nightfall at the supper table lit by a single light bulb hanging from the ceiling. The last time we met around that strange dinner table in the hotel eight years ago, he had said very little. When the Cultural Revolution ended, he and my father corresponded regularly, but he never told my father what happened to him after my father left Changsha. Now Mr. Ying tells me at least some of his story. His English is more accented than I remember, the words tumbling out as though a dam has broken, so fast that sometimes I find them hard to follow.

Eight years ago, he says, when he was in his seventies, he was living in a shed outside the city, where his job was to ladle sewage out of latrines into wooden buckets, which he then pulled in a cart to the fields, where it was dispensed as fertilizer. Mrs. Ying, who lived in the city, brought him his food.

I remember heavy carts with sloshing buckets of stinking human waste hauled by sweating coolies down the Ma Lou out of Changsha. I'm shocked. I can't imagine that Mr. Ying, who had studied at Yale, who had guided Yali through its most difficult years, who had spent long hours in meetings with my father, who had laughed and joked countless times at our dinner table, and whose children were my playmates—I can't imagine that he, an old man in his seventies, had been doing this when we last saw him in Changsha. I try to envision him straining forward as he pulls the cart; then I see my father kneeling on the railway platform in Changsha. Something surges through my heart like a gigantic sob, too deep for tears.

Mr. Ying goes on. One day, he says, a cadre—a Communist party worker—appeared at his shed and told him he must come to a dinner the next night at a hotel with Dwight Rugh's daughter and her family. "What?" Mr. Ying asked, bewildered. For over thirty years he had been continually punished for his friendship with us and his loyalty to my father. Now, out of the blue, he was to associate with us again? It sounded like entrapment. "I can't do it. I have no clothes," Mr. Ying said, looking down at his rags. But the cadre said he must be ready when a van came to pick him up the next evening, and he cautioned Mr. Ying against telling us about his present living conditions or his occupation.

The next day Mrs. Ying went around to her neighbors and borrowed enough clothes for Mr. Ying to come to our dinner decently dressed.

Now my eyes sting with tears. I want to cover my face with my hands and bend over to my knees, but I sit very still. *I didn't know*, I think, ashamed that I didn't know, wanting to ask his forgiveness for not knowing, wanting to apologize to him for causing such apprehension, for putting him and Mrs. Ying through such humiliation. But he keeps on talking, and somehow I can't get the words out. My apology would be, at best, trivial. I wonder about the rest of the people we had invited to that dinner. What fear, what embarrassment, what great trouble had we caused them with our naïve notions of hospitality and reunion? There was so much I had not known.

I had not known that Mr. Ying refused to testify against my father at the "trial" in the gymnasium. From then on he was made the target for all the anti-American feeling, paranoia, and propaganda that would have been directed at my father had he been there—only worse, because Mr. Ying was Chinese, one of their own, who ostensibly had betrayed them, an example to be made of. He was forced to sit at the head of classrooms at Yali and in front of endless meetings as an example of a "running dog" of the American imperialists and spies, where he was harangued and humiliated. Sometimes they would spit on him and hit him—"those ragamuffins!" he sputters indignantly whenever he talks about his tormentors, evidently using the worst English expletive he can think of. He does not say what happened to his family, but life must have been almost unbearable for them.

Things got even worse during the Cultural Revolution. Some other extraordinary men whose life work, like Mr. Ying's, had been with Western institutions, were so harassed and humiliated that they killed themselves. But not Mr. Ying. A devout Christian, he promised God two things: one, he says, leaning forward and holding up a gnarled finger, that he would never kill himself, and two, raising another finger, that he would never speak against my father. "I kept my promise," he says, and leans back deliberately in his chair. "I am still here."

We sit some moments in silence. With those four words, Mr. Ying has bridged the separation between the past and the present.

Finally I say, "I'm very glad you are."

His smile wipes out the inadequacy of my words. I am reminded again of my father. When my father smiled the lines at the corners of his eyes deepened like Mr. Ying's. Now I know why it is important that I came. Not only have I found a bridge to my past; I am here to span the distance between these two men, one alive and one dead, whose regard for each other held through time and space and most disparate circumstance and who survived extremity not only unbroken but enlarged in spirit.

Six years after this visit, Mr. Ying came to New Haven to receive the Yale Alumni Award for his service to Yali and Yale-in-China. When I saw him in New Haven I gave him my father's well-worn copy of a devotional book by John Baillie, *A Diary of Private Prayer,* with my father's notations and comments in the margins. His family tells me he read it every day until shortly before he died, at the age of ninety.

✍

After that evening with Mr. Ying, I have visited China every five or six years. I can't stay away much longer than that. I'm not sure why, except, perhaps, that I need to see with today's eyes what the past is becoming. I need to be with the people who were there when I was. I need to see the places I remember—or I think I remember—to make sure my memory doesn't lie.

Each time I return to China, the disjuncture between present-day China and my memories lessens, mostly because of the people I come to see. Students of my parents, now old men, offer touchingly generous hospitality whenever I come, some showing up at seven in the morning at our hotel to tell their stories as though they were talking not to me, the girl they had seen riding her bicycle through the Yali campus so many years ago, but to my mother and father. Somehow, with their telling and my listening, a violent dislocation is reduced, as though an injured shoulder were back in place, sore but functional and getting better.

But no account, no amount of listening or acknowledgment can do justice to the hardship they endured, to their courage and their spirit. One, You Dajun, who had found an excuse to be absent from my father's "trial," lived through seven years of prison for this and other "counterrevolutionary crimes." When his term was up, the authorities found other reasons to send him to labor camp for fourteen years more. During those twenty-one years, his wife had refused to divorce him even though her family strongly urged her to do so and she was publicly castigated for not repudiating him, as many other women did when their husbands were accused of crimes against the People.

The day You Dajun was released, he wrote a poem that, perhaps, speaks for all those who survived :

> *The East Wind is strong over the land,*
> > *The azure sky clear and empty of clouds;*
> > > *The world bursts into color and shouts in ecstasy.*
>
> *Hung by the feet for twenty-one years—*
> > *once untied, the nightmare vanishes;*
>
> *The heavenly steed races out of the stable*
> > *into the wind*
> > > *soaring across the sky.*

YUANLING

Of all the places I remember, Yuanling is the one I recall most clearly—even more clearly than places I have lived since. It is where I took shape, where my body grew strong, where I first felt the excitement of thought. It is where I made my first friends and first knew the loves and the fears that would last me a lifetime. It is where the vast mystery of everything was distilled into the enchanted solitude of Shi Qiao, the valley where just to be there was enough.

And so, at last, I come back to Yuanling. But when I arrive, it isn't here. The house we lived in is here, but the town along the river is gone. I stand at the railing of our sleeping porch, where I used to look down at the stone staircase and the housetops to the river beyond. The staircase is gone, the houses are gone; even the river is gone. Instead, I look down at wavelets of dirty water lapping lazily on a mud bank just a few yards below the house. It is the near edge of a lake whose metallic sheen stretches maybe two miles from here to the hills that used to rise on the other side of the river.

They have drowned Yuanling. I had been warned when I told my Chinese friends that someday I must return. They told me a dam had been built across the Yuan River, creating a lake over twenty miles long and over six hundred feet at its deepest. The place was completely different now, they said; there was nothing worth seeing. It was too remote, the trip was too dangerous (or tedious, depending on who was talking) for such small reward when you got there—all of which made me more determined to go. People are always saying that Yuanling isn't much of a place, but it is for me.

I refuse to feel sad about the drowned city—at least for now. I'll feel sad later. Right now I am back in our house—*our* house, with Jenny and Dave, who have accompanied me on this trip. Including Renee, who was unable to come, they are my family now. Having them in this house makes time fold in on itself, and for the first time since I've been returning to China, I feel as though I really am back and Jenny and Dave have come all the way back with me as well.

Except for the furnishings, the house is unchanged, as though I left only a few months ago. Excited and proud, I show it to Dave and Jenny.

232

Here is our dining room, where the pewter candlesticks on the sideboard wilted in the heat of summer; this is the living room where we held our Christmas plays; there is where I had my chapel, here is our sleeping porch, and there, down there between this house and the next, is where Daddy and I built the teepee. Yes. And here, here by the railing is the exact place where I had my bed. Even this railing where I rest my hand is the same—I recognize some of the worn places that were here fifty years ago.

This spot is so familiar that it feels like part of my body. Yet when I raise my eyes from the railing and look out, the view is totally alien. It's as though our 1944 house has been dropped by a tornado into 1996 and Yuanling has been left behind in space a hundred million miles from where we are now. A cement bridge on tall pylons spans the lake, where motorized sampans and launches swarm at random over the colorless surface. Traffic flows steadily over the back of the bridge to either side of the lake. The road from the bridge leads up to a different town by the name of Yuanling draped over the top of the hills behind us.

Again I look down at the railing under my hand; it is an old friend. But I can't stay here forever. I try to think about something else and turn to leave.

We thank the people living in the house for sharing it with us and walk out the back, where a path takes us into the new Yuanling. Here, where once we crouched in the rustling grass to hide from Japanese planes, now there are cement buildings six and seven stories high along dusty boulevards busy with trucks and bicycles and swarms of *ma li,* little three-wheeled conveyances pulled by a motor scooter with two passengers sitting in back under a fancy cloth roof with a fringe.

Our hosts are the Yuanling Yali Alumni Association, now consisting of four or five elderly men who out of their limited resources—for no one is rich in Yuanling—have welcomed us warmly. One of them is Liu Qing-guo, or "Rudy," the town historian, now retired and living with his son in Shenzhen, near Hong Kong. He has traveled with his wife all the way from Shenzhen to be our official guide for the two days we are here. The alumni accompany us as we walk around town, to a Tang Dynasty temple, a restaurant, and the main market, vibrant with life and produce punctuated by scarlet piles of chilies for which Hunan is famous.

A few of the old buildings are left, now near the water's edge. One is the Protestant church, a large stone building which I had forgotten, but I recognize its cavernous interior as soon as we enter its echoing precincts.

We meet Pastor Zhang, who is ninety years old. He is so bent over he has to twist up to look at us when he shakes our hands and when he stands up straight, he has to hold onto something to keep from falling over. He totters a bit as he leads us to a table at the side of the sanctuary, where we are offered hot water to drink while we talk (tea, I'm sure, being too expensive to serve). Pastor Zhang talks mostly to Dave, possibly because Dave reminds him of his missionary colleagues long since gone (perhaps he senses Dave's origins as the son of missionaries to Iran, although Dave, now a Quaker, never tried to convert anyone). Pastor Zhang has led his flock for over thirty years, after Liberation (when the Communists took over China), through the Great Leap Forward (which brought about a famine in which tens of millions perished), and through the Cultural Revolution. A Yali alumnus tells me quietly that Pastor Zhang has not retired because he is not eligible for a pension from the state. Evidently he depends for his income on the congregation.

How many are in the congregation? I ask. About thirty, Pastor Zhang says, and goes on to talk about the services he used to hold and those he leads now. Since the organist left two years ago for a bigger city, they don't sing hymns anymore. But he still has the organ. I ask him where it is, and he indicates a room behind the podium. Dave raises an eyebrow at me, and I signal a yes.

With Pastor Zhang's permission, Jenny and Dave carry out a small pedal organ and stool, which they dust off and position at the edge of the podium facing the rows of vacant pews. I slide onto the stool and pump the pedals to try out a few wheezing chords. I haven't played one of these things for years. But I soon get the hang of it and launch into a well-worn hymn, playing by ear. Behind me, Dave—who remembers every word of every hymn he sang during his Presbyterian childhood—joins in. Pastor Zhang, holding on to the side of the lectern, bellows out the Chinese words in stentorian tones totally out of keeping with his appearance. The members of the Alumni Association sit in the pews and applaud at the end of each hymn. We go through several numbers, ending with a rousing rendition of "Onward Christian Soldiers." Dave, Jenny, and I sing the words in English, Pastor Zhang in Chinese, and the men of the Yuanling

Yali Alumni Association ring out with the words of the Yali school song, which they haven't sung in forty years yet remember perfectly. The empty church reverberates with overtones from the final words: "going as before." My eyes are overflowing—not because our friends have sung that song for the last time, which they probably have, but because they sang it as though it were for all time.

We plan to search for Shi Qiao on our last day in Yuanling. The evening before, Rudy and Mr. Ding, who is the chairman of the Alumni Association, go to the lakeside where boats tie up for the night, three or four deep out from shore. The men walk along the waterfront asking if anyone recalls a village called Shi Qiao, but no one remembers it. Just as they are about to leave, an older chuan *lao ban,* master of a small motorized launch, comes walking over several boats from where his craft is tied up out on the lake. He thinks he remembers such a place, he says—a cluster of houses at the river's edge, now long lost under the water. But he probably could find the spot on the shore above the place where the village used to be.

In the morning we pile into his boat—Dave and Jenny, my friend Zhang You-qin, who came with us from Changsha, the Yali Alumni Association, several city officials, and me. The *lao ban* starts the motor, which settles into a soothing *putt-putt-putt* as we move out from the mooring. For a while we glide parallel to the shore and I imagine the old street deep below the surface, once bustling with all the activities of life, where I had trudged along the city's length so many times, and where the new year dragon danced his beneficent way through clouds of smoke and deafening noise. I picture the street as it must be now—dim and silent, wavering in the aqueous gloom. The deserted shops on either side are barely visible through the murk, a shroud of silt softening their stoops, obliterating the angles where walls meet the floor, here and there veiling some object on a counter, left forgotten.

I tell myself at least the old town is protected by the lake, allowing the buildings slowly to disintegrate and dissolve into the surroundings. That is a kinder end than shops being wrecked and replaced with grimy concrete boxes and the street torn up to make a featureless boulevard like those in the unseasoned city on the top of the hills. I suspect that the outlines and artifacts of the old Yuanling will remain, hidden deep below the surface, and someday will emerge when the water drains away. The old Yuanling has been here so long it was an inherent part of the landscape; it had accommodated to the river and the hills and lived in balance with them. The old Yuanling stood on millennia of its own history; countless numbers of people throughout the centuries had walked its length on the ancient stones of that single street. I, too, was part of that long procession, and I refuse to be sad. The old Yuanling doesn't deserve tears. It deserves respect.

Our boat moves to the middle of the lake and under the bridge with traffic rumbling overhead. We pick up a little speed when the way is clear, heading what would have been downstream when there was a river. We leave the new city behind, thank goodness. Houses by the lake and on the hills become sparse as we get farther from the city. It is a beautiful October day—cool clear sky, crisp air, and sunshine warm on our shoulders. Occasionally we pass someone in a sampan leisurely sculling across the lake, or a single fisherman standing in his boat to fling a black spiderweb net out over the water. Here the lake is quiet; the hills move past slowly, lower than I remember them to be, the shoreline unfamiliar.

I am caught between the serenity of our surroundings and the anxiety of uncertainty. I am suspended between the possibility that we will find the valley of Shi Qiao and the probability that we won't. I hang in precarious balance between anticipation and caution, between the fullness of discovery and the hollowness of disappointment. Even if we do not find the valley of Shi Qiao, I tell myself, I can still go there in memory.

> *The house sits tucked in at the top of the valley, shaded by a*
> *backdrop of pine trees rising high above it. When we climb past*
> *the sentinel pine and turn into the valley, we will step into a*
> *quiet so profound that it is like an ancient presence. . .*

Coming out of my reverie, I notice that our boat has turned toward the hills on the right. The *lao ban* stops the engine. In the ensuing silence we coast the last few yards to the end of a path that leads down through a fold in the hills to the water's edge. A woman by the path is washing clothes in the lake. A man, with buckets of water hanging from a pole over his shoulder, stands nearby. They stop their conversation and nod to us without speaking as we step off the boat. Is this Shi Qiao? we ask. The woman points up the path.

Between steep valley walls we toil up stone steps set in peach-colored clay until we come to a cluster of old wood and stone farmhouses arranged around an open area. A woman calls down from a second-story porch, but her dialect is so thick I don't understand what she's saying. Children and toddlers in split pants come out and stare at us. More people appear— middle-aged farmers and a few younger men and women. Rudy acts as our spokesman.

"Does anyone know of a place around here where foreigners built a house?"

People shake their heads. Never heard of it. They talk among themselves. What are you looking for? they ask us, as though they hadn't heard Rudy the first time. While he explains again, a man appears from the back—thin, with a weathered face and an air of quiet competence. It turns out he is the father, grandfather, or great-grandfather of most of the people who live here. His name is Deng—Deng Yong-zhang. Yes, he says. He remembers the house the foreigners built. That was when he was a boy. The house is gone now.

With his words I step into a fantasy where anything can happen. It is both incredible and inevitable that in the whole world we have found the one person who remembers from a half century ago a small house that no longer exists in a remote valley amidst the foothills of Hunan's western mountains. Or perhaps, instead of a fantasy, I am in the middle of a myth, for I dimly sense the immanence of some ancient, universal truth.

"What happened to the house?" someone asks.

"It fell down after the owner left."

"Didn't it burn down?" I ask.

Mr. Deng shakes his head. "That was another house."

But I had heard *our* house burned down. Maybe he's gotten it mixed up with another house.

"Can you tell us where it was?"

He says he'll show us. It's not far.

Our procession is longer, now that several villagers have joined us. We follow single file behind Mr. Deng, climbing a steep trail out of the cluster of houses, up the flank of the hill that forms the wall of the next valley. The air is still. The sun is hot on our backs. There are only a few trees, mostly scrub that has grown above my head, so I can't see over the open side of the trail. Finally we angle into the next valley. The bushes that obscure our view end up ahead. Jenny is in front of me. She stops and looks down from an open ledge of peach-colored clay. "Mom," she says, "is this it?"

I follow her onto the ledge and see a stretch of ground slanting down between two hills—a bare little valley, spanned by terraces of clay with clumps of grass and bordered by banks of wild vines and one or two dwarf palms.

"Mom?"

I would have known this valley anywhere—in any century, any millennium.

Everyone seems pleased that we have found the valley. There's a lot of talking and walking around, but actually there isn't much to see, except the view, which is the only thing that is the same from fifty years ago. After twenty minutes or so I realize the others must be wondering when I'll be ready to go. I gesture to them—please go first and I will follow. Their voices fade as they disappear around the bend of the valley wall. Now it is quiet. Now, finally, I can be here.

I ache with love for what this valley once held. This is where my mother and father and I sat on the terrace and looked out at the same view I am looking at now. This is where we watched a gnat lay a necklace of pearls more beautiful than any the empress possessed. This is where the gecko, the tree frog, and dear old Molly shared their small lives with ours for a time. This is where, in the evening, Mother and I heard my father whistle the oriole's song on his climb home past the sentinel pine, and I knew we would all be together again, safe at the end of the day.

How can I reconcile the past and the present? How can I bring together the two worlds I have known so as to form a single vision?

I walk up to the ledge and look down at this bedraggled little valley between two nondescript hills. The past is gone and the present is always changing, but the valley remains. There is a constancy under the changing surface of things.

I am comforted that the valley is here—here in this home world so different from the other one that I now call home. It occurs to me that I will never achieve a single vision, nor do I need one. I have been blessed with double vision.

The valley is quiet, basking in the golden sunshine of autumn, To have been here again is enough. I turn and walk away, around the side of the hill.

Our house is the right-most pillared building, Old Yuanling is under water (1966)

Dave with Pastor Zhang at his church in Yuanling (1996)

*In our search for Shi Qiao, the village patriarch,
Deng Yun-zhang, recalled our house*

Valley of Shi Qiao today

THE ORIOLE'S SONG

AN AMERICAN GIRLHOOD IN WAR TIME CHINA

BJ Elder

BJ Elder, born Betty Jean Rugh in 1933 in Hunan Province, spent most of her first sixteen years in China. Now retired, she lives with her husband in Philadelphia, where she raised two daughters, earned a graduate degree, and worked as a Nurse Practitioner.

EastBridge

Signature Books
Doug Merwin, Imprint Editor

Signature Books is dedicated to presenting a wide range of exceptional books in the field of Asian studies. The principal concentration is on texts and supplementary reading materials for academic courses, on Asian literature-in-translation, and on the writings of Westerners who experienced Asia as journalists, scholars, diplomats and travelers.

Doug Merwin, publisher and editor-in-chief of EastBridge, has more than thirty years experience as an editor of books and journals on Asia and was the founding editor of East Gate Books, an imprint of M.E. Sharpe Publishers. Mr. Merwin was born in Peking and lived in China off and on until 1950. He earned an undergraduate degree in Public Law and Government and a Master of Arts degree in East Asian Languages and Cultures from Columbia University.